Patricia Hills

Art World Feminist

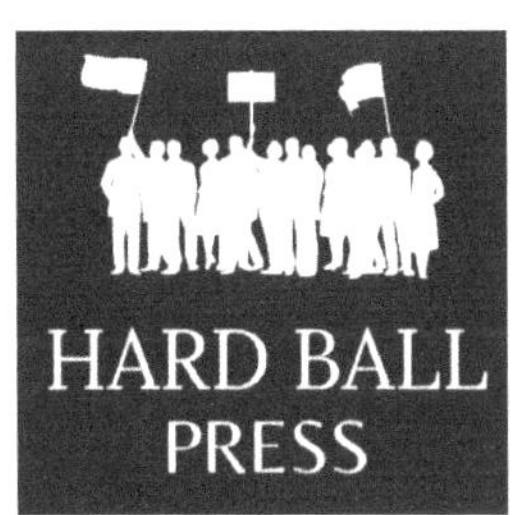

Praise For *Art World Feminist*

"This book is a lively mix of art and life, an intimate view of lived art history by a distinguished Americanist curator, professor, author, mother of three, and political activist—a unique and admirable combination. Defying convention as a 'combative feminist,' adamant leftist, and undaunted scholar of African American art, as well as a devoted family member, Patricia Hills recalls endless academic skirmishes, won and lost. Her life story provides a new model for all students and future historians." – Lucy R. Lippard, author of Moving *Targets: Feminist Essays on Women's Art 1970-1993.*

"*Art World Feminist* is a must read for anyone interested in entering the interconnected worlds of museums and art history. Its pages reveal a life committed to bringing together the personal, the professional, and the political, and to forging a new path for the study and display of American art." – Frances K. Pohl, author of *Framing America: A Social History of American Art.*

"Hills deftly takes us though a life dedicated to art, her family and social change. Rising to become one of the most influential scholars, curators and educators in the field of American Art History during decades, each filled with radical societal change as she shattered glass ceilings for herself and others in academia and museums. Living and curating in this period encouraged her to allow American art to tell our nation's stories as relevant to contemporary audiences. This memoir is a record of this activist historian's legacy as a scrappy champion of many overlooked artists shaping a field and opening so many doors for us to follow." – Kymberly Pinder, Dean, Yale School of Art.

"Rich in anecdotes, Hills's memoir tells the story of a bright, irrepressible female crafting a path through 1970s art museum jobs and cold war misogyny to become one of the leading historians of American art. Teacher, curator, rabble-rouser, organizer, writer, and advisor to generations of art historians, Hills here gives us the background story. Feminism would eventually discover Pat Hills, already practicing its creed. Her self-education in Left politics opened the realities of capitalist labor relations and the wages of being female, but expanded to a necessary embrace of labor-activist and Black art. Taking down "phallocentric Deconstruction," Hills's contributions to the social history of art are real – as are her rueful meditations on the contradictions of a Feminist working to make gorgeous exhibitions of the Veblen goods of art." – Caroline A. Jones, teaches modern and contemporary art at MIT.

"Jacob Lawrence once told me that you were the scholar he most trusted to tell his story. Now we see what happens when Lawrence's scholar of choice examines her own stories of personal and professional accomplishments. Your account blends scholarship and marriage and motherhood, the library and daycare, friendship and professional attainment with such integrity as if one could not be accomplished without the other, as only a true feminist would know. You take us behind the scenes of the most prestigious museums and institutions of higher learning. You navigated. We get to know your very renowned mentors and a few of your adversaries—in some cases, adversaries that you turned into allies. Your exhibitions and books have always been a guiding light to me. In looking back, you have shown us all a way forward." — Elizabeth Hutton Turner, co-author of *Jacob Lawrence: The American Struggle*

"There is properly no history, only biography."
Ralph Waldo Emerson, "History," 1841

Patricia Hills, Art World Feminist, by Patricia Hills

Published by Hard Ball Press, New York.

Copyright © 2025 by Patricia Hills, all rights reserved.

Library of Congress Cataloging-in-Publication Data: Hills, Patricia

1. Art Curatorship 2. Art History 3. Art Criticism 4. Feminism 5. Progressive Politics 6. Art Museums 7. Art Memoir 8. Patricia Hills

Front Cover Photograph of Patricia Hills, by Charles Giuliano, 2011.

Interior Photograph of Patricia Hills by Jeanne Hamilton.

Book design & formatting by Matthew Tallon

ISBN: 979-8-9898025-9-3

For information about the book and to request copies, email: hardballpress@gmail.com

Table of Contents

Preface

In writing this book, I realize that aside from the mentors who helped me along, the influences shaping my approach to life and art go back to childhood. That was the experience of growing up as an Army/Air Force brat. The military discipline, as well as the constant moving, were opportunities for new adventures. These factors helped me develop tenacity, as well as an openness to new cultures and new ideas.

I always enjoyed experiencing both abstract and representational art. Of seeing combinations of line, composition, color, and technique that conjured all the emotions that art elicits: delight and fear, peace and activism.

During the arc of my career, I have joined with others in making American art history a new and vibrant field. That focus brought resistance from a profession dominated by men who underestimated the capabilities of other women and myself. My experiences were probably not much different from the many women art historians of my generation who first achieved recognition in the early to mid-1970s. Although I approached subjects with a more overtly feminist and political outlook, each of us had our own styles and together, along with some very smart men, we published and mentored a new generation of art historians.

1

Dead End Jobs in San Francisco, 1958-60

My adult life began when I severed ties with my father. I was 21 years of age, standing on the tarmac of the Air Force airfield near Tokyo.

After begging, arguing, and cajoling, I persuaded Hartwin to sign the necessary military papers allowing me to fly back to San Francisco from the Air Force Base in Gifu, Japan, where we had been living after I graduated from college in June 1957. He wanted me to stay as his housekeeper and drinking buddy. While I treasured having new experiences there, I wanted to marry Fred Hills, my Stanford boyfriend. We were crazy about each other. Fred proposed in a letter from the States, and I accepted.

In mid-December 1957 my father relented and the Air Force approved my flying on a military plane (a refitted old "Flying Tigers" cargo plane) to Travis Air Force Base, just north of San Francisco. As I was about to board my father gave me $200 in cash [$2100 in 2025]. That seemed generous to me and enough, I thought, to launch myself as an independent woman making her way in the world.

I was eager to begin my new life. Having moved around for twenty-one years as the kid of a career military doctor and having had many adventures, I felt confident in my ability to live an independent life. I had picked up the skills of an anthropological researcher by probing and experiencing the cultures and legacies of different peoples. I was free of commitments to any specific geographical place, and I had absorbed the military discipline that had shaped my military father. I knew I could cope with anything that life threw at me.

I took the train from Travis AFB to Palo Alto looking for Fred. He never got the message that I was returning. I finally found him at a party with friends. Somewhat woozy with alcohol, he looked surprised at my sudden reappearance in his life, and I wondered whether committing myself to marriage with this quirky guy was a good idea. But we jollied ourselves into believing we were doing the right thing. We spent Christmas at a friend's vacant home in San Mateo.

In early January, we hiked all over San Francisco looking for a place to live. We finally found a garden apartment on Pierce Street, half a block down from Alma Vista Park, with a small kitchen, small living room, and small bedroom with a three-quarter bed not much bigger than a twin. The bed was tight, but we liked to snuggle. Our favorite meal was tuna casserole: a can of mushroom soup, a can of tuna fish, and some Minute Rice. I discovered San Francisco sourdough bread.

My old college friend Yvonne Irwin lived in San Francisco. She worked in the girdle department at Macy's and Fred and I hung out with her and her new SF friends. We were quite poor in terms of money in our pocket, but felt rich in terms of prospects. After all, Fred, was a Columbia man, and I had graduated from Stanford.

However, in January 1958 a moderate recession hit the country. Jobs froze for an unskilled, inexperienced, and unworldly young woman who looked about 15 and whose only background was studio arts and literature. I was also afflicted with *spasmodic dysphonia,* a speech impediment brought on during the last stressful month before my college graduation. How would I present myself verbally?

Finally, I landed a job in mid-January at Kaiser

Insurance. After getting the offer, I came home to the apartment and told Fred we had to get married immediately because I was starting the job the following Monday. We got married on January 17 at the Court House in San Francisco. Our best man was a clerk named Jack. We never saw Jack again.

I wore my trench coat to the ceremony. Fred insisted. He reminded me that in my senior year I had announced to everyone that I would get married in my trench coat. That was my reaction to the silly girls rushing about the cafeteria tables in my dorm, showing off their engagement rings, and talking about wedding dresses and exotic venues for their weddings. Marriage and children seemed to be their immediate goal.

Even during the 1950s, while becoming aware of my individual strengths and hoped-for accomplishments, I willingly conformed to the general expectations that middle-class life in America demanded. The script was: I would graduate from college, get married to a promising man, and have children—and let's throw in the house in the suburbs, station wagon, and Irish Setter dog. For most of my teen years I assumed this was my path, and I developed skills to cater to and finesse the male ego. I was clearly interested in medicine, but there was never encouragement to go to graduate school or develop a professional life. My father often said to me: "A medical education is a waste of time for a woman who just gets married and has children."

In contradiction to that was the independence and freedom middle-class parents back then gave to their children—both girls and boys—to play when and where they wanted. No helicopter parents charting their children's every movement. They encouraged self-reliance and trusted us, an attitude I later passed on to my own children. Typical was my parents' admonition: "Just be home when the streetlights go on." They had no idea how far we roamed.

So my trench coat (now sleeping in an old Air Force locker I own) was my answer.

&

At first, Fred did not look for a job because he was finishing his master's thesis on William Butler Yeats. A year later, like a dutiful wife, I typed his thesis. Many theses filed away in dusty libraries include this sentence in the acknowledgments: "And I thank my loyal wife for typing my thesis." Never a mention of the *name* of the "loyal wife." That was the 1950s. But I made certain that I included my own acknowledgment. I had adopted Fred's last name, but insisted my name, Patricia Hills, also be listed in the telephone book.

My job at Kaiser earned me $45 per week [$510 in 2025]. The job was awful. As a filing clerk I spent long days with rubber fingers as I filed away claims and judgments in tall filing cabinets. By mid-afternoon I would go to the restroom to smoke a cigarette in a stall and try to settle the nausea brought on by the boredom of such repetitive tasks. This experience introduced me to alienated labor—a concept I did not then know.

But computers were coming in. Kaiser had a huge computer installed in a room about half the size of a basketball court. Since it was clear that human repetitive labor was soon to be replaced by computers—and the technicians to run them—my boss offered to send me off to learn how to program. I declined. I wanted to get out of there.

One morning, three over-crowded busses went by on Sacramento Street without picking up passengers. I considered that a divine sign. From my bus stop I walked three blocks to Stanford Hospital, a small facility then located in San Francisco. After I assured the personnel chief that I believed workers should *NOT* have to work for a union if they did not want to, I was promptly hired. I later learned that I had capitulated to the anti-union *"Right to Work"* movement. What did I then know about unions and union solidarity? I was placed in the X-Ray Department as a receptionist and received a slightly better pay. I was not a particularly efficient receptionist, and the doctors snubbed me. But I didn't care, I was out of the insurance business.

We were still broke, never traveled, and went to the 25-cent movies in the Fillmore district. We had to save up through the credit union to buy a $19 FM radio—a vast improvement over our AM radio. Because I still had a military ID, we went to the Post Exchange (PX) in the Presidio Army Post (later the post became a part of the San Francisco parks system) and bought cigarettes for $2 a carton.

But we never went into debt, and later we began saving up for a decent hi-fi system. We also had good friends, like Yvonne and her new boyfriend, Ken Rand, who later became famous for his cool restaurant, the *Minimum Daily Requirement*, in the North Beach area. We had neither the resources nor the inclination to be proper beatniks who, I then thought, must have been living on their trust funds or mooching off friends.

The Army rescued our finances. Fred had drawn a low number for the draft, which would soon mean two years of active duty. Facing that outcome, he signed up for the "six-month program": six months in basic training at Fort Ord, California, and then a five- year commitment to the Army Reserves, which included an annual two-week summer camp. Off he went to Fort Ord. I visited him there, and his commanding sergeant gave me special respect when I let on that my father was a colonel in the Air Force. Not sure how that helped Fred. The long-term benefit of Fred's Army experience was his conversion to being extremely neat in his appearance and habits.

When not at work, I was alone in the apartment, reading novels, entertaining my divorced mother and father when both came on separate visits, and hanging out with my friend Yvonne.

When Fred was discharged from the Army in fall 1958, he scoured San Francisco for a starter job that would lead to a better position as a book editor. He landed one at *The Daily Pacific Builder,* a trade journal for the construction business.

We bought a Brooks Brothers suit for Fred to wear, and he became a meticulous dresser. Even though he had only one suit, he had lots of ties and shirts. He shined his shoes every day (no doubt inspired by his Army training). His boss liked him and offered to send along a good recommendation to the parent company, McGraw-Hill, should he decide to relocate to New York. In our small family it was Fred who was going to have a career. I was merely looking for a "fun" job before kids would arrive—like the script I had accepted from the 1950s playbook.

However, I had nursed a secret ambition to work in an art museum. How did that ambition creep into my consciousness and encourage me to shift gears?

It took a sophomore boyfriend to wake me, a nineteen-year-old science-major, to the reality of my pathetically low-level post-graduation prospects in the sciences. One day, having lunch in "the Basement" (a Stanford student eatery), we stood up to leave the table. "I know what will happen to you," my boyfriend said. He conjured up the image of my future self, working as a technician in some pharmaceutical company, wearing my white lab coat, and pouring chemicals from one vial to another. He laughed. I did not think it funny—not the optics I had in mind for my future self.

Hence, in my junior year I jettisoned my major in biology and switched to a major in Modern European Literature, even though I loved the sciences. As a child I had poured over my father's medical books with their pictures of skin diseases and broken bones. My senior photo for my High

School Annual included a caption stating my ambition was "to find a cure for cancer." Indeed, by changing majors, I was leaving behind the beautiful precision of chemistry, the messy logic of biology, the epiphanies of a math solution, and the imaginative problem-solving and practical application of physics.

With my new major I focused on German literature. The department would be less intimidating than the English Department, which was brimming over with East Coast preppies. This new major would allow me to take more courses in studio art, art history, philosophy, and other challenging advanced courses.

In the realm of the humanities I could sink myself into the pleasures of reading British and American novels, Russian and French novels translated into English, and untranslated writings of the great German-language authors, including Johann Wolfgang von Goethe, Thomas Mann, Hermann Hesse, Rainer Maria Rilke, Bertolt Brecht, and Franz Kafka. I also took a course on Existentialism, a European philosophic outlook then in vogue. The approach at Stanford was to combine close readings (necessary when translating German into English) while probing an author's intentions and exploring the full import of literature's ideas on historical change. I now realize how much these readings also shaped my attitudes, identity and approach to art.

Just before my graduation in 1957, I found myself in the office of Professor John LaPlante, who taught Asian Art. I told him I wanted to work in a museum. I had completed seven studio courses in drawing, painting and design, along with three art history courses, and had decided I was interested in "bringing art to the people." I do not recall his precise response, but it seemed friendly. All I remember is telling him my modest ambitions. He later gave me an "A" in the class, which I did not expect. That one "A" in a transcript full of mostly B's, some other A's, and occasional C's, would later help my admission to graduate school. Thank you, Professor LaPlante!

&

One year later, submerged in my second awful job, my thoughts turned again to my dream of working in a museum.

On a dare to myself, I wrote to Grace McCann Morley, director of the San Francisco Museum of Modern Art, saying that I hoped to meet with her for advice. I did not realize at the time that she was one of the first women to lead a major museum. She agreed, I went. She met me in the lobby, and we talked. She suggested two paths to take towards my goal of working in a museum: first, I could go back East and enroll in the curatorial MA program at Harvard, or second, I could learn shorthand and get a job as a secretary in a museum and advance my way up.

The first option was out of the question. I would never get into elite Harvard with my mediocre college grades and no one to write letters vouching for me. Besides, it would be expensive to pull up stakes and move to Cambridge, where Fred might have difficulty finding an editor's job. In those days, I knew well that a woman's career path often began in the typing pool—and she "worked her way up."

I thought to myself: *I can learn shorthand.* I knew touch-typing, so how hard would shorthand be? I promptly signed up for a night secretarial course in the Market Street area of San Francisco. The creepy building was in a crime-ridden neighborhood. Bare light bulbs dangled from the ceiling and the teachers were indifferent. But I learned Gregg Shorthand Simplified. I even got a certificate that verified I could take dictation at 120 words/minute.

However, I soon learned that it was not easy getting a secretarial job at one of the San Francisco museums. Such jobs were structured like government jobs and required test after test for beginners to move up the salary grade. I decided I did not have the patience for that. But I now had the skills (so I thought) to test out jobs in the non-profit sector.

I landed my first actual secretarial job in the Personnel Department at The Asia Foundation. Not a museum, but a non-profit that helped people in Southeast Asia. I thought: *How wonderful that they hire basketball coaches to go to Kuala Lumpur to set up sports programs.* Little did I know then that The Asia Foundation was a CIA front.

After working the first week for the assistant personnel director at The Asia Foundation, I was sure I would be fired. The secretary at the desk next to me helped me get into the swing of things, opening my boss's mail, placing the most important letters on top, and sitting while he read the letters and dictated his replies. I took shorthand with my spiral notebook and then typed out the letters. The boss would sign the originals and the carbon copies went into a file. Seemed easy. But it was not. Although I could take shorthand, no one had trained me how to translate my shorthand into proper business letters.

The first three days I had produced perhaps three final letters satisfactory to my boss. But there were many, many rejections. Type was either too scrunched up at the top or the bottom. Margins wavered from side to side. Too embarrassed to reveal my mistakes, I stuffed the messy pages into my desk drawers, making them invisible. This was before the advent of *Wite-Out* correction fluid to brush over mistakes, so my only recourse was vigorously erasing typewriter ink from the letters. That, of course, made another mess. The retyping took time, and another bunch of rejections went into the dark recesses of my desk. I was terrified, but they did not immediately fire me.

Everything at the Asia Foundation was super secretive. One of my tasks entailed shredding many of the incoming and outgoing confidential letters. I puzzled over the fact that no one asked me to shred the easily read individual carbon paper sheets (an invention of the 1950s) attached to each sheet of the typing paper. Those one-use-only carbons were thrown into the wastepaper basket. I realized that anyone up to poking their noses into Asia Foundation business just had to look at the carbon paper in the trash. No doubt those Commie Russians were doing just that, but I never dared to suggest a different protocol for shredding.

Meanwhile, government security officers investigated my background to determine whether I was a Communist. Friends told me that men in trench coats would show up at their homes at 7 a.m. and want to know their opinions of me. I never questioned the rightness of being investigated. It was the 1950s, the Cold War was still raging, and writers and movie stars had been blacklisted. Many people applying for jobs found themselves scrutinized as to whether they held "subversive" communist ideas.

Often in those years when a person applied for a job she had to sign forms saying that she "was not now and never had been a member of the Communist Party."

Moreover, we were often required to take "personality" tests. Think of the legions of psychologists who had to read those. Fred took a test for a job in which the questionnaire asked him whom from the past he would wish to be. Fred wrote down: "I would like to have been Jonathan Swift just before he went mad." He did not get that job.

Pundits called us the Silent Generation who conformed to rigid norms of behavior and thinking. Sloan Wilson's novel "*The Man with the Grey Flannel Suit*" caught the "yes man" spirit of the corporation age. Again, I want to emphasize that we had no money except for what we earned. No trust funds. Not even a check from a parent to help tide us over. Today we all realize that just being white conferred some privileges. But back then, we weren't conscious of "whiteness" being a privilege.

Back to The Asia Foundation. The personnel director was a woman who conducted many hush-hush closed-door conferences with outside staff (probably CIA agents) coming and going. I admired her imposing figure, a real alpha female. I even considered going into the personnel field, now called "Human Resources" (HR). I even took a night course in Personnel Management down in the don't-go-there-at-night area of San Francisco, where I had previously been for my shorthand classes. But I found the classes simplistic and boring. Personnel Management was not for me.

Athough after a year I did become a good secretary at TAF, my immediate Mr. Milktoast boss continually blamed me for his own incompetence in performing his job. Perhaps it was also that his boss, the formidable personnel director just mentioned, was suspicious of me. They rewrote my job description so that I no longer qualified for my job. At the time I thought that was very clever. But good riddance to me and to them.

I turned to making art as a serious pastime, painting in our apartment. In spring 1960 I enrolled in a painting studio course at the San Francisco Art Institute, but I had to quit before the semester ended because we were about to relocate. The instructor understood and gave me a "B" in the class. Although I would be absent for the last few sessions, he saw I had some talent as a painter. I don't recall having any favorite artists to emulate—except for Vincent Van Gogh, whose anthologized letters I had read. I was simply there to improve upon the basics.

By that time, Fred and I had managed to save some money. We could have bought a new hi-fi system to replace our $19 FM radio, or even a car. However, I still daydreamed of working in a museum, and Fred wanted to break into the book publishing field as an editor. We jettisoned the car idea and chose instead to relocate to New York after taking a trip through Mexico with a stop-off in Cuba, which had just undergone a successful revolution that piqued our curiosity.

This plan was a well thought out move, and we anticipated success in finding jobs at one of New York's many museums and book publishing houses. In the few months before we left, I worked for a temp agency—Western Girls—which dispatched me to short-term secretarial jobs. One was at a market research firm, another for a billboard company. I got jobs through Western Girls again after we got to New York, where they had a small branch office. They enticed me to join their firm permanently as a recruiter, but I turned them down. I wanted to keep my focus on museums.

Fred was a good candidate for a job at McGraw-Hill in New York, thanks to his boss at *The Daily Pacific Builder*, and I was seasoned enough as a secretary to qualify for an entry-level job at a museum.

We were eager to move to New York, but wanted to have fun on our trip there. We traveled through Mexico on the cheap, knowing nothing of the country or the language. With our savings converted into American Express checks, we boarded the bus from San Francisco to Los Angeles and then to Nogales, New Mexico, where we crossed the border.

The Mexican buses we rode provided a terrifying experience as they crossed the mountains in northern Mexico. Sheer towering cliffs on one side and a plummet into a gorge on the other, all while the bus driver and a friend drank beer and chattered away in front. People in the back had baskets of live chickens. It's a wonder that Fred and I got any sleep. We stuck to our budget of $8 per day for all expenses with the proviso that we would sleep on buses at night.

Traveling through Mexico measured up as a fabulous adventure, learning street Spanish, finding piles of skulls in church basements, attending bull fights, walking through the plazas of cities and villages, exploring the architecture, seeing the murals, and swimming in the warm Pacific waters.

Buses remained our favorite mode of transportation, except for flying into the fishing village of Puerto Vallarta, then so isolated—right before Richard Burton and Elizabeth Taylor arrived to make a movie. For lodging and two meals a day, we stayed in pensiónes along with retired US servicemen who could live comfortably in Mexico on their Army pensions. We wanted to go on to the Yucatan to see the ruins and, of course, Cuba, but we were running out of money. We took the bus from Mexico City to San Antonio, where my mother, Glennie, lived. We never got to the Yucatan or Cuba.

After a few days in Texas, Glennie, Fred, and I drove to Washington, D.C. in her two-toned, wing-tipped, turquoise Oldsmobile. We spent a week with Fred's brother Carter in a charming Georgetown ex-carriage house. A smart, well-traveled, and suave sophisticate, Carter had moved from his working-class neighborhood to Columbia College, where he learned Arabic, earned a Master's degree, and worked as a career officer for the U.S. State Department, with a stint in Egypt. He introduced me to hummus and kalamata olive dip. And to intriguing colleagues and friends. I understood why Fred admired him and had followed in his footsteps to Columbia.

Two things struck me about Washington: First, I was not prepared for the racism—right there in the nation's capital. It reminded me of Selma, Alabama, where I had summered during my college years. Grown men were dismissed as "boys," treated rudely, and denied entrance to some restaurants. And second, the Old Master paintings in the National Gallery of Art overwhelmed me with their dazzling, assured brushwork and intriguing subject matter. I spent the most time transfixed by the Rembrandt paintings gathered in one gallery, more than ever determined to plant myself in a museum.

Glennie, Fred, and I finally said good-bye to DC and pointed the big Oldsmobile north. New York here we come.

2

Working at MoMA, Oh My! 1960-64

In July 1960, my mother, Fred and I arrived in East Orange, New Jersey. Not exactly New York City, but a mere ferry boat ride and a bus to the City. My mother returned to San Antonio in her Oldsmobile. Fred and I camped with Fred's mother, Mildred, in a four-room walk-up apartment over a store. The somewhat deserted and dreary working-class neighborhood had been her home for decades. She lived on small amounts of money sent by her ex-husband, as well as monthly stipends from her three sons. No air conditioners but lots of fans. She kept her home charming and immaculate.

That summer, John F. Kennedy ran for president. We were transfixed by the suspense of the Democratic National Convention, which we watched on Mildred's TV. In those days, candidates were not decided in advance of the convention—far more exciting than now. We cheered when Kennedy won the nomination, deplored "Tricky Dick" Nixon, and pledged our votes to JFK. My parents had been Republicans. When I first voted in San Francisco, I had registered Independent. I switched to the Democrats because they all seemed honest, hardworking, ethical, and promised reforms.

Fred had his interview with the McGraw-Hill publishing company, set up by his San Francisco boss at the *Daily Pacific Builder*, a McGraw-Hill subsidiary. No surprise, Fred got a job as editor. Intelligent, well spoken, and witty—Fred knew his English grammar and syntax. No doubt it helped that he had a Columbia BA and a Stanford MA.

A few weeks later we relocated to a hotel room in Manhattan with an electric burner and small refrigerator located at Broadway and 104th Street. We next moved into a spacious one-bedroom apartment on Riverside Drive at 103rd Street after bribing the tenants and the real estate office clerk.

We were thrilled to be living in Manhattan. Fred and I explored the old restaurants and bookstores he knew from his Columbia days. We walked all over the city—even taking the Circle Line around Manhattan. We noticed a different demographic from San Francisco. A substantial percentage of subway riders were Black or brown. I met so many people raised in the Jewish faith and traditions that I decided to assume anyone not Black, Asian or Hispanic must be Jewish. It was only when I moved to New York that I began to learn about the Holocaust. I became aware of people with numbers tattooed on their arms, including the beautiful older woman who worked in the drugstore across from MoMA, and the "Fuller Brush Man," a Jewish survivor who would knock at our apartment door, and was later painted by Alice Neel.

The energy of working people was more palpable in New York than in San Francisco. It struck us that here in New York, people "lived to work, not worked to live." Moreover, in the early 1960s, the promisc of change and a better life for ordinary people promoted a general feeling of optimism. I applauded JFK and his brother Robert, who seemed to have new attitudes towards race and social issues. A different side of America was emerging as Black protest movements in big cities across the country increased in visibility. The Harlem Riots of 1964 took place not far from our Riverside Drive apartment. Many of these riots coincided with anti-Vietnam War protests. But I am getting ahead of my story.

Before we left New Jersey, I got in touch with the

New York City temp employment agency Western Girls, for whom I had worked in San Francisco. They found me palatable short-term secretarial jobs. During my lunch hours, I methodically scoped the museum scene and made appointments with personnel directors. The Frick showed interest, but insisted I return for a shorthand test. But I wanted first to interview at the Museum of Modern Art before making decisions about the Frick.

Thus, in early September, I showed up at MoMA's personnel department, pitched myself as someone who had secretarial skills and emphasized that I wanted to bring art to the public. The next day, the personnel director called me to say that William S. Lieberman, the curator for the Drawings and Prints Department, needed a secretary. His previous secretary had taken a leave of absence and her return was doubtful.

This changed my life. Lieberman didn't so much as dictate letters to me as he allowed me to write final responses to letters he received. I learned to say, "Dear Fluffy" (or some such nickname that tagged rich people) and to write effusively whatever the content. My talents amused him and he would jokingly say, "That's just the way I would say it." Tall and debonaire, Lieberman had a good sense of humor. His loud laugh often prompted heads to turn. He had graduated from Harvard University's museum training program directed by Paul Sachs of the Fine Arts Department, and was Alfred Barr's protégé at MoMA.

Barr had been the first director of MoMA, founded on the eve of the Stock Market collapse in 1929, and famous for his innovative, scholarly exhibitions. He was a professional colleague of Grace Morley, the director of the San Francisco Museum of Modern Art who had, as mentioned in Chapter 1, suggested that I should enroll in the Harvard program. Little did I then know that I was stepping into a tradition of great art curators.

Three weeks after I had joined the department, the ex-secretary showed up. As Lieberman and I had already bonded, he convinced Personnel that I would be the perfect curatorial assistant for the Max Ernst exhibition that Lieberman was organizing to open in the spring of 1961.

I plunged into working on all aspects of the show, watching Lieberman draw up a checklist that made sense, securing permissions for loans, shipping and insurance, registering art works, and observing the catalogue creation process with exacting editing and an appropriate design. I helped bring in conservators (if necessary), arranged for reframing, installation plans, watched the art handlers hang paintings in the galleries, as well as large photostats of artworks not available for loan. I was busy crafting wall labels and editing press releases, and being charming to patrons at the gala opening. Organizing and implementing such an operation required a lot of teamwork—but exhilarating work—and I loved it. I felt I was finding my community.

Lieberman painted the walls in various colors and hung most of the pictures low— about 54 inches from the floor to the midline of the frame. Museums often choose 57 inches, unless the paintings are very large. To Lieberman, viewing a work of art merited an intimate experience. One in which the viewer must look down to study the work. Moreover, he designed each wall with variations, such as hanging three on the 54-inch line and a fourth raised higher, like musical notes on a score. He also ordered and carefully placed clusters of plants to help set a mood. Part of my job entailed touring the exhibition every morning before the museum opened to see if anything was amiss, and make sure the plants were watered.

Lieberman was a great boss. He once insisted I walk with him through the exhibition. "I want you to know how to do an installation because one day you will be doing this," he said. He explained the ways he had crafted the hanging. What better encouragement could a young woman get? Especially one who had not even imagined one day being a curator installing her own "cutting edge" large exhibitions. Being a curator! This meant I would have the responsibility of presenting artworks to the public and conveying information so that a museum visit would be both pleasurable and educational. That would be a responsibility to which I looked forward.

Max Ernst, who came to town from Sedona, Arizona with his wife Dorothea Tanning, was a darling. He approved every decision Lieberman made. Tanning was fiercely protective. Once, I had to deliver a package to Ernst at his Manhattan hotel. Max wanted me to stay and chat, but Dorothea rushed me out as soon as she suspected Max might get sweet on me. Lieberman thanked me in the catalogue's Acknowledgments as "Mrs. Frederic W. Hills." I was irritated by that, but it was 1961, and women were either "Miss" or "Mrs."

At some point I met Lucy Lippard, who served as the researcher for Lieberman on the Ernst show. She later became one of the great critics of the late 20th century, spotting trends long before others and writing significant books, including *Mixed Blessings* (1991). She developed personal relationships with many of the avant-garde artists and has served as a model for me.

When the Ernst show closed, Lieberman and I knew I would be out of a job. Peter Selz, the head of the Department of Painting and Sculpture, eyed me as a secretary for himself—not a position I relished, as he had the reputation as being a womanizer who "chased women around the table." He was handsome and dynamic, but a bit overbearing. However, I did not want to go back to being a secretary. I wanted to continue doing curatorial work with Lieberman. He persuaded Personnel to create a new job for me as Curatorial Assistant for Drawings.

As to Peter Selz. I recalled that no one really seemed to

like him at MoMA. In his teens, Selz had escaped the Nazis and later returned to Europe to get his doctorate degree. He insisted on being called "Dr. Selz." Flaunting a higher degree (even though the degree was an enviable benchmark and carried prestige) went against MoMA's culture.

Moreover, forty years later I realized another reason for the less than warm feelings toward Selz. He was perceived as being out of touch with changes in the art world. The year before, in fall 1959, he had mounted the exhibition "New Image of Man." The theme centered on an existentialist approach that interpreted the art of the time as being profoundly influenced by the irrationalities and horrors of World War II. Selz invited the renowned Christian existentialist theologian Paul Tillich to write the preface. The exhibition showcased a mix of American and European artists: Leonard Baskin, Richard Diebenkorn, Leon Golub, César, Alberto Giacometti, Balcomb Green, Willem de Kooning, Rico Lebrun, Jan Müller, Nathan Oliveira, Eduardo Paolozzi, Jackson Pollock, and Theodore Roszak, among others. Not surprising for the time, women artists were not included.

I later summed up contemporary critical reception toward Selz's exhibition in my anthology, *Modern Art in the U.S.A.: Issues and Controversies of the Twentieth Century* (2001):

> From the vantage point of today [2001], the *New Images of Man* exhibition ... brought to an end a fifteen-year period of intensely expressionist art. There was no doubt that it gathered together a stellar group of both American and European painting and sculpture ... What the exhibition meant to do was to give a name—'new image of man'—to the direction which the pessimistic side of humanist painting had taken since the war. What unified the artists was

less a style, a technique, or an iconography than what Selz perceived was a shared sensibility that drew on the ideas of Existentialism. But the critics were not convinced.

I then quoted the artist Fairfield Porter, who wrote in *The Nation* (October 24, 1959) that "the common superficial look of the exhibition is that it collects monsters of mutilation, death and decay. It is less an exhibition for people interested in painting and sculpture than an entertainment for moralists." Such criticism must have been crushing for Selz, who was personally touched by the Holocaust and did not realize that others found him clueless of the newly emerging Pop culture. Especially to his colleagues at MoMA, Selz and his European sensibility did not jive with the New York of the emerging '60s.

Back in the early 1960s, I, too, was only vaguely aware that the art world and art market were experiencing a paradigm shift toward a newer kind of seemingly unproblematic (and un-existential) art. MoMA Curator Dorothy Miller's 1959-60 winter exhibition, *Sixteen Americans*, which followed *New Images,* brought a younger generation to the forefront. Jaspar Johns, Ellsworth Kelly, Alfred Leslie, Robert Rauschenberg, and Frank Stella were five of the young artists displayed. With her large black wood sculptural abstractions, the much older Louise Nevelson, also fit in well with the new sensibility. Soon there would be exhibitions of minimalist, assemblage, and installation artists.

In my new position as curatorial assistant, my career in museums was growing. I plunged into art historical studies of drawings and prints, and learned how to sort the differences between different kinds of paper and media and the conservation issues of paper. I had learned some of that by taking studio courses at Stanford. Nevertheless, I went downtown and enrolled in the Pratt Graphic Workshop and learned etching with artist Michael Ponce de Léon.

Lieberman was always in a tug of war with Peter Selz as to which department could claim stewardship of the watercolors. I remember Lieberman mostly won on this, because I vividly recall admiring Paul Klee watercolors in the Department's solander boxes—or storage boxes. Perhaps, in MoMA's table of organization, watercolors were under the control of Selz, but if stored in our solander boxes, we considered them not paintings but "works on paper."

Alfred Barr, Jr. was still at MoMA as Director of Museum Collections (as listed in the Ernst exhibition catalogue), but I did not comprehend what exactly he did, except to support everything that Lieberman did. Thin and wobbly, Barr wafted about the halls like the Ghost of Christmas Past. I was afraid that he might stumble, but he had a loyal assistant, Betsy Jones, who kept Barr focused on his walking and whatever museum issues he should be thinking about.

Back in the early 1960s, long before email, when administrators or curators wanted to get in touch with another staff member, they picked up the phone or, when the content had to do with work plans or money, they wrote out a memo and directed a department assistant to deliver it to the other party. I loved that part of my job. Delivering memos got me a break from the office chair, and I could chat with the recipients, mostly women.

One day someone will have to write about these talented MoMA women who sat in their desks and gave their lives to MoMA. From my observations I decided that these women did most of the work of their celebrated male bosses, such as the Director René d'Harnoncourt, Alfred Barr, Monroe Wheeler, Edward Steichen, Porter McCray, as well as Lieberman and Selz. Besides Betsy Jones, there were Mildred Constantine in the Department of Architecture and Design. Alicia Legg, who served as Assistant Curator under

Selz. The male-boss exception was Sara Mazo, widow of the artist Yasuo Kuniyoshi, who assisted Dorothy C. Miller, a person too lofty to ever speak to me. Moreover, since Lieberman and Miller were on the same level in the table of organization, he had little reason to write memos to her, as each did their own projects.

Some women ran their own departments. The formidable registrar Dorothy Dudley codified her techniques in her book *Museum Registration Methods,* 1958 (co-authored with Irma Bezold), long considered the Bible for registrars. Another forceful woman was Helen Franc, the daunting editor who oversaw the texts and design of catalogues, and I suspect, wrote all important museum statements. Except for Elizabeth Shaw, head of public relations, these women were friendly and encouraged me. When I came around to their offices to deliver Lieberman's memos, I always felt they were metaphorically patting me on the head.

My actual role model was Elaine Johnson, a curator who seemed to be assigned to Fairfield Porter, the mastermind behind exhibitions that traveled abroad. Johnson spent time in our department conferring with Lieberman. Perhaps she was even a curator in our department, but she did not have a desk. Well dressed and elegant, she always wore a trim suit, white gloves, and a net snood over the upper part of her face. I tried to emulate her but somehow always got the netting wrong or was missing a glove.

Working at MoMA had its perks in terms of learning. The Museum offered visitors a comprehensive film series that ran in the afternoons and early evenings: Howard Hawks, Greta Garbo, all the greats. I made a habit of seeing the first half of a movie during my lunch break, and then the final half after work. I liked that the museum celebrated all the visual arts, including painting, drawing, sculpture, photography, film, design and architecture. MoMA had become the model for other contemporary museums, and we all basked in that reputation. The bookstore sold books with a huge discount for employees. MoMA also had an excellent library, and eventually a first-rate archive, which I used later when writing about Alfred Barr.

Bill Lieberman, who was encouraging me to find my own path and identity, informed me that MoMA had another perk: MoMA gave scholarships to their staff to study for MA degrees at the Institute of Fine Arts (IFA), the graduate art history division of New York University. He urged me to apply. I did and was accepted, but since I had not worked at MoMA the required six months, I delayed my admission until fall 1961. Meanwhile, for the spring 1961 semester I enrolled in the MA program at Hunter College. I took a 20th-century art course from Dustin Rice, a sometime art critic and indifferent teacher. Finally, in Fall 1961 I had permission to take a course at the IFA.

Overwhelmed and even terrified by the neo-classical building and by the atmosphere of serious *Kunstgeschichte* (art history) taught by émigrés from Nazi Germany, I began my IFA education. The building had been the Fifth Avenue home of heiress Doris Duke, with a large central hall, marble floors, a great chandelier, and a magnificent curving staircase originally meant to display beautiful ladies descending to greet their rich and socially celebrated friends.

My first course at the Institute was *From Mengs to Manet,* taught by Professor Walter Friedlander. Still legendary at 90, Friedlander had been a student of the great German art historian Heinrich Wölfflin.

For my first term paper I chose a topic that Lieberman wanted me to research for a potential exhibition: the prints of the English artist Walter Sickert. I generally communicated with Friedlander's teaching assistant, but toward the end of the semester, I bravely climbed the great stairs to Professor Friedlander's small, dark, second-floor office to talk about my finished paper. He patted me on the knee, lingering over the thigh, and declared me a "very clever girl." I was too dumb to understand his other comments, since I did not yet have command of the high-culture art history lingua franca. His teaching assistants ribbed me on this. One said to the other, "She must be a scrubby." I asked what they meant, and they only grinned. I did not know then what "scrubby" meant. Per Google it means, "inferior in size and quality; stunted." But the TAs made me think I appeared to be some kind of adorable furry animal.

The second course, Spring 1962, was an Introduction to Museum Studies taught by Colin Eisler. A great course, it gave me background on the history of museums, dealers, and the art world. Eisler taught me to see the big picture of patronage and of a collection, rather than focusing only on one painting or artist. He treated us to wonderful field trips, including to Philadelphia to see the Rittenhouse Square townhouse that contained Henry McIlhenny's collection of 19th-century French masterpieces, and to the suburban Barnes Foundation with the impressionist paintings and African art collected by Albert C. Barnes. Other MoMA staff who got MA degrees at the IFA included critic/writer Lucy R. Lippard, MoMA curator Kynaston McShine, and Hirshhorn Museum curator Phyllis Rosenzweig. I was pleased with my job and my new life.

What stalled my career at MoMA was getting pregnant in spring of 1962—not planned, but eagerly anticipated. MoMA had a rule that a pregnant woman could not work past her fifth month of pregnancy. So, those of us in that situation naturally lied about our due dates. Fortunately for MoMA, I stayed on because that fall the Cuban Missile Crisis turned MoMA upside down. Orders were issued to move the collections to a storage facility on Long Island, far away from the threat of any nuclear rockets striking Manhattan. As I lifted heavy solander boxes, I recalled thinking, *MoMA cares about the collection but not about its staff?*

I went to the Clinic at Cornell University Hospital after I discovered the steep costs of having a private doctor. The clinic only cost $200 [$2,100 in 2025] for everything. I read up on natural childbirth and breast feeding, which turned out to be novel ideas in early-1960s America, even though females have had babies naturally since before the beginning of Homo sapiens. I prepared by going to Lamaze classes, practicing my breathing, and exercising the muscles for the baby's delivery.

When I broke my bag of waters and went into labor, we rushed to the hospital. I endured a long labor, but wanted no anesthesia and insisted on adjusting the mirrors over the birthing table so I could see everything happening. I told the doctor, "I want to have a natural childbirth." His sarcastic reply, "Whatever turns you on!" I stifled a retort.

Baby Christina finally arrived in the early hours of January 3, 1963, and I fell in love with her. The next morning the nurse came into the room shared by four of us clinic patients and handed out pills. I asked: "What are these for?" She replied, "Oh, they are to suppress your milk." I exploded. I resented that hospital staff would refuse working class clinic women the option to make their own decisions about their babies' nutrition. The late '60s era that saw a growing interest in women's health issues had not yet arrived.

My mother Glennie volunteered to come help when I left the hospital, but I declined her offer. I told her that during these early weeks Fred, Baby, and I needed to bond. My actual reason, which I kept from her, was that I did not want her to come in and boss me around. My father, on the other hand, did not visit from Japan, where he had retired and remarried. He did send me a Harvard rocking chair so that I could comfortably nurse Christina. I was pleased when my sister Gail stayed with us over holidays and semester breaks during the years 1962-66 when she attended the University of Connecticut.

Although I had planned to return to MoMA six weeks after giving birth, Fred and I realized we could not afford a nanny. Lieberman, however, asked if I could come in on Saturdays and work for $20 a day [$212 in 2025]. I accepted and helped him on various projects. I was there on the Saturday after John F. Kennedy's assassination. Visibly shaken—as were we all—Lieberman insisted on continuing to work. Fred watched Christina on Saturdays but rarely changed her diapers. However, I still felt connected to MoMA, even with only a Saturday schedule.

The reality of babies in pre-feminist America blocked most women from developing careers. I was no exception. When the next fall I got pregnant again, I quit working on Saturdays at MoMA. Lieberman had little enthusiasm for my having more babies. He must have thought a woman could have one child without her career suffering. But Fred and I had planned for another child. Bradford was born on July 27, 1964. He, like Christina, was adorable. I threw myself into my new identity as a mother, priding myself in washing all diapers in our apartment's washing machine. Without a dryer, diapers hung all over. I was always exhausted from pregnancy to breast feeding to another pregnancy to another round of breast feeding.

Not working and to save money, I made my own clothes. I also belonged to a neighborhood babysitting club. All the member-mothers saved money by babysitting for each other's kids using chits for money. To keep up appearances because of Fred's ambitions, we still had dinner parties for which I prepared Julia Child French dishes for Fred's co-workers, bosses, and their suburban wives. These women all seemed to be leading boring alcoholic lives in Tarrytown and Yonkers. I, a stay-at-home mom like them, felt sorry they were imprisoned in middle-class suburbia from where there seemed no exit, while their husbands had challenging jobs in NYC.

The babies took so much of my time. I had little energy other than to keep things going: shopping, changing diapers, taking the babies outside, feeding them, making play dates, and falling exhausted at night into the pull-out couch in the living room, which we called our bed. I still managed to see art in museums. Gail Keller, my best "mom friend" at the time who lived across the street, and I consolidated babysitting to allow each of us a weekly afternoon off. I spent those hours visiting new exhibitions in Manhattan and transporting myself back to my beloved world of color, line, images, and ideas.

Nevertheless, I could feel myself becoming strangely passive and not standing up for myself in the marriage. Although I saw some exhibitions, I did not have the focus to read books. I barely glanced at the newspapers but did watch TV with the babies. Fred would come home after work, and immediately after coming through the door would scan the apartment and say, "The place is a mess. What have you been doing all day?" Moreover, his eyes were drifting toward other women. He proposed we have an "open marriage," which had come into vogue in the mid-1960s. Although I didn't want that, I did not probe or protest whatever he may have been doing.

Later, I recalled those two years, 1963 and '64, as my "little brown mouse days." Fred began to worry about me. That I had deteriorated into an empty-headed and boring woman with a flip haircut whose friends were other "sandbox moms." One day he barked at me during an argument, "Why don't you do something about yourself? Why don't you go back to graduate school?"

A lightbulb went on in my head! I could pull myself out of it. I could restart my career.

I could find my identity.

3

Coming of Age, 1965-68

When I returned to Hunter College's MA program for the spring 1965 semester, my self-confidence had hit a low ebb. In contrast, my husband Fred had an enviable job as Acquisitions Editor for McGraw-Hill. He traveled across the country visiting universities and signing up famous authors to write textbooks. He went to parties and hippie spas in California and seemed to relish his life. He dominated discussions about household decisions, and I went along. Although times were changing and I would in time look at the world through a feminist lens, we were then stuck in patterns that had emerged after I gave up working full-time and was contributing less to the household income.

Fortunately, Hunter graduate classes were all offered in the evenings or on Saturday mornings, and Fred promised to babysit. Nevertheless, I was fearful of signing up for an art history class. I thought it would be too challenging for my mushy brain. Instead, I opted to take an advanced design course taught by sculptor Richard Lippold. Many of the class assignments required painting in tempera. I went from cheap poster paints to expensive Windsor and Newton gouache tubes, fine brushes, and the best paper. Lippold seemed a towering figure who could reduce students to tears in the class critiques, but he liked my work.

The course was a good transition, as it encouraged me to look at the world and think like an artist, and thus maintain that important identity. Lesson from Lippold: All artwork is about something. Its content has its origin in an idea, an experience, a feeling, or a formal relationship between colors, three-dimensionality, two-dimensionality, and/or time. It is not fingerpainting.

For my second round at Hunter from 1965-67, I came into contact with some great and provocative teachers. I will highlight three.

Moonlighting from Columbia, Professor Howard Davis taught two courses on Saturday mornings, which I attended: Renaissance Art and Post-Renaissance Art. He was always late to classes, but it was worth the wait. A thin, ascetic-looking man, he guided us through close examination of forms in space as if reading scripture. Through him I discovered John White's *The Birth and Rebirth of Pictorial Space* (1958). I began to understand that many artists in the Renaissance-Baroque period focused not only on the pictorial space within the canvas, but also the vantage point and sightlines of the viewer outside the canvas, such as Caravaggio had done, and Mantegna before him. Severe foreshortening—*anamorphosis*—also began to fascinate me, and I almost picked Hans Holbein's *The Ambassadors* (1533) as my MA thesis topic.

A critic and freelance curator but not an art historian, Gene Goosen taught two courses on American art, both of which I took. A rugged-looking guy, he could easily have split logs at his Upstate New York summer farm. He arrived at our 5 p.m. classes on time and was all charm (its seemed to me) after having belted down one or two cocktails. Believing strongly in American exceptionalism, he advocated these ideas to the students. To him, flatness and frontality were the shared elements of both folk colonial art and of Barnett Newman and other Abstract Expressionist painters. These words, derived from the influential critic Clement Greenberg, were his main descriptors for American art.

I argued with Goosen over what seemed to me to be crackpot theories of American "exceptionalism." He seemed to enjoy our sparring but never wavered in his stance. Later in my own scholarship, I would argue vigorously against simplistic interpretations, and for an art history that contextualized complexity and embraced the cultural and political forces engulfing art production and distribution.

In spring 1966, I took a lecture course on *Classical Art* taught by Leo Steinberg. He was then only teaching one semester a year at Hunter, leaving him time to write. Already famous as a teacher and scholar, Steinberg had a fascinating past. He was born in Moscow in 1920. His father had been politically engaged as a lawyer but had fallen out with the new Bolshevik government. The family moved to Berlin, and then moved again to London to escape Nazi fascism.

In London, Steinberg attended the Slade School of Fine Art. He immigrated to the United States in 1945, took a turn at teaching studio art, and wrote art criticism, for which he became famous. The art magazines began giving Steinberg a platform for his art criticism, and people were soon contrasting his criticism to that of Clement Greenberg and Harold Rosenberg. During the 1950s, he enrolled at NYU's Institute of Fine Arts, where he wrote his doctoral thesis on Italian Renaissance architect Francisco Borromini. Steinberg was also handsome, with intense eyes and a Van Dyke beard. When he walked, he seemed to dance.

Like many others, I was fascinated by Steinberg's intellect. For me, Steinberg made art history an exciting, exacting, intellectual and visual endeavor that could encompass issues of space, of pose, of iconography, of patronage—and still be informed by period documents. He emphasized boldness in interpretation.

I thought to myself, *If Columbia teachers such as Howard Davis could come to teach graduate students at Hunter, why couldn't a Hunter MA student go to Columbia to audit their classes?* So I walked up to Columbia, about twelve blocks from our apartment, to experience more great teaching. Professor Davis let me audit his Columbia course on *Early Netherlandish Painting.* From that I learned about the beginnings of genre painting and patronage, and even took the take-home final exam to assure myself that I had learned. Then I went to petition Professor George Collins, who was teaching *19th Century Architecture.* He said, "No problem," to my auditing his course.

Professor Meyer Schapiro had a different response. He was teaching a course on *Abstract Contemporary Art*, and I was determined to audit it as well, mostly to get the experience of his teaching style, the subjects were familiar to me. I had admired him ever since I read his book on Cézanne (Abrams 1954), the first art book I ever owned, given to me by my high school boyfriend's mother. I was too much in awe of Schapiro to ask beforehand if I could audit his class. I just figured I would sneak unnoticed into the large amphitheater and sit in the back.

Schapiro had an outsized reputation as a scholar who commanded a wide range of subjects. During the 1930's, he had been active in leftist political groups, wrote Marxist art criticism, and went on to get his doctoral degree at Columbia focusing on early Christian and Medieval art. He had been a presence among contemporary abstract artists throughout the 1950s, and allegedly told Willem de Kooning to stop painting one of his famous *Woman* pictures even when the artist protested it was not quite finished.

At Professor Schapiro's first class, in the amphitheater packed with students, he announced that only registered students would be allowed to stay. The rest of the people there should leave immediately. I took my position at the back of the hall and held my ground. Every week he continued his order that all unregistered students must leave. I stayed put on my radiator under the back windows.

Without notes, Schapiro spoke in paragraphs. One could feel the pauses as indentations to paragraphs. He never digressed from the smooth flow of his information and arguments, and provided a great learning experience for all of us.

Fast forward: Fred and I are visiting Europe the summer of 1968, and at one point spending time in the National Gallery in London. Whom do I see in the empty galleries? Meyer Schapiro and a companion. Naturally, I did what an admiring former student would do: I approached him and thanked him for the stimulating course he taught a few years back. His first words to me: "Were you registered?" I explained, no, I was not, but I never took up a registered student's seat, sitting instead on the back window ledge or a radiator. The conversation was getting awkward, so I quickly changed the subject and told him I knew his daughter Miriam, a neighborhood mom friend who taught mathematics at Albert Einstein. He then warmed up, we chatted some more, and I left the galleries.

Two weeks later: Back in the United States I am walking home on 103rd Street when I hear a woman's booming voice behind me: "I heard you took my father's course and were not even registered!!" That was Miriam speaking. I turned to face her and thought: *What is going on with these people? Why are they making such a fuss about my auditing?* Perhaps draconian measures were going to be levied against Schapiro if he permitted auditors? But I doubt it. However, the incident did not change my mind about his brilliance.

&

At the same time, while I was taking Steinberg's class, Fred's father died of cancer. Then a surprising turn of events occurred: Fred's mother, Mildred, who had long been divorced from her husband, Fred Senior, went into a deep depression. She felt she could not cope, could not walk or care for herself. She made frantic calls to Fred pleading for him to come help her in her New Jersey walk-up apartment. For three weeks he traveled to East Orange after work, cooked her supper, spent the night, and then early in the morning would come home to Riverside Drive, shower, shave, dress, and go in to work. It was a grueling schedule for Fred, but he did not complain. He and I shared the strong ethic that you take care of family. After three weeks I said, "This is crazy. She needs a psychiatrist." A psychiatrist neighbor in our building agreed to see her.

During Fred's next trip to East Orange he told her she was coming to live with us. She said, "I cannot walk down the stairs." He replied, "Yes, Mom, you can." She moved into our one-bedroom apartment, sleeping in the bedroom's double-bed, while Christina and Brad slept in bunk beds. Fred and I slept in the living room on a small pull-out couch. The psychiatrist we brought her to see recommended a colleague, but gave us parting advice:

"The first thing you must do is to get a full-time helper for Pat." Mildred spent each day of the first few weeks curled up in the fetal position on our large couch in the living room, taking her meds, and seeing the new psychiatrist three or four times a week.

Money from Fred senior's estate paid for a hired home aide—a wonderful woman from Harlem who always dressed in a long white gown because of her religion ("Not the Nation of Islam," she insisted). She took care of the house, doted on "Master Bradford," and made the most wonderful Parker House rolls. She relieved a lot of my stress. I will be forever grateful. After three months of talk therapy and medicine, Mildred eventually became well, even cheerful, and returned to East Orange.

The Mildred episode transformed what would have otherwise been an ordinary classroom association between me (as a student) and Leo Steinberg (as a teacher) — into an extraordinary and long-lasting relationship beneficial to us both.

I was finishing Professor Steinberg's Classical Art course at the time and could not find enough hours in the day to complete the research term paper. I wrote to Steinberg asking for an extension. He sent me a warm note complimenting me on the outline of my paper and approved the extension. With a home aide now sharing my daily caregiving, I could spend full days researching at the New York Public Library.

I wrote my paper on the representation of water in Greek art. In July, I delivered the paper to Steinberg at his elegant Central Part West apartment. He insisted I stay while he went into his study and read the paper. He emerged an hour later—all smiles. He was pleased with my efforts. He kindled in me the conviction that I could continue beyond the MA toward a PhD. When I went home to fetch Christina and Brad from the Riverside Park playground where my friend Varda had been babysitting them, she recognized my transported enthusiasm and declared: "*You* are going on to get your PhD!"

Leo Steinberg was my first intellectual friend with whom I felt I could share my ideas on art and art history. My husband Fred could not do that because art history was out of his field. Moreover, he was too busy editing his authors' manuscripts. My fellow students at Hunter also could not help because most had full-time teaching jobs outside classes and would not want to revisit concepts already discussed in class. I hoped to nurture my relationship with Steinberg.

After my term paper, I wrote him several letters that July laying out my thoughts on art history. I was particularly focused on the "oblique point of view" in Caravaggio's *Conversion of St. Paul*" and wanted his opinion. He responded with a long letter. He invited me to audit his Hunter undergraduate course on Baroque art. After class he sometimes invited me to accompany him to the Metropolitan Museum of Art. Together we studied paintings in detail. He gave me his opinions and listened to mine. I ran into him at the opening of William Rubin's 1967 *Surrealism* exhibition at MoMA, and we went through the galleries together. He introduced me to Salvador Dali, who kissed my hand and then flung it away when he concluded that I and Steinberg were both nobodies.

Steinberg later asked me to conduct research for him at the New York Public Library, which I and some of his other students did without pay. He credited me for my assistance in the Acknowledgments of *"Other Criteria"* (1972), his classic book of essays on contemporary art. I urged him to hire a regular research assistant, and he did. In December 1968, Sheila Schwartz became his assistant and worked with him for more than forty years. Like me, she went to Hunter College with Leo as her advisor, and then on to the Institute of Fine Arts.

In *Other Criteria* Steinberg opposed Clement Greenberg's reductive theories of art and championed the "other criteria" crucial to interpretations of art. I joined the community of young anti-Greenbergians because of Steinberg. His attention and encouragement were exactly what I wanted and needed.

In the Fall semester of 1967, Steinberg recruited me to be one of three art history teaching assistants (TAs) for a special experimental freshman course that the CUNY graduate center was initiating. This—my first teaching job— was exhilarating and exhausting. Every week Steinberg would give his typically brilliant lecture on a specific painting, such as Leonardo's *Last Supper*, and then we TA's had to fill in the blanks by lecturing to our three sections of students meeting twice a week. They needed to learn not only the transitions between Steinberg's lectures, but the rudiments of art history. On the days I taught, I had to retire to the pull-out-couch bed at 8 pm—shortly following my kids' bedtime.

I got to know Steinberg quite well. Not only did he share with me some of the ideas that would eventually be published, but also his quirks, his pet peeves, and his dismissal of most of the art critics of the day. He could not stand people who did not look closely and intensely at art and who closed their minds to new ideas and associations. He grew angry when he thought that the art history establishment was ignoring his scholarship.

Once he had established a thesis for a particular interpretation, he did not like to be contradicted. He focused on the "crossed leg posture" of the Virgin as she holds Christ close to her in a lecture he gave on Michelangelo's *Medici Madonna*. It was a pose never done before in Christian art. I thought about the pose and remarked to him that based on my experience as a mother, I found it easier to cross my legs when holding a wiggling baby. The baby would be less likely to fall off from the pitched cross legs than from the sloping decline created when legs are not crossed. "Do you think that Michelangelo makes decisions based on mere naturalism?" he responded. I thought, *Of course ... why did I even bring up my observation? Why would I challenge a man's interpretation by my own woman's experience!*

Sheila Schwartz recounts Steinberg's version of the conversation in *Michelangelo's Sculpture: Essays by Leo Steinberg* [p. 101]. "I once put the question to a young mother. She answered predictably that it's a comfortable way to perch a baby, especially if he's nursing. Helps to bring his lips up to the breast. She thought the situation so natural that even an art historian should be able to tell when he's not needed. But some of us are incorrigible." He did, however, make a convincing argument for his interpretation of the intimacy achieved by the "crossed leg posture."

His reading of an artwork was thorough. He told me that when writing on Michelangelo's tondo *Doni Madonna*, he would go every day for six weeks to the Uffizi and spend an hour looking at the painting. He once told me that he had spent a whole day thinking about the right word to use in a sentence for an essay. He raged against editors who dared to change his prose. Brilliant but arrogant, Leo taught me to take risks in thinking and writing.

In 1967, I naturally wanted him to be my MA thesis advisor, and he agreed. I had a ruse. I presented a Renaissance topic to the Chair of the Art Department and wrote letters of petition for him as a Renaissance scholar to serve as my reader. That was approved, but I actually began research on an aspect of American art, which had been my plan all along.

As my subject I chose Thomas Eakins, whom I researched while functioning as a TA. I decided my topic would be the current 1960s critical reception of his work, when most writers on Eakins emphasized that his approach was scientific rather than artistic.

I was determined to challenge the received wisdom and argue the opposite, as Steinberg might have done. The title became "The Portraits of Thomas Eakins: The Elements of Interpretation." Under Steinberg's guidance and his close reading of my drafts, I pulled it off.

In spring 1968, after I had re-enrolled at the NYU Institute of Fine Art, which was then the highest rated graduate program for art history, Steinberg and I still met frequently. I would lay out my ideas for seminar projects, and he continued to advise me as to how to negotiate the IFA culture. We enjoyed each other's company, and I think he was happy with our very gentle relationship.

In April 1969 I was to meet him at the New York Public Library for a coffee and chat about my progress at the Institute of Fine Arts. I was disappointed when he did not show up. He wrote me a letter that speaks volumes about the texture of our relationship:

Dear Pat – The week just past has been a real dark night of the soul for me. You don't know how desperate I often feel, for you cheer me up so that I seem a much more sunny person in your presence— like the moon, reflecting your own light. Today I feel a little less of that agony of mine which kept me from inflicting myself upon you last Wednesday at the NYPL. I know your pride and how mad you must have been. Please forgive me. What fun we would have had studying together. But then you would have missed Goldwater & Rosenblum ... & Schiff etc. etc. You've really been very lucky to have escaped and you were lucky not to have had to put up with me ... I am / Your very fond friend, Leo.

A week later I received another letter from Istanbul describing his travels and his love for the architecture. He ended the letter: "What a pity our lives were so directed that we can never take a trip like this together. See you soon." The relationship continued as a long-lasting friendship that I treasured. I seemed to cheer him up and change his mood when I visited him late in his life.

In spring 1998, I organized a three-day visit for Steinberg to give a lecture and meet with students for two seminars at Boston University. The students were mesmerized by his intellect and sensibility, and the deans treated him like royalty.

Visiting New York in later years, Leo and I would meet for dinner at a French restaurant or connect at his Lincoln Center apartment. I often brought him the recent books and catalogues I had written. He would talk, share some details of his private life, and show me his recent scholarly work. A few years later we could not go to restaurants because he chain-smoked, and restaurants refused smokers. He would order in Chinese food. In his final years Steinberg had the same mentor/student relationship with several former students, as well as with young art writers who sought him out. He always performed long, mesmerizing monologues for us all. And we all learned.

I visited Leo about two months before he died—in 2011. He explained how he had suffered a seizure in 2009 and had called his assistant Sheila Schwartz in the early hours of the morning. She responded and called an ambulance. He reflected that during his convalescence he would look out the window from his hospital bed and watch the morning light pour onto the sides of buildings, bringing shadows as the sun got brighter, and then dim again in the evening. His telling was an elegiac moment. I felt he had become a man who had finally achieved some peace from his demons.

4

Who Cares About American Art? 1968-70

In January 1968 I returned to the NYU Institute of Fine Arts with Robert Goldwater as my advisor. He almost did not re-admit me because of what he considered "unsurmountable family issues." Today we would call his response prejudice against women. Here's what happened. When I went to his office in mid-December 1967 for my application interview, I told him of my activities—teaching, writing my MA thesis, caring for children. I thought he would be impressed. Instead, he started to wag his chin from side to side. He lectured me that a woman with small children could not both teach and be an IFA student. I thought, *I must fight this—not only for myself but for other women in my situation.*

When I returned home, I immediately wrote Goldwater a letter telling him I would not be teaching, my babysitting needs were covered, and I would be a serious student. He admitted me with the proviso that I spend the first two semesters taking independent reading courses and then take an oral general history of art exam before I could claim to be an IFA doctoral student. I did and passed. I was ready to plunge into a community that took seriously art history and its methods of interpretation. Leo Steinberg had prepared me for the intellectual challenges I would face.

That spring I was notified that my application for a multi-year Danforth Foundation Fellowship for Women had been granted. The Fellowship's trustees (St. Louis Ralston-

Purina executives) had seen a need to support women with families. This unique fellowship covered not only tuition and fees but babysitting expenses up to $1000 each year [$9550 in 2025]. This meant I could afford babysitting for daytime classes. With these funds I partnered with a neighbor to share babysitting costs for five days of after-school childcare for her kids and mine. Leta Arnett was the babysitter—a wonderfully warm and unconventional Canadian woman who lived in my neighbor's building. Another aspect of the fellowship were my bragging rights: the fellowship gave me credibility with the IFA faculty.

At the time I thought, *What better way to study these masterpieces of art than to go to Europe and see artworks first-hand?* My mother came to babysit, and Fred and I spent three weeks visiting London, Venice, Florence, Rome and Paris. I flew home sated with the art I had seen and the art history I had absorbed from direct experience.

My courses and reading assignments this second time around at the IFA did not intimidate me as they had in the early 1960s. I realized the benefits of being exposed to excellent teachers and scholars—the older émigrés from Nazi Europe, as well as Goldwater, and younger scholars such as Colin Eisler, Donald Posner, Robert Rosenblum, and Gert Schiff. All of them encouraged students, including me. I avoided the few misogynist teachers, whom all universities tolerated in those days. My IFA training would give me time to reflect on the trajectory of serious art history scholarship. I realized that learning about European art and culture would draw me out of the parochialism that had generally characterized approaches to American art.

During my years in the MA program at Hunter, I had become familiar with the concept of "Cultural Nationalism"— which means the glorification of the United States through the celebration of its art, music, and culture. We see cultural nationalism as being activated by chauvinism (*we are better than anyone else*), xenophobia (*we don't like anyone's art other than our own*), or anti-European sentiments (*we don't want the art of the controlling European mother countries to direct our standards*). Cultural Nationalism becomes political when it serves nation building—(*only American artists can produce a great art reflective of a great nation*).

To win over the people, the architects of nation-building also depended on the concept of American exceptionalism (*we are different and freer than anyone else.*) I sketch in these various approaches to American art because in the 1960s to 70s, when my generation of Americanists entered the field, the books available on American art were generally premised on American exceptionalism. I was then unaware of the concept's tie-in with Cold War rhetoric.

A study of American history shows that cultural nationalism and its driving force of nation building rose to primacy and then retreated several times during the centuries from the 1850s to the 1950s. Writers such as Ralph Waldo Emerson pleaded with US artists to paint American scenes worthy of the greatness of the nation. In the 1920s, as art writers recoiled against the savagery of World War I, many urged Americans to turn away from the decadence and bohemianism of Europe and look, instead, towards America's own "usable past."

During the 1930s, cultural nationalism became virulent in many quarters. Those writers, particularly Thomas Craven, reacting against the internationalism of communism and socialism exerted great efforts to define what was uniquely not European and not communist in American art. Craven and others sought, instead, the patriotic and the "good."

Nevertheless, 1930s leftist artists pushed back and took a more internationalist approach, focusing on class and racial diversity. Scrappy artist Stuart Davis rebuked the narrow-minded Americanism of Craven and his ilk, and wrote a screed for *Art Front* (the artists' monthly journal) against

Time's celebratory paean. To Davis: "Painting the American scene is not a new manifestation ... George Bellows, John Sloan, Glenn Coleman, John Marin ... had the advantage of not being burdened by the vicious and windy chauvinistic ballyhoo carried on in their defense by a writer like Thomas Craven whose critical values may possibly be clouded by a lively sense of commercial expediency ... Craven's ideas are unimportant, but the currency given to them through the medium of the Hearst press means that we must not underestimate their soggy impact."

Artists of the 1930's influenced by a Marxist outlook, especially those employed by the Federal Art Projects (FAP), boldly continued to draw, paint, and sculpt images of the American scene with a diversity of class, gender, race, and ethnicity in their choice of subjects. FAP artists tended to paint working-class struggles—caring for children, farming, constructing buildings, riding the subways, relaxing at home and at restaurants—and going on strike.

Scratch below the surface of art writing in the 1950s-1960s and one might find another version of American exceptionalism: not one based on subject matter, but one based on style and on Cold War cultural propaganda. Critic Clement Greenberg's chief legacy includes directing art writers toward an emphasis on style alone. He declared in a series of articles written for *The Nation* and *Partisan Review* that the analysis of color and line was the only legitimate way to judge art. Greenberg wrote in 1944: "Let painting confine itself to the disposition pure and simple of color and line, and not intrigue us by associations with things we can experience more authentically elsewhere."

Greenberg did not favor illusionism—too literary. Not pure art. The take-away from Serge Guilbaut's 1983 critical book, *How New York Stole the Idea of Modern Art: Abstract Expressionism, Freedom, and the Cold War*, pointed to the political ramification of Greenberg's art-for-art's sake approach. The CIA seized on the theme of the freedom of American artists to paint abstractly when circulating government-funded exhibitions abroad.

Alfred Barr, Jr., the curator of the Museum of Modern Art agreed. Barr merged abstract expressionism with national chauvinism in the small booklet *What is Modern Painting?* which he wrote and revised during the 1940s and 1950s. Thousands of these booklets were sold at MoMA's bookstore. Barr argued that abstract art was an "art of freedom" suited to the democratic freedoms of America, as opposed to the socialist realism dictated to artists by the art apparatchiks of the USSR.

No doubt influenced by Greenberg's flatness theories, those writers exploring the roots of contemporary "flat" painting pointed to the inspiration of American folk art. This came at a time when collectors such as Jean Lipman and dealers such as Edith Halpert were promoting the collecting of American folk art. Indeed, we see a conflation of folk art and contemporary art when writer and curator Lloyd Goodrich wrote "What is American in American Art," published in Jean Lipman's *What is American about American Art* (1963).

That same year, John W. McCoubrey published his slim book *American Tradition in Painting*. McCoubrey argued that European art had traditional skills which aided the European artist "to convey not just a convincing image, but a heightened awareness of objects or figures in an illusion of ordered space." Whereas American art, done by artists perhaps not as well trained as their European counterparts, "is possessed by the spaciousness and emptiness of the land itself ... Spaciousness is at home in America not only in our landscapes but in all of our painting."

Critic Gene Goosen continually reiterated these theories in his Hunter College classroom. I don't mean to suggest that all of this was bad, it is just one more example of how trends in the art world celebrated by art writers connect to enhanced sales and to the politics of building national hegemony.

Critical thoughts swirled around me in the late 1960s, as they swirled in the zeitgeist of 60's political turmoil.

&

At the Institute of Fine Arts, dialogues about *"what is American in American art"* were nonexistent. The IFA did not teach American art, ignored its importance, and dismissed concepts such as cultural nationalism. So, I steeped myself in the study of European art from the Renaissance to contemporary times. The professors gave us no reading lists. We were supposed to know what we should read—guided by advice from more senior doctoral students and periodicals like *The Art Bulletin* and *The Burlington Magazine*.

Irwin Panofsky's ideas, tacitly encouraged by IFA professors, helped guide me to the kinds of art historical questions I wanted to probe. Panofsky had taught at NYU and later joined other émigrés, such as Albert Einstein, at Princeton. Even today I return to his book, *Meaning in the Visual Arts,* (Anchor Books, 1955) with its introduction, "The History of Art as a Humanistic Discipline." The original essay, published in 1940, served not only as a guideline for young art historians of the 1950s and 1960s, but went far to explain the mindset of a 1940's intellectual toward the world situation. Panofsky's was a plea for a humanistic approach to life and culture during the year when the Nazis took control of Paris, were preparing to invade the Soviet Union, and were persecuting and murdering Jews, Communists, gays, lesbians, Blacks, the Roma, Catholic priests, and left-leaning intellectuals.

Panofsky, like Leo Steinberg after him, presented the

history of art as a dynamic undertaking. Panofsky spoke as much as a scientist as a humanist: "Every discovery of an unknown historical fact, and every new interpretation of a known one, will either fit in with the prevalent general conception, and thereby corroborate and enrich it, or else it will entail a subtle, or even a fundamental change in the prevalent general conception, and thereby throw new light on all that has been known before." In other words, every new bit of evidence always reshapes our knowledge. He continues the thread: "An art historian, then, is a humanist whose 'primary material 'consists of those records which have come down to us in the form of works of art." The next issue is: How do we interpret those works of art?

His second essay, "Iconography and Iconology: An Introduction to the Study of Renaissance Art," begins with the simple definition: "Iconography is that branch of the history of art which concerns itself with the subject matter or meaning of works of art, as opposed to their form." Meanings, for Panofsky, must rest on correct identification of objects. "Iconography is, therefore, a description and classification of images."

Panofsky himself saw the bigger picture: "So I conceive of iconology as an iconography turned interpretative and thus becoming an integral part of the study of art instead of being confined to the role of preliminary statistical survey ... Iconology, then, is a method of interpretation which arises from a synthesis rather than analysis." Then Panofsky interjects the necessity of exploring the history of style with the goal of the humanist's "search for intrinsic meanings of content."

In my path through my IFA years, I continued in the footsteps of Steinberg's pedagogy: close-looking first and then turning to the contemporary cultural documents for evidence. One needs to be thorough in one's scholarship before issuing an interpretation.

The IFA as a whole advocated no particular theory—but the study of iconography, the writing about "masterpieces," and maybe a little social history were tacitly encouraged. I appreciated the faculty who respected me and my developing ideas. I learned also from the other graduate students. My buddies at the time were Maddie Fidell (who later moved to Paris), Brooks Joyner, John Hunisak, Tom Wolf, Marc Miller, and Marie Tanner. I am still in touch with many of them today.

Later I would re-shape my writing of art history. But that only came after years of critical study, along with learning a dialectical analysis of art and the culture that produced it.

5

Art Dealers, 1969

My life was filled to the brim with the chores of motherhood and research for my seminar classes. Even so, I still hoped to get as much experience in the art world as I had at MoMA in the early 1960s. In 1969 I took a part-time summer job with the well known gallerist Paul Bianchini, a tall, charmingly handsome, and rich Frenchman who liked to claim credit for advancing the careers of Pop artists with his Great American Supermarket gallery show. My pay was $4/hour [$35/hour in 2025]. Bianchini and I had a good relationship. One summer weekend he even invited my family out to his mansion in Stonington, Connecticut.

My job was to gather information for a catalogue *raisonné* focused on Pop artist Roy Lichtenstein's works on paper. My job entailed going to Roy's studio and measuring the works, noting the medium, assigning a date, and placing them in logical sequences. I also spent time at the Leo Castelli Gallery, Lichtenstein's gallery, to record the prints held by the gallery for sale.

To tell you something of Lichtenstein's character: One day when I was working downtown at the gallery, a Castelli employee rushed up from the basement to tell Ivan Karp, then Castelli's manager, that Lichtenstein was going berserk. Roy was tearing up all the prints in the basement that had not been numbered. Apparently, the artist was adamant that when prints were published in limited editions with each print differently numbered, dealers should honor that protocol and not print up extra unnumbered prints for sale. I recall that Karp just shrugged his shoulders and let the tearing in the basement continue. I was impressed with Lichtenstein and Karp.

Bianchini had a limited edition deluxe boxed book in mind with all the artworks in color—plus a specifically made "Real Estate" bonus print. I found my work exciting, and I would get credit in the published catalogue raisonné—a welcome addition to my thin CV.

At one point, I asked Roy (who was frequently in his New York studio) whether I could do further clerical work for him in exchange for one of his sketches. At that time, he dismissed the sketches as valueless—mere working studies for his large, dot-filled paintings. He told me to choose three works and he would decide which to give me. I did so and met him again over lunch. He looked at the sketch *Leda and the Swan,* which was my favorite because of its art historical subject, and said: "Don't you want this one?" I was delighted. Then he added: "You don't have to work extra for me."

Bianchini, however, turned out not to be so generous. He wanted his book to include an essay by Diane Walden, a Guggenheim curator then organizing an exhibition of Roy's work. Waldman kept missing her deadlines. Worried, Bianchini asked me to write three essays of about 750 words on each of the categories: sketches, drawings, and prints.

I did so. Roy loved the essays when he read them, and I submitted them to Bianchini. He wrote me out a check for $225 [$665.00 in 2025]. The check bounced. A few days later I returned to his gallery to wave the bounced check at him. He wrote out a new check and said, "You'll have to change your name or add a middle initial, because readers will confuse it with my wife's name, Pati Hill, who's an artist." I told him that I was *not* going to change my name "Patricia Hills" by adding an initial, the names were different. He seemed to be fine with that. The check cleared.

When the deluxe boxed book arrived, my essays had been edited out and my name excluded. Apparently, Waldman objected to including another author (and a graduate student at that) in the book, and Bianchini still wanted to get rid of my name. However, Roy gave me the *Real Estate* print from his "artist's proof" stash and signed it "For Pat." That print has hung for many years in our home, along with *Leda,* which I loaned out to exhibitions. I would sell *Leda* in 1989, bringing my family a life-changing bonanza.

6

Change Is Gonna Come, 1965-72

The late 1960s saw a tidal wave of movements that affected my friends and me: the counterculture movement, the Civil Rights movement to end racial segregation, feminism and equal rights/opportunities for women, the student movement to reform the universities, the anti-war movement, and unionization of museum workers. As Sam Cooke sang, "A change is gonna come." We saw people from the various movements flooding the streets—marching, protesting, and demanding new solutions. Whatever a grad student like me might think of the evolving trajectory of art history, we saw the protesters from all those movements on the streets. Today we would call them activists.

There had been street protests since the 1930s organized by left-wing groups, including the Communist Party. There were also Ban the Bomb protests during the 1950s. But this time differed because of the confluence of the reformist issues cited above. A few of these groups agitated and leafleted with the goal to end the economic system of capitalism, but I think most activists called themselves liberals.

My generation wanted to part of this paradigm shift. The counterculture of drugs, free love, Beatles music, and Bohemianism was a vital force. It helped to create a more relaxed style of living that challenged the buttoned-up style of 1950s Cold War company men. Counterculture folks began to realize the destructive power of the state and its media to manipulate consent. They embraced writers such as philosopher Marshall McLuhan and his books *Understanding Media, The Extensions of Man* (1964) and *The Medium is the Massage* (1967). His paradigm-shifting collection of insights was powerful, but I never became a McLuhan acolyte. Like other young mothers living in urban America, I participated as best I could—sometimes in leadership, but more often as a support soldier in the background.

The counterculture was pushing back against the conforming sensibilities of the 1950s Cold War. Allen Ginsburg, Jack Kerouac, and other Beats in New York and San Francisco responded to the lethal absurdity of world politics. They wrote poetry that spoke to a new generation of youth who felt no need or obligation to conform to stultifying and repressive social norms and dictates.

The Hippies inherited that outlook in the 1960s—many following their guru, Timothy Leary, the Harvard Professor who popularized LSD and who famously advocated "Turn on, tune in, drop out." Whereas the Hippies were somewhat passive—smoking joints and retreating to communes—the later anarchistic Yippies were all over the place as street militants—drawing attention to serious issues through their own antics.

Fred and I were faithful readers of the *New York Times*. Like other young New Yorkers we wanted to be part of the scene, and were savvy about avant-garde art happenings. Even with our strong work ethic we became quasi-hippies.

One of Fred's prospective authors, New York University professor Richard Schnechter, ran a performance workshop in the Village focused on immersive theater. His group previewed Schnechter's *Dionysus in '69* at New York's Performance Garage in July 1968. Fred and I were invited. At one point in the performance, the actors plucked me out of the audience to participate in the actors' bacchanal, which consisted of rolling on the floor along with a dozen or so other audience members—seeing, touching, and smelling each other. To me it was sensuous, not sexual. The idea was that audience and actors would merge into one performance organism/orgasm.

We had tickets to the famous 1969 Woodstock festival and had borrowed a car to drive there. But weather reports of rain and mud gave us second thoughts. We were reluctant to leave our kids at home with neighbors, and even more reluctant to take them with us. So, we bailed out, loaned our borrowed car to another couple, and babysat their kids while they went. My sister Gail and her boyfriend rode to Woodstock on a motorcycle and had no problems with the mud. Sorry I missed the event.

Other memories recall how our heads were turning toward the counterculture. We visited our friends in San Francisco and went to concerts at Fillmore West. We tacked to our walls posters of Lenny Bruce, The Jefferson Airplane, and Big Brother and the Holding Company. My sister Gail, who went to Cuba to help harvest the sugar cane, gave me Cuban posters, including one of Che Guevara.

Fred and I had friends who liked to go dancing with us at nightclub dives that used strobe lights. At one small club, Fred spotted Timothy Leary at a nearby table and said, "Go ask him to dance." So, I did. Leary's version of dancing, however, was to sway from side to side, face blank, no affect, no small talk. But at least I could now brag I had danced with Timothy Leary.

In the art world, I had become friends with a sand box mom, artist Bici Hendricks. Bici was part oft the Fluxus movement, an international quasi-anarchist group of 1960s artists that rejected establishment practices. When she and her husband Geoffrey broke up, they had a Fluxus divorce. This entailed inviting their friends to their home, including Fred and me, luminaries Yoko Ono and John Lennon, and other artists. With a large whirling chainsaw they put on a performance, cutting in half all the furniture in their apartment. Plus serving wine, of course.

Meanwhile, the urgency of the Civil Rights movement—focused on racism, segregation, and voting rights—came to us through TV. The movement had already gained momentum with the 1955-56 bus boycott in Montgomery, Alabama, under the leadership of Dr. Martin Luther King, Jr. and the Rev. Ralph Abernathy. In May 1961, James Farmer of CORE (Congress of Racial Equality) began to reach out to civic leaders to organize an integrated group of antiracists known as the Freedom Riders. They entered segregated restaurants as a group and demanded service. They also boarded segregated interstate busses. The racist reaction against them proved violent: smashed glass, broken bones, blood, and yes, even death.

When A. Phillip Randolph, head of the Brotherhood of Sleeping Car Porters, Bayard Rustin, civil rights leader, and others organized the September 1963 March on Washington, Martin Luther King delivered his famous *I Have a Dream* speech. Although Fred and I did not participate, I always felt connected to the march because we babysat two toddlers for neighbors who did attend. It was another event I wish I had witnessed. But even babysitting can contribute to a cause.

Other groups and figures, including the Black Panther Party, SNCC (Student Nonviolent Coordinating Committee), and Malcolm X (both before and after he broke with Louis Farrakhan of the Nation of Islam) were more politically radical. These leaders urged students and citizens to join them in moving beyond just carrying placards in street demonstrations.

During these early 1960s, second-wave feminism came to the fore, and modern medicine contributed to the changes by developing the birth control pill. By the mid- 1960s the pill was widely available to prevent conception and, thus, unwanted births. This removed worries that had plagued women for decades. They formed consciousness-raising groups and organized marches for women's rights. Women reconceived themselves as potential leaders in the civic and political worlds, the professions, and in the arts.

The National Organization for Women (NOW) formed at this time. My feminist friends and I were focused on our own communities and our childcare responsibilities. We all rejoiced when the Supreme Court gave us the Roe vs. Wade ruling in January 1973, finally allowing women the right to have control over their own bodies and their own family planning.

The main focus for both Fred and me during the 1960s was joining the anti-war movement. Too many young men were being drafted and dying in Viet Nam, the citizenry of a far-away country was being massacred, and money that could be put into social programs in the US was being diverted to the military machine.

As the war killings intensified, Fred and I joined with friends on November 15, 1969, to drive down to the massive Anti-War Demonstration in Washington, D.C. The day was freezing cold, but being a part of a community of protestors was exhilarating. Participants came from a broad spectrum of political views: anti-draft advocates, pacifists, liberals, socialists, communists, New Left radicals, anarchists, and religious groups. At many of the big marches we witnessed small groups of people supportive of US foreign policy who heckled the marchers, but they were far unnumbered.

As a graduate student from 1965-1972, I was limited in my active participation and often on the sidelines because of child-caring responsibilities and juggling babysitters. I also needed to attend classes, do research in libraries, and write seminar papers. But I still wanted to focus on activism as much as possible. In those days, I did not think much about theories for or against Capitalism, Marxism, etc. I did not belong to a specific group, but felt it my duty to get my body in motion to join with other protesters for good causes.

In grad school I was naturally drawn to the student movement that erupted across the country. I knew that the Free Speech Movement was launched at the University of California Berkeley campus during the 1964-65 academic year by students demanding a liberalization of campus rules, the right to free speech, changes in the curriculum, and the hiring of young faculty to teach subjects ignored by the University.

In April 1968, Columbia University witnessed the storming of the administrative offices by angry students. Students wanted reforms in the curriculum and the curtailment of university real estate purchases as Columbia attempted to gobble up the adjacent working-class neighborhoods. Students also supported unionization among cafeteria workers and cleaning staff.

I began to rethink *New York Times* liberalism after reading the newspaper's coverage of hundreds of students protesting at Columbia. The *Times* trivialized student complaints and focused on property damage. A few weeks later, Columbia art history graduates organized a forum, "Wither Art History." I went, eager to join the activists who were raising issues in my own field.

When four protesters in Ohio were killed by National Guardsmen at Kent State University on May 4, 1970, fellow grad students at IFA insisted on a moratorium. I attended a large evening meeting of grad students and faculty to reach a consensus as to the actions IFA should take for making visible our condemnation of the massacre. Another issue was deciding whether IFA students should continue accepting fellowships funded by such industry giants as Krupp, which in the 1930s had funded the Nazis. One student from New Zealand renounced his Krupp fellowship, and no one ever saw him again.

Faculty stood in solidarity with students. Professor Colin Eisler revealed to the group that for some time he had counseled conscientious objectors. Students proposed and got the go-ahead to affix a black funeral drape outside of Duke Mansion, the Fifth Avenue building that housed the Institute. To us the black crepe would symbolize both mourning and protest.

I participated in another small select meeting of student leaders and faculty to review criticisms we students had about the curriculum. It was held in a seminar room with a long table covered with a tablecloth and caterers serving tea and petit fours. I said to myself, *How can one hammer one's fist on the table when there is a tablecloth and petit fours?* Imagine the mess of little French pastries bouncing around. I believe the faculty took a new, more respectful view of students. The reforms we had in mind, which were mild to begin with, came to fruition. Eventually.

We grad students now knew each other in ways we had not before. Those of us at IFA linked up with the grad students at Columbia University, plus some New York museum curators to form the New Art Association (the NAA). We met and issued a newsletter.

I hosted one of the big organizing meetings in my Riverside Drive apartment. The people involved included Carol Duncan and Alan Wallach, who were associated with Columbia; Stephen Pepper from Johns Hopkins; Eunice Lipton and myself from the Institute; John Walsh, then a curator at the Metropolitan Museum; and Edward Fry, a curator from the Guggenheim Museum then involved in the controversial Hans Haacke's show. The NAA later had a large conference in Buffalo.

One of the NAA's actions included a demonstration that I attended on April 3, 1971 on the inside ramp of the Guggenheim to protest the director's cancelling of the Hans Haacke show. The reason? A group of the artist's works—

large photostats of the facades of rental buildings, and data highlighting addresses, ownership, and mortgages—referred to the real estate holdings of slum landlords and inferred their complicity with politicians and major financiers. The Rockefellers, who held the mortgages for some of the most notorious slum landlords, were a particular target. It was a spirited protest as we chanted and shouted across the circular atrium at the highest ramp.

Unionization was in the air by the late 1960s. The Professional and Staff Association at the Museum of Modern Art (PASTA/MOMA) was formed in 1969 and recognized as a union two years later when it held its first strike. In 1973 many of us at the Whitney identified in solidarity with the MoMA workers, as we were then protesting the Whitney's new decision to implement admission fees. We argued that museums should be free, especially free for artists. Another Whitney staffer named Helen Ferrulli and I drew up a petition addressed to the director, John Baur, to protest the new admissions policy. Most staff members signed. When the PASTA/MOMA went on strike in 1973, we joined with them on their picket line.

We talked among ourselves at the Whitney about forming our own union. Curator Marcia Tucker was opposed to any staff union that did not include the director! But I could understand. She was close to some of the trustees at the time—people who later helped her found the New Museum.

A Whitney union did not immediately happen, but we did form the Museum Workers Association, which included MoMA and Whitney staff, as well as a trickle of staffers from other museums. We held one large city-wide meeting, which Hans Haacke videotaped.

In 1974, I moved on to teaching, but managed to secure my affiliation with the Whitney as Adjunct Curator. The Whitney staff did eventually unionize without the curators, who were considered supervisors. Even though there have been successful union drives in the last fifty years, museums are still resistant to unionization.

The fight to organize never ends.

7

Becoming a Feminist, 1968-72

My embrace of feminism came in the late 1960s—a time of social and political ferment. I was ready.

In 1949, Simone de Beauvoir published *Le Deuxieme Sex*. Four years later, it appeared in English as *The Second Sex*. While this book or other studies about women's inequality written before the 1960s did not show up on my radar, I had been living and thinking about that inequality since the 1950s.

Two of the most influential books that jolted me toward feminism when I was a senior in college were Virginia Wolfe's *A Room of One's Own* (1929) and Henrik Ibsen's play, *A Doll's House* (1879). The Doll's House brought tears to my eyes as I realized how universal was the heroine's situation.

Men in the 1950s were considered to be the sole bread winners and heads of the family. Check out Turner Classic Movies to see the ways period movies reinforced the ideology that the home was the "natural" place for women. She could achieve fulfillment only through raising children, creating a nice home, being a loving wife, and sometimes—like Lucile Ball—showing spunk.

However, there were sexist humiliations and shames we women had to endure without speaking out. No one would believe us, and our trauma would only increase when parents, husbands, and the police rejected our statements.

My own experiences are probably much like others. When five-years old I was molested by a group of neighborhood boys. They called it "playing doctor." I never told my mother until I was 12-years-old, and then I wept and wept.

In my early 20s living in New York, an ambitious lawyer/politician I had met at a political meeting tried to rape me. We had gone to his apartment to return some folding chairs. It was a surprise attack, and I resisted. So, the rape was, one might say, a botched one. Able to free myself, I ran out of his apartment. I took my soiled little black dress to the cleaners, hung it in my closet, and some time later threw it away. I never told anyone until a few years ago during a *"Me, Too"* conversation with a woman friend.

But progress was on its way. The early 1960s began to present different opportunities for women. The impact of the birth control pill should not be underestimated. For the first time a woman could be in control of her own health. She could take a pill, and no one would know. She could guarantee that sexual play would not be interrupted by fumbling with contraceptives. She felt free, as men had always been (or so she thought).

One does not want to dismiss the idea that women's relaxed inhibitions were not also due to the social climate, where mind-altering drugs (LSD, marijuana) were easily available. However, one did not have to take drugs to witness and emulate young uninhibited women accepting the culture of protest and rejecting what they saw as their parents' uptight values. This social climate urged many of us toward an embrace of greater sexual freedom.

American women in the 1960s were ready for another book: Betty Friedan's *The Feminine Mystique,* published in 1963 and credited with launching the "second wave of feminism," the first movement being the late 19th- and early 20th-century drive for women's voting rights. A great number of articles, books, and anthologies soon appeared to raise issues about the validity of traditionally assumed gender differences, patriarchy, and the opportunities for women in political life, civic life, the professions, business, education, and sports.

My feminist friends and I were not much interested in Gloria Steinem, who co-founded *Ms.* magazine in 1972. Our problems were local, with husbands, bosses, and babies to tend to. What really changed us were the consciousness raising (CR) sessions happening across America, where groups of women met together weekly to share their thoughts and experiences about sexual harassment, gender restrictions and lack of opportunities for working women and at-home moms.

Some artists say that consciousness raising among artists started in a parlor in California. Wherever it started, for me it began in the lobby of my Riverside Drive apartment in 1970, when a neighbor suggested that women in the building get together to air our experiences as women. She had been active in the Free Speech movement at Berkeley and knew how to organize.

She gathered about twelve of us to start up a CR session. Each week we chose a different apartment, sat in a circle and each spoke for about five minutes about her own situation—with males in the workplace or with husbands who expected adherence to traditional gender roles, and with changing attitudes regarding sex. We soon realized how common our stories were, and that they were not unique to one person.

One of the women in our CR group talked about her job at an advertising agency. At one office planning session the ad men came up with the idea: "Let's do a 2CK." The other men laughed, and my friend, who had no idea what they were talking about, fell silent but went along with the men. She soon discovered that "2CK" is short for "two cunts in a kitchen." To the men, that was a joke, but ads with 2CK sold refrigerators.

Although I admired the women in our building's CR sessions, after about a year, the meetings devolved into a coffee klatch with more gossip than substance.

I looked around for another CR group—one that would include women in the art world. Marcia Tucker, then a Whitney curator, called a meeting to advocate for and bring new people into CR. I attended along with so many others that some of us decided to form our own smaller CR group. Individuals in this group were artists, curators, museum staff, and a dancer. The artists included Barbara Zucker, Toba Tucker, Susan Williams, and Hermine Fried.

With the encouragement of our consciousness-raising group, Zucker and Williams founded the first independent, all-women, artist-run cooperative art gallery, renting street-front space at 97 Wooster in SoHo. The group of women artists called themselves A.I.R. (presumably the acronym for "Artists in Residence"). As part of a collective, members spent time as gallery attendants, bookkeepers, and curators. They organized solo and group shows for their own members. In the early years, my name graced their masthead. SoHo 20, another similar artists-run collective, formed somewhat later, and included my soon-to-be friends Sylvia Sleigh and May Stevens.

When Linda Nochlin published *Why Have There Been No Great Women Artists?* in the January 1971 issue of *Art News* there was a firestorm. Nochlin, a well-established and innovative professor of art history at Vassar, was about to publish a major book, *Realism,* and had also organized exhibitions of American realist paintings for Vasser's art gallery. A great stir occurred in the art world, including curators, academics, and artists. She began her essay:

While the recent upsurge of feminist activity in this country has indeed been a liberating one, its force has been chiefly emotional—personal, psychological and subjective—centered, like the other radical movements to which it is related, on the present and its immediate needs, rather than on historical analysis of the basic intellectual issues which the feminist attack on the status quo automatically raises.

Her essay continues to elaborate on the intellectual, sociological, and cultural restrictions that historically had stifled the development of great women artists. In 1971 Nochlin was calling for a deeper and more critical analysis of culturally influential artworks that trumpeted or slyly approved of sexist ideas, misogynist attitudes, and the rewards of patriarchy. Hers was a needed clarion call.

Women in the art world—artists, curators, academic art historians—had already learned through the CR meetings the importance of coming together. Nochlin was now pointing the way that we could refocus our art and scholarship.

Shortly thereafter, the Women's Caucus for Art (WCA) within the College Art Association was launched with art historian Ann Sutherland Harris as its first president.

As a graduate student, but also a fledgling museum curator, I attended that first mass meeting at the 1972 CAA conference in San Francisco to see what was happening. I recall standing in the back of a crowded, overheated hotel ballroom and admiring Harris for speaking out on women's issues in academia. Linda Nochlin, Muriel Magenta, and others commented from the panel table. I found myself excited to be there and participating in a mass event where light bulbs were popping on in all of our heads. All of us had the common goal of redressing the gender inequities we found in the art studios, in museums and commercial art galleries, and in academia.

A few years later Nochlin and Harris curated the

extensive 1976 exhibition *Women Artists, 1550-1950*, which opened at the Los Angeles County Museum of Art and traveled to The Brooklyn Museum. It contained a breathtaking range of production by women artists equal to the Old Masters. Again, another eye-opener.

I became an enthusiastic feminist—not yet leaning toward Marxism. The book that gave me a greater understanding about the situation of women in the modern period was Friedrich Engels' *The Origin of the Family, Private Property, and the State* (1884). His message: capitalists need a working class and especially lower paid working-class women to create generous margins of profit to sustain their industries and their own privileged lives.

Patriarchy (looking to the father to make all decisions) can be a powerful tool to develop and maintain the ideology that "inferior" peoples (such as uneducated women) should be grateful that a man (husbands, fathers or uncles) supports them. Or they can, if lucky, subsist on low wages, standard for the growing work force. Eventually, I came to understand that a class analysis and a gender analysis should go hand-in-hand. Hence, my growing radical feminism needed to include a class outlook.

Some people blamed feminism for the breakup of my marriage. Through participating in consciousness-raising groups I came to question the dynamics of my one-sided marriage. In some cases, husbands, work colleagues, and bosses caught on and began to accommodate themselves to new and more equitable relationships. Some women in my second group (mostly artists) learned to ignore their husbands' resistance to feminism. They took a big step by opening their own galleries, organizing their own exhibitions, and promoting their own art.

I was beginning to discover myself—as a person, as a feminist, an activist, and an intellectual. I wanted to focus on my studies and my children. Moreover, Fred was constantly picking on my perceived inadequacies and insisting that I needed to do better housekeeping. He never suggested that I get a mother's helper or that he could help do household chores. His small acts of cruelty had the effect of sabotaging my self worth. In retrospect, I am not convinced such acts were calculated. More likely, he was simply clueless.

Around 1971, Fred joined a "men's consciousness-raising group." To describe its influence on Fred is to tell a short anecdote: Fred came home late one evening from the group with an announcement.

"My men's group is going to have a potluck supper with the wives invited," he said.

"Oh, that's nice!" I replied.

"What are you going to make for the supper?" he retorted.

I rolled my eyes. When he realized the contradiction we decided to bring deli takeout to the supper.

I felt I could no longer sustain any enthusiasm for the marriage. Fred was simply not budging from his patronizing, patriarchal position. I began to be attracted to men who respected me and were interested in my opinions. If I was flirtatious, I rarely acted on such impulses. But sometimes I did. I have always believed that affairs outside of marriage are not about an infatuation with a new lover, but rather a reaction toward the spouse from whom one is already trying to distance oneself.

During this time, 1971-72, Fred did begin to recognize my changes toward our marriage. He suggested we go to a couples therapist. We made three attempts. First, we went to a therapist's office on a high floor of a Park Avenue building. The therapist was tall, blond and glamorous and looked like the 1940s film star Alexis Smith. At the end of the session, she bent over and looked me in the eye: "You will have to change."

That remark was less than helpful. The suggestion that

I should sweep my grievances under the carpet and adapt Fred's preferred "open-marriage" lifestyle was not going to happen.

A second attempt at therapy occurred when Fred took me to a weekend ashram retreat in upstate New York. That also didn't work for me, although I enjoyed sitting cross-legged and saying "Om" with the group. We tried yet a third group therapy session, located in the Village. Fred and I agreed they were sleezy charlatans. Their technique involved selecting one person or a couple in the group, bully them, and invite the other attendees to do the same. Usually, the victims broke down and cried. I suppose the technique aimed to make the rest of us feel good that we had not been targeted, and perhaps to be cathartic to the victims.

I finally suggested a trial separation, which commenced a few weeks after the Eastman Johnson opening in March 1972. The separation puzzled the children. It soon became clear that we were not going to get back together. We discussed divorce and hired a hippie lawyer to draw up the papers.

Neither of us had any taste for an acrimonious divorce. We had no property except furniture, rugs, kitchen equipment, and phonograph records—so we set aside funds for Fred to purchase furnishings for his own apartment. The only stressful moment came when we divided our record collection. Who would get Bob Dylan? Joan Baez? Christina and Brad were to live with me with visits to Fred on weekends. He gave me child support money and some modest alimony until I had a full-time job at the end of 1972. We wanted to lessen the stress that our children were experiencing. The optics dictated that the parting be amicable and cordial.

Feminism, however, had not prepared me for coping with living without a man. Lonely that early summer of 1972, I focused on my children. I brought them on a trip to California. We went to Disneyland and museums in LA, then drove up Highway 101, stopping off to see the William Randolf Hearst mansion. We ended our trip in Muir Beach, where we visited with my friend Martha, who was then an active member of the Zen Center.

Back in New York, the artist Jane Kaufman took me to Max's Kansas City (a hangout for the Andy Warhol crowd) to cheer me up. But I was uncomfortable with the idea of sitting at bars and picking up men. The drug scene also made me uneasy.

However, I did have a couple of boyfriends in 1973. One was a married neighbor, but he decided he wanted to try to make his marriage work. I was supportive of that. Next came one of my political friends. But he turned out to be crazy (possessive, paranoid) and I finessed a breakup. Finally, I had an art historian boyfriend whose intellect I admired, but he was too tethered to his ex-wife to commit to a relationship. I considered giving up on men: too many problems. I felt they would cork me up in a bottle. I needed to explore my evolving identity.

In the early summer of 1974, Fred's mother told her family she had cancer. Mildred had discovered a lump in her breast years before but chose not to seek medical help. She only told her chiropractor. She wanted to die after having lived a life in genteel poverty in East Orange, New Jersey. To her family, the news came as a shock. When she began to fail rapidly, Fred took her from her home to a hospital in the Bronx.

I visited her. She seemed happy to see me, but I became distressed by her total lack of will to live. Her puréed lunch came, and I attempted to feed her with a spoon. She spat it out, murmuring, "No, I don't want it." She leaned back on her pillow and faintly whispered, "Take me, Jesus." She dozed off to sleep, and I left.

On the subway from the Bronx down to my stop at West 103rd street, I saw two teenagers sitting and affectionately patting, hugging, and kissing. That perked up my spirits. I contrasted the dying woman who welcomed death, with these teenagers full of life and promise for a future. I envied them.

Then came a marvelous moment. One of the subway riders standing close to my seat recognized me as having been on the same jury panel with him a year or so earlier. He stood there hanging onto a strap with a friend. The friend was so handsome, I could not take my eyes off him. We were instantly attracted to each other. We chatted. I gave him my phone number. A day or so later, he called me suggesting that we get together for a date. I welcomed the call and what seemed to me like a promising romantic relationship but felt it only fair to tell him that I had two children. He paused and said that perhaps it made sense for us not to start a relationship. I agreed. We hung up. I have always wondered what might have been. But I knew then that men were still attractive to me.

8

Becoming a Radical, 1972

There's a difference between activism and radicalism. During the 1960s, people participating in marches, demonstrating outside city halls, and sitting in government offices called themselves protesters. Today we call them activists.

I felt that many of the the sixties activists were not looking for the root causes—the word from which radical comes. I did not see them develop a radical anti-capitalist theory of how society could be re-organized. They were not thinking through the issues at a deeper level. Instead those activists wanted immediate action. When the government or a corporation offered small concessions, many of these activists stopped protesting.

During the 1930s, the Left advanced Marxist, socialist, and communist ideas that critiqued capitalism and that warned against fascism in the US and abroad. A great number of the radicals were members of the Communist Party USA. Many left the Party during the anti-communist repressions—job firings in the late 1940s and 1950s, Cold War witch hunts, and incarcerations.

By the early 1960s, a younger generation of mostly college educated women and men defined themselves as the New Left. Often they were reformers in friendly opposition to the Old Left which had always advocated class struggle as primary. The New Left protesters became *activists,* but generally not *radicals* committed to the capitalist critiques written by Karl Marx, Frederick Engels, Vladimir Lenin, Mao Tse Tung, and others.

As an art historian, I first turned to the revisionist history writings of the tenured radicals at universities who had rejected the great men theory of history. Instead, they proposed a new "bottom up" history featuring the struggles of the working classes. These young historians, many of them Marxists, also challenged the old Dixie historiography and emphasized the agency of enslaved persons, their victories, and their Black and white abolitionist supporters. Meanwhile, art world people had their own work-related protest movements, such as unionization and structural reforms. For them we needed reform, not revolution.

During the late 1960s and 1970s I witnessed new groups springing up with artists in the leadership, such as the War Resisters League and Artists and Writers Protest Against the War in Vietnam. During Angry Arts Week in 1967, protesting artists showed anti-war artworks at New York University. More artist demonstrations appeared on the West Coast. Because artists were creative people working in their studios and removed from establishment jobs, many had the freedom to probe more deeply the inequities and injustices of capitalism and the military-industrial complex. And many did.

In step with the times, activist organizations grew beyond anti-war issues of the 1970s to embrace artist's issues, women's issues, and racial disparities in the arts. The Art Workers Coalition, Guerrilla Art Action Groups, Artists Meeting for Cultural Change, the New Art Association, the Black Emergency Cultural Coalition, and the Guerrilla Girls organized sit-ins, protest marches, and manifestoes. Their goals were: hire more women and people of color as staff in museums, mount exhibitions of women and underrepresented people, provide studio space for artists, and persuade museums and galleries to buy their work.

Another radicalizing influence was learning about the Black Panther Party, which I saw and heard up close.

In the fall of 1970, my husband Fred was called to jury duty in New York. Twenty-one members of the radical and community-oriented Panthers had been indicted on conspiracy charges for having planned in 1969 to blow up police precincts, in addition to other "acts allegedly committed in furtherance of the conspiracy" and the "crimes of attempted murder." However, many months passed before the case was brought to trial. In the meantime, the number of defendants dropped to thirteen.

Fred had a demanding job as an editor at McGraw-Hill, but was intrigued by being on a jury deciding the fate of the New York Black Panther Party. Two weeks before the trial hit the news and before we knew Fred would be involved, we both had gone to a fundraiser for the Panthers at the large apartment of poet Adrienne Rich and her economics professor husband Alfred Conrad on Central Park West.

Arriving at the courtroom dressed in a Brooks Brothers suit, Fred carefully evaded questions from the Panthers counsel or the district attorney as to whether he had had any dealings with the Panthers. Nor did he volunteer such information. He passed the *voir dire*, became Juror Number Five, and braced himself for a long-term commitment of time.

The trial lasted about eight months. At the end he remained the only juror with a full-time job. He did that by going to his office early in the morning, leaving at 10 a.m. for the trial to begin, then leaving the court at 4 p.m. to return to his office. The Court did not convene on Fridays. The official reason was because the Panthers were Muslims, but one assumes they needed a day off for defense lawyers to regroup and district attorneys to collect more "evidence."

A few days after Fred's *voir dire* questioning, when walking home I saw a tall man on the sidewalk in front of our apartment building aiming his camera at our apartment. As I drew near to confront him, he abruptly turned and walked down the street towards Riverside Park. Shaken, I went up to our apartment, scooped up the one scrabbly marijuana plant we had in the bathroom window, and took it to a neighbor for safe keeping. The possibility that the stranger was an informer seemed very real. In those days when we picked up the telephone, we would hear—instead of a buzz—a strange silence and then a click. We speculated that all our phones were being tapped. Even in our *New York Times* liberal circles, we always joked about the FBI's bungling wiretapping.

More than anything, the Panther trial radicalized me to a new understanding of the realities of police informers, agents provocateurs, the court system, and to the good sense of the jury citizenry. Since my children were in school, I found time to attend many of the morning sessions, after officials gave a thorough search of my handbags. This time would normally have been my library research time. Needless to say, I justified my immersion as "experiential" research.

One day at the trial I learned that the New York chapter of the Panthers had been organized by three men—two of whom were undercover agents. One of these agents, Gene Roberts, frequently took the stand. He would say things like, "And that day we decided to 'off' the pigs." (The Panthers always referred to police as pigs.) I thought: *What do you mean? You are one of the pigs!*

I later learned that Roberts, who subsequently had managed to infiltrate the inner circle of Malcolm X to become Malcolm's bodyguard, was the one who gave mouth-to-mouth resuscitation to Malcolm when the latter was mortally shot at the Audubon Ballroom on February 21, 1965.

As the Panthers grew in New York, there would be more undercover agents infiltrating their organization. Defense lawyers argued that these agents—acting as provocateurs—supplied the guns and explosives to the Panthers.

Unlike the flamboyant attorney William Kunstler, who had recently defended the Chicago Seven, the Panthers lead counsel was Gerald Lefcourt, who had the most nimble mind, and who patiently argued to discredit the testimony of informers. I recall him saying, "You have to understand that informers are paid to find something, and they will report on those findings that they themselves have manufactured." That's the way informers keep their jobs.

Margo Adler, one of the news reporters at radio station WBAI, spent 20-30 minutes each evening reprising the trial, while Fred gave me other details. But in respect to the court, Fred never revealed to me whether he had sympathy for the Panthers, and I did not press him. However, the evening before the jury was sequestered, we took a walk along the Riverside Park sidewalk, and I blurted out my belief that the Panthers were absolutely not guilty. Fred took my remarks "under advisement."

Before the jury went into deliberations, Judge John M. Murtagh leaned down to charge the jury. He reminded them that the Panthers were being charged with conspiracy. "And what does conspiracy mean? It means 'co-spire,'—'to breathe together.'" The implication is that anyone within hearing distance of a proposal to commit a crime, is as guilty as those who might carry out the actual crime.

When they convened on May 13, 1971, everyone anticipated that the jury would take days to deliberate. They returned to the courtroom after 90 minutes. The foreman read the verdicts: Not guilty ... not guilty ... not guilty ... He continued through the entire 150-plus charges. Fred told me that when courtroom attendees realized that *all* charges would be rendered not guilty, the Panthers and their friends began dancing in the aisles. When the final verdict was read and the court adjourned, Fred telephoned me to ask whether I could join them all—Panthers, defense lawyers, and jurors—for a celebration. Alas, being home alone with two young children prevented my participation.

During the many marches, people representing various political groups—such as the Socialist Workers Party (SWP), Revolutionary Communist Party (RCP), and the Progressive Labor Party (PLP)—would be buzzing around leafletting, selling their newspapers, and engaging other protesters in talk. Curious about such groups and their analyses of the current state of politics, I developed a friendship with my neighbor Jake, a building contractor who lived across the hall from us on Riverside Drive. I knew Jake was politically engaged. When Fred and I moved to a two-bedroom apartment one block away in the fall of 1971, we hired Jake to divide our second bedroom into two spaces for our Christina and Brad. In one of our had many long conversations about politics, Jake introduced me to the Progressive Labor Party.

I joined a reading group and read not only PLP literature, but also basic works by Karl Marx, Frederik Engels, Vladimir Lenin, and 20th-century Marxists. The big issues discussed were racism, sexism, poverty, inequality, immigration, uprisings around the world, protests in the U.S. and the failure of capitalism to improve the lives of the working classes. PLP deplored terrorism as a tactic to bring about change. Still involved with my second woman's consciousness raising group (1971-72), I also read feminist writers who analyzed all aspects of patriarchy and proposed new rights for women. The theories dovetailed.

Jake drew me into political practice. In April 1972, he drove me and my sister to one of the last big Students for a Democratic Society (SDS) conventions held at Harvard. SDS was by then still allied with PLP. The convention was held in a huge auditorium, where I recall Harvard philosophy professor Hilary Putnam, who had been connected to PLP for years, giving a rousing speech at the last plenary session.

For PLP's May Day 1972 celebration (about six weeks after the opening of the Eastman Johnson exhibition), Jake persuaded me to help build a float for the PLP Fight for Communism march in Washington, DC. I attended, riding in the cab of the rental truck pulling the float.

By early September, Jake proposed that he and I join the 1972 reelection campaign of Sidney Von Luther, a progressive New York State representative from Harlem. Sidney had previously led the union fight to raise the wages of cafeteria workers at Columbia University. Also, in 1972, protests erupted in the public schools over the gross inadequacies of New York City public education. Jake reasoned that Sidney could forge a connection between Black and white parents in the area. His presence at meetings about the schools would draw both groups. I jumped in, even though I had to focus on finishing my dissertation. Jake's exciting proposal was an opportunity to experience working for a good cause.

The Von Luther campaign needed a treasurer. I volunteered. I raised all of $26 for the campaign—collected in contributions of $1 to $5 at an open house campaign party we had in one of the projects—the only fundraising event we had. Why only one? Because, unfortunately, Sidney declined to mount a vigorous campaign. He had no real rival, and he was lazy. He typically got out of bed in the early afternoon, even though we often scheduled meetings for him in mornings.

Other contradictions we had to deal with: Sidney proudly sent his own son to private school, but we hoped he could still argue vigorously for more aid for public schools. Not surprisingly, he got reelected by a landslide because the Harlem machine backed him. He didn't really need us, but we needed him to consolidate an organization that united Black and white parents. That multi-racial organization lasted for years.

Before the November election, Basil Patterson, borough president of Manhattan, held a large fundraising party in his swank Harlem apartment for Walter Mondale, the presidential contender running against the incumbent Richard Nixon. Almost giddy about being invited to the party as Van Luther's staff member, I enjoyed talking with Harlem's elite.

The food at the party was delicious and the liquor flowed. At one point Patterson clinked a glass to pause the party. He announced: "Now I would like you all to write $25 checks [$190 in 2025] for Walter Mondale." Or maybe it was $50. Even Sidney was appalled. He leaned over and whispered to me, "Each one of these people could write checks for thousands of dollars." It was a party for the optics—that Mondale had the "support" of Harlem. The Nixon campaign had already made inroads by making promises to Harlem that the politicians did not want to jeopardize. My optimism tanked that the Democratic Party could make a better world.

But there's more: Sometime later that fall, a bomb destroyed Mondale's Harlem headquarters. I saw the damage myself. The bomb made a hole in the middle of the block. I could find nothing in the *New York Times* about it. Curious, I hurried over to the Democratic Party Headquarters in Harlem and asked if they were going to issue a press release on the bombing. The man who seemed to be in charge nodded vaguely and said "not yet." There never was a press release. Harlemites knew what was going on, but not the rest of New Yorkers. Yes, Nixon had Harlem sewn up. And as we know, he won in November.

&

The radical practice, I was doing. And then there is theory—developed from reading, discussion, and thinking through issues to discover patterns.

In 1973 I joined a reading group of five women art historians—two finishing their dissertations at Columbia (Deborah Gardner and Barbara Braun)—and three of us (Josephine Gear, Julie Schimmel and myself) finishing or just having finished dissertations at NYU's Institute of Fine Arts. We began by reading cultural and feminist history and soon gravitated to political writings. Our group lasted until the summer of 1975, when we finally finished reading Volume I of Marx's *Capital.* Marx's theory of surplus value explained so much to me about why worker exploitation is critical to the advancement of capitalism. Not surprisingly, Marx's theory is rejected by tenured academics in the field of economics. In any event, I finally came to an understanding of the ways theory and practice interacted.

Regarding Marxism, the bugaboo for both Republican and Democratic politicians, this philosophy has three different applications. First, Marxism is a *theory*—the theory that the working classes have been the engine of history and economic development. Worker and slave revolts have changed the historical landscape.

Second, Marxism uses a *method* of historical and dialectical materialism— analyzing history based first on the material conditions of a given epoch at a given place and the subsequent ideas that arise from those material conditions. The method entails studying contradictions between opposing classes at a moment in history. For example, why is there vast poverty alongside a small group with extreme affluence?

Third, Marxism is a *call to action*: "Workers of the world unite. You have nothing to lose but your chains." In our own day these actions would mean working for better education for the working classes, decent housing, nutritious food, protection of immigrants, and job opportunities. In short, being not only a vocal critic of capitalism, but uniting with others to achieve these goals.

But the current governing powers view Marxism only in its third application. They see Marxism as a dangerous threat to liberal capitalism and are willing to censor, disappear, and even murder dissenters. Moreover, they point to a history of Marxist values being corrupted, as happened in the Soviet Union and China. This means radicals have even more work to do.

9

Four Whitney Exhibitions, 1972-74

During my last three years at the Institute of Fine Arts (from 1970-1972), I turned to the final tasks of a doctoral student: pass the comprehensive exams (which in my case focused on European and American art from 1660 to the present), research and write a prospectus, have that prospectus approved, finish my dissertation and defend it before a select committee of professors.

Although my IFA courses exclusively focused on 19th-century and modern European art (along with contemporary American art), I decided to become an Americanist: one who studies American art and its history. I was intrigued with my own culture and how American history has been written. Having lived in Europe and America, I decided it was time to probe the origins of my mother country and their continued relevance to the issues besetting the USA in the early 1970s. I would embrace the community of Americanists—no matter my disagreements with them—to help me become aware of my own emerging identity.

But there were also practical concerns. I would not have to master a foreign language and would not need to spend years abroad with children in tow, since most research archives would be in this country.

As I searched for a fresh dissertation topic in the field of 19th-century American art, I kept circling back to Eastman Johnson (1824-1906). Although Winslow Homer, Thomas

Eakins, Mary Cassatt, and John Singer Sargent were well known, hardly anyone knew of Johnson, the most celebrated genre painter of the Civil War era. Johnson's work forged a link between the generations of the 1830s-1850s (William Sydney Mount and Lily Martin Spencer) and the realism and impressionism of the 1870s-1890s (Eakins, Cassatt and Sargent). His depictions of women were notable and modern—being one of the very few American 19th-century male artists who showed women reading newspapers. Like many European artists in the 1870s, he also attempted to capture the interior lives of women lost in thought, enjoying quiet moments of reflection looking out windows, dressing themselves, and feeding their pets.

Moreover, I felt he handled the subject of Black Americans with a compassion unlike the other artists who relied on the stereotypes of watermelon-eating boys and grinning mammies. Although I considered *Negro Life at the South* (1859) as rife with stereotypes and a bit sentimental, my dissertation would give the paintings the needed analyses of its social context and message. Johnson had also painted three versions of *A Ride for Liberty—The Fugitive Slaves* (1862), an image depicting the agency of Black people in freeing themselves. Johnson's motivations needed to be unraveled, as did the surrounding culture and contemporary commentary in period newspapers.

Like my mentor Leo Steinberg, I determined that my approach would not only deal with style, but also be a contextual history of Johnson and his cultural surrounds. As evidence I would include contemporary readings of the paintings that reflected or rejected the art world ethos of Johnson's time. Although not yet influenced by Marxist texts and ideas, my feminism and anti-racism made me pay attention to Johnson's depiction of women and Black people. But my basic approach was consolidating in the 1970s: to see and write about the blending of subject matter/

iconography, style, context, and the relevance of our findings to our current era.

I began my research about the time the Metropolitan Museum was celebrating its 100th anniversary with an expansive exhibition of American Art, *19th- Century America: Paintings and Sculpture.* The exhibition included many of the best paintings by Johnson, a founding trustee of the Metropolitan Museum of Art. I went to the opening in 1970 and chatted with fellow students and faculty. IFA Professor Horst Janson, the influential author of a major and widely used history of art textbook, turned to me when the dinner bell rang, held out his arm and said, "Shall we dine?" That confirmed my hunch that I had faculty approval, and that the study of American art had arrived. Johnson and I were ready.

About a year into my research, I went to see John I. H. Baur, director of the Whitney Museum of American Art, and pitched the idea of the museum mounting an Eastman Johnson retrospective. He enthusiastically embraced the proposal, handed me a contract, and provided funds to travel across the country to museums and private collectors with Johnson holdings. I also asked Baur, who had an MA degree from Yale, to be my second reader for the dissertation, and he agreed.

I was ready for the challenge of curating my own exhibition for a major museum.

&

Leaning on my 1960s training at the Museum of Modern Art (MoMA), I recorded information about each artwork on 5 x 8 inch cards modeled on MoMA's accession cards—even including a small recognition photo (cut out of a photo proof sheet) pasted on the upper right of the card. I also relied on the scholarship of John I. H. Baur, who had organized the first large Johnson retrospective for the Brooklyn Museum in 1940. Baur's catalogue contained a checklist of about 472 drawings and paintings. With the exhibition on the calendar and my status as a guest curator, I would now have easier access to private collectors, galleries, and public museums. I advertised my search for Johnson's works in the *New York Times*, and collectors began to contact me.

My husband Fred drove me, along with Christina and Brad, to collectors all along the East Coast where most of the Johnson paintings were. My Whitney travel budget paid for the gasoline and lodgings. John Wilmerding, then teaching at Dartmouth, and William Gerdts, then working at Coe Kerr Gallery, cheered me on. My Institute of Fine Arts (IFA) advisor Robert Goldwater read the final draft of my 40-page manuscript. So did Baur of course, as well as the Metropolitan Museum curator John Walsh, one of our neighbors on the Upper West Side. The major New York City gallerists, especially Gerdts and Ira Spanierman, were supportive. It truly takes a village to produce a major exhibition.

My responsibilities included designing and installing the exhibition on the 3rd floor of the Breuer building on Madison Avenue. I enjoyed the challenge of hanging paintings that would work as pairs or as part of an ensemble on a particular theme, or would provide sightlines to associative paintings hanging in adjoining rooms. Like my former MoMA boss Bill Lieberman, I instructed the art handlers to hang some of the paintings low, used color for the walls (forest green, dark red, and a light beige color), and included standing potted plants. I placed text labels (at that time not common for exhibitions) throughout the galleries. The installation could not have been more perfect.

Alcoa stepped in to sponsor of the exhibition, *Eastman Johnson*. This represented a new trend: corporations funding museum exhibitions—and a first for the Whitney. Alcoa also sponsored a gala dinner after the opening. Baur, who had probably never attended a corporate-sponsored opening dinner, awkwardly gave me the news that I was not invited. To Alcoa, I functioned as the hired help. So I celebrated with my friends. Today's directors understand that curators can be excellent social assets, as we curators know how to look stylish, talk to collectors and sponsors, and make them feel special as patrons of the arts.

There was nothing controversial about the themes of the exhibition. Good reviews came quickly after the March 1972 opening. To the critics, a young curator had brought before the public a 19th-century artist who did remarkable paintings and should be taken seriously. The show got similarly good reviews from critics across the country where the exhibition traveled: the Detroit Institute of Arts, the Cincinnati Art Museum, and the Milwaukee Art Center.

Following the exhibition tour, collectors began bringing alleged Johnson paintings to show me, as they previously had to John Baur. He provided me guidelines for my examinations and told me I should not charge, since I worked for the Whitney. Hence, I became the new expert on Eastman Johnson.

By early 1972, John Baur offered me the position of Associate Curator for the field of historic art. I came up with a better title, Associate Curator of 18th- and 19th-Century American Art—a mouthful, but crystal clear as to my area of expertise. Arthur Altschul, a Whitney trustee and Chair of the Committee on Historic Art, seems to have been the patron underwriting my salary.

After we had put to bed the catalogue for the Eastman Johnson exhibition, John Baur gave me a new assignment— to organize a collection of primarily 19th-century paintings from private collectors in the New York area. I now call this a propinquity exhibition—cobbled together from art owned by patrons in the neighborhood.

This was Baur's way to introduce me as the new Associate Curator. He also wanted to create a broader patron base. He said as much in his Director's statement published in the exhibition's slim brochure/checklist: "Five years ago the Committee on Historic Art was established for the purpose of helping the Whitney Museum to strengthen its collection of 18th- and 19th-century paintings and sculpture, especially through gift and bequest. It was the Committee's belief that the present exhibition would not only be an event of aesthetic value to the public, but might also help to notify collectors of our very real interest in acquiring fine examples of historic American art."

Like the Johnson show, nothing emerged as political about the Collectors' exhibition. It was simply what the title tells us. In the months before the opening I had visited about three dozen collectors—many members of Altschul's Committee on Historic Art—and they were equally enthusiastic. One rich Long Island collector even loaned her treasures. But my access to her home and collections, as the maid told me when I rang the front door, would only be through the back servant's entrance, as was usual for vendors, construction crews, etc. Many times in the 1970s I entered wealthy homes and private men's clubs through the servants' entrance. That shows the stature of curators in that era. Or perhaps only women curators?

In the end we mounted 76 paintings by 46 artists—a handsome show for the 2nd floor of the Breuer building. My only regret is that we borrowed an "Asher Brown Durand," that I later concluded was not by Durand. *Oh, well!* Often we curators will borrow a work that doesn't fit, looks funny, or is physically in worst shape than we remembered. If we could, we would return the work. But in those days, we usually didn't make a fuss, but hung the unwelcome painting in a corner and lived with it.

As to my Whitney Associate Curator position, I asked

if I could work part-time until I finished my Johnson dissertation. Baur agreed. I also had a two-month leave of absence during the summer of 1972 to wrap up the dissertation.

After having organized a monographic exhibition, I decided I would take on the challenge of a theme show. In 1972 at our weekly curatorial meetings I proposed an exhibition based on paintings representing the American frontier: landscapes, genre paintings of everyday life, and Mexican War pictures. I had previously researched the theme for a paper on "The Noble Savage" for an IFA seminar conducted by Professor Robert Rosenberg. I admired art historians like Rosenberg who took on projects that others had overlooked. The American West had been the focus of only a few monographs and shows. I felt my exhibition could present a new interpretation of the art of the American West.

Again, Baur agreed. With Whitney travel funds, I managed to find the time to travel to museums on the West Coast, even though immersed in finishing my dissertation, neighborhood politics, the dissolution of my marriage, and caring for my kids.

Previous exhibitions focused on white artists painting wilderness scenes, stereotypically placid indigenous peoples, or—the opposite—fanciful concoctions of Indian battles by John Mix Stanley and Charles Ferdinand Wimar. I wanted my Whitney exhibition to be critical of the ways that the white man, guided by Manifest Destiny ideology, stole the lands and systematically slaughtered the buffalo and killed the Indigenous peoples of the Western States.

As I groped toward a thesis, my readings included: Frederic Jackson Turner's famous address, delivered in 1893, *The Significance of the Frontier in American History*; Henry Nash Smith's *Virgin Land: The American West as Symbol and Myth* (1970 edition); Matthew Josephson, *The Robber Barons: The Great American Capitalists, 1861-1901*

(1934; 1962); and Kevin Starr, *Americans and the California Dream: 1850-1915* (1973).

The first paragraph of *The American Frontier* introduced my thesis:

> Beginning with the westward migration of Anglo-Europeans across the Atlantic, America took on the dimensions of myth. Confronting the early settlers was not just the reality of a different geography and climate, but the promise of a *new* world—where man could shed the corrupting influences of an over-refined society, forget his previous mistakes, and be reborn into innocence. Both the reality and the myth of America as a frontier—as a new, only partially civilized, land would become a major theme in American painting in the second and third quarters of the nineteenth century.

In other words, my thesis would be a critique of westward expansion and settler colonization, and I wanted my audience to know that. The tally came to eighty paintings by 51 artists.

When planning the exhibition I followed the method I had learned from Leo Steinberg and the Institute of Fine Arts professors. First, I looked at paintings that were intriguing, beautifully painted, and that took as their subjects aspects of the frontier theme. Then I went to the books and archives to read about these artists and the circumstances under which they had painted.

The subthemes emerged: wilderness paintings by East Coast artists Thomas Cole and Asher B. Durand; artists of the journey west during both the pre- and post-Civil War years, such as Titian Ramsay Peale, George Catlin, Karl Bodmer, Alfred Jacob Miller, John Mix Stanley, Seth Eastman, Charles Wimar, Albert Bierstadt, Henry Farny, Emanuel

Leutze, and Thomas Moran. William Ranney invented and painted some of the most engaging images of the European Americans trekking west in his New Jersey studio without, apparently, feeling the need to travel West.

I expanded the subthemes. Having traveled to California museums and private collections and been amazed at what I saw and learned, I included many California artists not familiar to a New York audience, such as Thomas Hill, Joseph Harrington, William Keith, James Walker, and Ernest Narjot. I also had a section on images pertaining to the Mexican War, a war that drastically changed the contours of the U.S.

All of these themes contained images that had a wide audience during the 19th century through national exhibitions and reproductions in magazines and newspapers. I wanted to enable the viewer to do two things: visualize the indigenous peoples, their historical circumstances, and the frontier landscape, and grasp the facets of Manifest Destiny ideology—an ideology that proclaimed that it was God's will that the European Americans appropriate the lands and resources of all the western lands.

Given the overreaching ways that Manifest Destiny ideology justified itself, I purposely chose stereotypical images of "the cunning Indian," "the vicious Indian," "the dying Indian," and the "Indian damsel-in-distress-rescued-by-white-man." I wanted the viewer to understand the role that these false images played in justifying settler colonialism.

One of my favorite paintings was a counter Manifest Destiny image, attempting to tell the story from a Native American perspective. Theodor Kaufmann's *Railway Train Attacked by Indians* (1867) depicts Native American warriors dismantling railway tracks before an oncoming train. Apparently, such incidents actually occurred later during the Indian wars of the late 1880s.

I included wall labels with critical and sharp texts. Steven Weil, the associate director of the Whitney and occasionally acting director when John Baur vacationed, called me into his office and asked me why I had used the words "racism" and "genocide" in the wall texts that discussed western expansion. My response: "Because that is true—there was racism and genocide." He mumbled, "Far be it from me to censor your text, but you have to sign the introductory wall label with your own name."

His point was that the public needed to know it was my judgment about history and not the institution's. That pleased me. I was taking the risks, not the institution. When two United States Information Agency (USIA) people came by to view the show in advance of proposing that I curate an abbreviated version for European travel, they were not at all disturbed by "racism" or "genocide" in the texts. The issue of wall texts and whether curators should sign them still elicits controversy, but seems to be tilting toward written acknowledgment of curators.

The American Frontier did not end when the exhibition closed in New York. The smaller USIA version functioned as a tool for the United States Cold War efforts to convince European countries of U.S. democracy. USIA printed 19,000 copies of the catalogue with my original essay, but we cut the checklist and illustrations to reflect only those works in the traveling show. Months elapsed before I heard from USIA again.

Finally, I got a telephone call from Washington in 1973. The USIA caller wanted to share with me the line-up of countries where they planned to send the exhibition. He included Spain. "You cannot send it to Spain," I said. "That's a fascist country ruled by Franco, a dictator." He responded, "O.K. we won't send it there." I was amazed by his remark. I didn't realize how easy it was to influence American foreign policy. The final schedule brought the exhibition to

Helsinki, Bristol, London (at the Courtauld), Manchester, Copenhagen, and Dublin.

I pressed the caller: "Since you are sending all these paintings all over Europe, why not send me to lecture about the show?" The caller liked the idea. A few more months passed, and then I received my orders. I was to be a Short-Term American Grantee (STAG), paid by the State Department, for a two-week tour of the exhibition sites. My salary grade was $50/day [$335 in 2025] with all travel, lodging, and food expenses. Embassy officials would be greeting me at every airport.

At the time, spring semester 1974, I had been teaching as an Adjunct Professor at the Institute of Fine Arts, so I chose spring break (no classes) and cancelled class for the second week. I packed my light box and slide tray with about 500 slides—as no two lectures would be the same—and flew off to Europe. First, I went to Oslo, not on the exhibition schedule, but where USIA had arranged for me to lecture to "friends" of the US Embassy. The USIA staff were terrific, providing a great hotel room and delicious meals. They gave me a tour of the city and took me to see the Sonja Henie Museum, with its artifacts and memorabilia, including her ice skates and letters installed in glass cabinets. I became an instant fan of the iconic figure skater.

Basically, what I did in each city was attend parties and give lectures. Few of the USIA people really engaged with the lectures. They needed me as the occasion to invite civic leaders and businessmen to their embassies. My job entailed smiling, being charming, and talking about American culture and our "freedom." The other cities I visited as a STAG included Stockholm, Copenhagen, Dublin, and London—the last three of which were on the exhibition schedule.

Eventually, I caught up with the *American Frontier* exhibition in Manchester, England. My lecture addressed the students at the local polytechnic school. *Perhaps,* I thought, *some of these sharp students will get my message.* My text labels calling out racism and genocide were up on the walls, and I discussed those issues. I did not censor myself. The reaction of the USIA folks was split. Some became visibly nervous about my remarks about settler colonialism (a term not then used).

But they were not the smart people. The smart people—I assumed they were actually CIA—loved my using those terms in front of a European audience. Their thinking: "Only in America, can a professor like Patricia Hills be critical of her own government." Freedom of thought and speech was an important message to deliver during the Cold War. I realized that by devoting two whole weeks to this STAG assignment, I had become complicit in American Cold War propaganda.

US Government apparatchiks had a different reaction in 1991 when *The West as America* was shown at the Smithsonian American Art Museum.

In September 1974, my third big traveling exhibition, *The Painters' America: Rural and Urban Life, 1810-1910*, opened at the Whitney Museum and then circulated to the Houston Museum of Fine Arts and the Oakland Art Museum.

This exhibition presented an opportunity to explore another theme. I had already shown genre paintings with frontier themes in 1973. Now I wanted to explore the so-called everyday life of America's Black and white habitants in the East and Middle West. I wanted to burrow into issues of gender, race, and class—subjects that I knew would be controversial—and push toward a radical interpretation—a re-presentation—of the classes, races, and genders of 19th-century America.

"Re-presentation" rather than "representation" became an important concept for me: "To present again an image." It meant addressing what purports to be real people and then visualizing them—which could be condescending and racist, or empathetic and heroizing—but never neutral. Artists of re-presentations might parade them as objective, but we realize that the vantage point of the artist, their subjectivity and positionality, often determine the final image. The image can then be harnessed by opinionated writers and critics to "illustrate" the fictions passing as history.

For the catalogue I created sections, one of which was "Black People in Pre-Civil War Painting." I believe this was the first exhibition of genre painting to single out images of Black people as a separate category to be seriously considered. In that section I contrasted Eastman Johnson's *Negro Life at the South* (1859) to Eyre Crowe's *Slave Market in Richmond, Virginia* (1852).

I wrote:

Not offensive to public taste—whether pro- or anti-abolitionist—was Eastman Johnson's *Negro Life [at] the South* ... In this work Johnson portrays blacks in a variety of activities which we have come to recognize as racial stereotypes: playing banjoes, shuffling to music, courting idly, and tending to children. Compared with Eyre Crowe's painting, Johnson's work is a fancifully staged concoction.

As Jeffrey Stewart has observed, Johnson's work was doing the cultural work of appeasing northern industrialists that a new Black workforce would be compliant.

New York Times art critic Hilton Kramer slammed the show in his September 29, 1974, review. His banner headline declared: "Artistic Excellence Loses Out to Social History at the Whitney." Kramer states my premise and quotes me from my opening page of the catalogue: "'In the century from 1810 to 1910, most scenes of everyday life in America were synthetic constructions, reflecting the cultural ideals and social myths of the picture producers and picture consumers—the painter's America—rather than the actual social circumstances of the majority of the people.'"

But his real criticism was that I had neglected art appreciation in my selection of works. Kramer's words: "We are urged to blind ourselves to aesthetic distinctions in order to participate in some of the social myths of the 19th century [and] some of the ideological scenarios of the 20th." He then states his fear that others will follow my misguided direction.

I was, in fact, introducing the best examples in terms of color, composition, and technique of works physically in the exhibition. I also reproduced in the catalogue the art of less skilled painters and contemporary prints to strengthen the points I was making. An example was James Goodwyn Clonney, *Politicians in a Country Bar* (1844), which Kramer discussed as if it were in the show. My point was to exemplify the ways Blacks were marginalized by always standing by the door, rather than centered in the room where the main action is occurring.

In a letter to the *New York Times* editor, published October 27, 1974, the critic Max Kozloff rebutted Kramer's ideas and came to my defense: "'The Painters' America,' with its catalogue, is one of the very few examples of the scholarship and vigorous criticism needed to dissent from the prevailing conservatism of our museums. It should have been celebrated, not reproached." Thanks, Max!

The star of the show was Robert Koehler's *The Strike* (1886), owned by Lee Baxandall. As I researched genre paintings and visited museums throughout the US in preparation for *The Painters' America,* John Baur received a letter in the mail from the writer and self-taught historian, Lee Baxandall, informing Baur that he, Baxandall, had recently purchased Robert Koehler's large painting *The Strike* (1886). Baur handed the letter to me to "take care of."

The tone of Baxandall's letter was belligerent as he opined that we would probably *not* be interested in his painting because the subject featured working-class strife. To him museums would by their nature shun images of class conflict. However, he had the painting in New York and said he would be happy to show it to whomever showed interest.

I immediately got in touch with him and explained that, *au contraire*, I was *very* interested in such pictures, although not familiar with Koehler's work. We agreed to meet at Lowey's, a well-known New York conservation studio. When I saw the painting, I was stunned.

Baxandall explained that he previously knew the painting only from an 1886 *Harper's Weekly* illustration. He had planned to use it as an illustration for an anthology he was editing. He became curious as to what happened to the painting that had been exhibited in 1886 at the National Academy of Design. He did some sleuthing and discovered that it belonged to the Minneapolis Library, but was physically in storage at the Minneapolis Institute of Art.

He got in touch with the Director, Samuel Sachs II, of MIA and inquired whether he could have a photograph. The MIA responded to Baxandall. They had no photograph. Further, it was too much trouble to make photography arrangements as the painting was rolled up and stored in their basement.

Baxandall prevailed, and finally Sachs said that the museum would sell the painting to him for, as I recall, $2000 [$13,400 in 2025], rather than spend the money on photography. I believe Baxandall paid another $2000 for the restoration. According to Baxandall, after the painting left Minneapolis, a reporter asked Sachs why he had sold the painting. Sachs allegedly replied that the painting had "no aesthetic merit." Each year when teaching the painting to my students, I passed on the quote.

Baxandall agreed to lend the painting to my exhibition, and I decided to reproduce it in color—one of only eight color reproductions in a book illustrating 167 works. Baxandall kindly provided me with copies of his research notes, which I incorporated into my catalogue essay. On opening night a TV crew who came to film the exhibition made a beeline for the picture. I was not surprised and surmised that they were familiar with strikes. In any event, they no doubt had decided it would function nicely (if not ironically) as backdrop for the interviews between the Whitney's director and me.

Baxandall and I became friends. I appreciated his research on art and Marxism. He, in turn, found it fascinating that he had found a *rara avis*—a radical museum curator (albeit "in the closet"). Our families (spouses and children) soon became friends. Baxandall's book became one of the first popular anthologies in English devoted to Marxism and art. We stayed in touch for years, until he returned to Oshkosh, Wisconsin to run the family business making overalls. He later turned his energies to advocating for nude beaches at Truro, Cape Cod.

However, he put *The Strike* on long-term loan to the building headquarters of 1199, the Hospital Workers Union on West 43rd Street in New York City. It hung in their lobby for years. The painting inspired 1199 Executive Director Moe Foner, and he asked me to participate in *The Working American*, a traveling exhibition being curated by Abigail Booth Gerdts. I wrote the lead essay. The exhibition traveled under the auspices of the Smithsonian Institution in 1979.

All of this, you might say, came about because Lee Baxandall wrote a letter challenging the Whitney to risk showing a painting with working-class subject matter.

Baxandall eventually sold the painting to Richard Manoogian, a Detroit businessman and collector of American art. At one point, I believe Manoogian offered to sell it to the Smithsonian American Art Museum (then called the National Collection of American Art). Instead, Manoogian sold it to the German Historical Museum in Berlin. That's a pity because I consider *The Strike* to be a part of our national patrimony. Although painted in Germany, its subject resonated with the Chicago Haymarket incident of 1886—when many striking workers returned gunshots from Chicago policemen sent in to break up the workers' strike. Museums in the United States, not surprisingly, have generally shunned the topic of class conflict.

The other paintings in *Painters' America* provided me with the visual evidence for a working thesis summarized in my conclusion:

> By and large the painters' America represented neither conditions nor events, neither the typical nor the specific, but an artful blend of fact and fantasy, of realities and dreams. The genre painting that has survived and has been treasured reassured its select audience of a continuity between the past and the present. But the paintings did not simply serve their patrons as nostalgic respite from the pressures of the day. Widely exhibited and reproduced, many also contributed to and perpetuated nationalistic and elitist attitudes which are with us still.

That's the dialectic between past and present. I was hitting my stride and hoping other art historians would join me.

10

A Busy Time, 1974-78

In the summer of 1974, a political friend, Ellen Tremper, who taught English at Brooklyn College, telephoned and said she wanted to introduce me to a friend of hers, Kevin Whitfield, who taught Classics at Brooklyn.

We soon met at the Whitney for a blind date on a sunny July day, walking from Madison Avenue to Central Park with sandwiches. He was a broad-shouldered, large, handsome man with a shaggy grey beard and mustache. Arriving at the Park, he noticed I had tucked under my arm Georg Lukács's *Marxism and Human Liberation*, a book familiar to him. We talked about the intersection of culture and left politics. Both of us had been separated from our former spouses for two years and both had two pre-teens at home. Immediately, and not surprisingly, we took a liking to each other. We had many things to talk about.

Our personal histories had common features. Both of us had lived in families constantly on the move before and during World War II.

My military father was stationed at the army post Schofield Barracks in Hawai'i on December 7, 1941, when the Japanese bombed Pearl Harbor.

My mother and I were living with him. That evening the post commander ordered all dependents to board a bus and evacuate to Honolulu. I witnessed the ships on fire in the Harbor, a memorable event for a five-year old. Within a month my mother and I flew to Rochester, New York. My father stayed in Hawai'i, came back to the States, and less than a year later was deployed to Europe to accompany the 9th Army as it charged through France, defeated the Nazis at the Battle of the Bulge, and crossed the Rhine. At war's end, we moved some more. By the time I graduated from High School, I had attended twelve different schools—from New York to California, Texas, then Cambridge, Germany and Southern Illinois.

Switching to Kevin: On a lark, Kevin's father Guy, who played in jazz bands (clarinet and saxophone) took his family to Venezuela to pan for gold. Soon Guy, along with his wife Helen, Kevin, his sister Marianne, and little brother Michael, moved to Panama where Guy played in American touring bands. Panama was soon declared a war zone, and Kevin's parents got government jobs related to the war effort. When the war ended, they moved back and forth between Brooklyn and Florida.

To Kevin and to me, home was where one spent the night. Home meant family, not a geographical site. No roots to the soil. When friends asked where we were from, we both replied, "from all over." We were both more open to alternative living options and different people's cultures. We knew the military phrase "FIGMO," the acronym for "Fuck it, got my orders."

I regret that my father died at 67 of aplastic anemia before Kevin came on the scene. Hartwin would have liked that Kevin had been a naval officer. I believe his death was due to radiation exposure during atomic testing in Nevada. He most likely traveled there from Hill Air Force Base in Ogden, Utah, and was exposed to the testing. I wrote to the Air Force for information but was denied: the government keeps its secrets forever.

Kevin and I blended our families: my children Christina and Brad became good friends with his daughters Mary and

Emily, who visited on weekends. Along with Polly the dog, we often vacationed at my grandmother's empty house in Ocean Grove on the Jersey Shore.

That September would bring big changes in my professional life. When *The Painters America* opened at the Whitney in late September, I had just begun teaching art history full-time at York College, part of the City University of New York (CUNY), in Jamaica, Queens. Kevin reasoned that we had to live together, or we would never see each other because of his commute to Brooklyn, and mine to Queens. Moreover, cohabiting would make our separate family lives easier when we combined resources. I was not quite ready to live with a man again, but agreed he had a sensible plan. Kevin turned out to be a wonderful, supportive, devoted and faithful partner. One of the best decisions I ever made was to live with him. Moreover, he was to become an astutely critical reader of my manuscripts—a welcome bonus.

Teaching that first year at York while continuing as an Adjunct Associate Curator at the Whitney proved to be intense. My application to the York job had consisted of one interview that summer with Arthur Anderson, Chair of the Performing and Fine Arts Department. No hiring committee met with me, no campus lecture, no letters of recommendation requested, no interviews with the Dean or Provost. My qualifications—that I had taught an undergraduate course on American art at Hunter College (CUNY) in the spring of 1973 and a graduate course as an associate professor at the Institute of Fine Arts in the spring 1974—satisfied the Chair, who hired me on the spot as an associate professor.

He approved my maintaining connections to the Whitney, which would bring luster to York College. The only other art historian on faculty was Jane Schuyler, a fellow graduate student friend from Hunter. Hers was probably the sole recommendation. The Chair offered me a one-year, renewable contract teaching four courses per semester. Jane and I were expected to teach the entire history of art.

Founded in 1966, York opened in 1967. Community leaders from Black and Latinx neighborhoods pressured the CUNY system to designate York a four-year institution that would accommodate all of New York City's high school Open Admissions students who had been guaranteed entrance to CUNY. The problem with the policy, as I came to understand it, was that no efforts were made to limit class size or provide remedial courses for those students undereducated by the NYC public school system in terms of writing, basic math, and science. Even then, there were many great students in our department: curious, bright, eager to learn.

The job challenged me: lecturing in four large classes each semester and tutoring students on how to write papers. My standard courses were: two sections each semester on a survey history of art, along with two advanced courses: 19th-century European art and 20th- century American art, or 20th-century European and 19th century American. Sometimes, I dropped one of those courses for a focused course, such as "Media, Culture and the Visual Arts." When Jane's contract was not renewed, I also taught Baroque Art—focusing on my favorite artist, Caravaggio.

The students struggled, as did I to keep one jump ahead of them. During the cutbacks of the 1977-78 school year, when tech aides were laid off, I taught a "jumbo" survey course on the history of art to over 100 students in a basketball gym. I hired my student Vytautas Sakalaukas (aka Vytas Sakalas, still a close friend) to help set up chairs and projectors since the tech aides were all gone. Grading papers and exams took days. I tried to remain positive, but Kevin said I "was pissing against the stream."

The students were largely first-generation college attendees, of Asian, African, and Latinx descent, generally smart, but overworked by their outside jobs and ill-prepared by their high schools. One student told me that the only place where he could study in his family's hectic apartment was the bathroom.

I dreamed about my students all the time and fretted about how I might make a difference. I passed one faithful attendee—on the borderline of failing—when I decided to add his body temperature (98.6) to the 1000-point system I had devised. I taught a graduate seminar as an adjunct Associate Professor at Columbia in spring 1975, while trying to keep up my Whitney work. I felt exhausted.

Faculty in the CUNY system, including Kevin and myself, then belonged to the faculty union—the progressive Professional Staff Congress. With or without the blessing of the PSC, Kevin, our colleagues, and I staged protests—going so far as having a sit-in in the City Comptroller's office in Manhattan one afternoon. I remember our friend Tony picking up one end of a huge conference table and letting it bang on the floor as he made a point to the Comptroller. We wanted more resources for students, smaller classes, more funds. The city pushed back, citing no money. The city faced bankruptcy charges, tried getting loans, and counted on a federal bailout. Faculty were laid off for three weeks without pay in spring 1978. Years later the City paid us back with interest for those three weeks of missed pay.

Meanwhile, our political friends up in Boston were literally fighting—with baseball bats and hockey sticks—against the racists opposed to busing, led by Louise Day Hicks and her South Boston neighbors. One of the biggest marches occurred on May Day, 1975, organized by the Progressive Labor Party (PLP) when we New Yorkers and people across the country rode busses to Boston to demonstrate. Some of my York students learned about it independently and came. We expected violence, as the Freedom Riders in the South had experienced. But the march went smoothly thanks to the pre-planning of Boston comrades. That summer, however, witnessed continuing battles of young PLP members and their friends against the racist South Boston contingent.

Family life settled in. Getting married seemed like a good idea, as it would reassure the children that our liaison was going to be permanent.

Kevin and I had a hippie marriage in our apartment on January 3, 1976, the same day as Christina's 13th birthday. I bought a pale rose-colored, Victorian style gown from a small Madison Avenue shop. All three girls—Christina, Mary, and Emily—looked beautiful in their long party dresses. Brad and his friend Juan, both wearing blazers, served as ring bearers. Handsome Kevin wore his tweed blazer.

The Episcopal minister from the Cathedral of St. John the Devine, who had been active in housing homeless people in the Columbia University area, performed the ceremony. We all laughed when he pronounced us husband and wife "by the power invested in me by the *provisional* government of the State of New York." That indicated that he believed we all would one day have our workers' revolution. We invited Bill and Abigail Gerdts, Milton and Blanch Brown, Alan Wallach, Eleanor Bernstein, Michael Goldman, and other friends. A chamber group of friends played music. Homemade roast turkey, ham, and a French wedding cake were served. The champagne flowed.

I wrote a short-term grant proposal for the National Endowment for the Humanities to spend two months traveling to visit museums holding collections of art of the West. I had ambitions to expand the Whitney's *American Frontier* catalogue into a proper scholarly book. The grant came through, and we immediately made plans for me to fly to several cities with museums and private collectors I needed to visit. Kevin would rent a Dodge station wagon, pile all four kids into the back, and meet me five days later in Tulsa, Oklahoma.

I flew off to the Midwest. The highlight of my solo travel

was visiting the Busch mansion and grounds in St. Louis, home to August A. Busch III, then the CEO of Budweiser, the family beer company.

The mansion looked like one of those Gilded Age mansions of Newport, and he had the art of the West I wanted to see. After I looked and took notes in his mansion, Busch invited me to swim in his pool. I was enjoying myself, when Busch's young blond wife, sartorially decked out in splendid riding clothes, rode up to the pool on her horse. In her heavy German accent, she reported to her husband that another riding horse had been badly injured. They discussed shooting the horse, and she rode off to execute the task.

Later in the afternoon a security guard gave me a ride in a jeep to inspect the gardens and the stables quartering some of Busch's famous gigantic Clydesdale horses. The guard also explained the security of the Busch compound and the various thieves and potential murderers that had been caught climbing the high barbed wire fence. I thought, *Ah, the travails of the rich!*

Traveling on to Oklahoma City, I met up with the family, who at 2 a.m. came tumbling into my hotel room. I still had many more Texas museums to see, so we drove on to Dallas and Ft. Worth. We stayed briefly with my mother in San Antonio, who by then had her own flourishing private law practice, and then on to Houston. We drove further south and camped on the beach at Galveston, where some nighttime hooligans stole our portable burner.

As we drove east through hot and sticky Louisiana, Mississippi, Alabama, and Florida, we also camped next to busy highways, grilled our food using flashlights, and saw what museums and tourist sights we could. In Jacksonville, we spent a few days with Kevin's parents before heading home. I never wrote the longer, scholarly book, but I had amassed dozens of slides of paintings by George Catlin, John Mix Stanley, Karl Bodmer, and others to use teaching.

In the new job I had created for myself at the Whitney as Adjunct Curator, I wanted to show my face as often as I could. I scheduled my York classes so I could attend Wednesday morning Whitney staff meetings, where Director Tom Armstrong presided.

In the periods when I worked both full-time and part-time as an adjunct, I was assigned to supervise pre-20th-century exhibitions traveling to the Whitney from other museums. One traveling exhibition showed American Impressionist Painting, an exhibition organized by the High Museum in Atlanta. Another small show focused on the American Art-Union of the late 1840s. When the Pennsylvania Academy of the Fine Arts closed their building in Philadelphia for restoration, I made several trips there and organized a show of its collection that we brought to the Whitney.

The most controversial outside exhibition I mounted was *American Art: An Exhibition from the Collection of Mr. and Mrs. John D. Rockefeller 3rd,* organized by the de Young Museum in San Francisco. Although Director Armstrong knew the Rockefellers planned to give their collection to the de Young Museum, he wanted to host the exhibition in hopes of currying the favor of the Rockefellers for future gifts. In charge of making the installation look elegant and at Armstrong's suggestion, I borrowed 18th-century pier tables from the Metropolitan Museum of Art. The show looked gorgeous when it opened.

My leftist art historian and artist friends, some affiliated with Artists Meeting for Cultural Change (AMCC), objected to the show. On November 3, 1975, Rudolf Baranik of Artists and Writers Protest, Lucy Lippard of the Women's Slide Registry and formerly of the Art Workers Coalition (AWC), and Benny Andrews of the Black Emergency Cultural Coalition (BECC), wrote a joint letter to Tom Armstrong demanding a meeting.

Armstrong did not want to meet with those he considered

troublemakers, so he called me into his office for my advice. I persuaded him that he had to meet with them. In Armstrong's office, he and I listened as the three of them made their demands: 1) the Whitney had made a mistake to feature elite art as its Bicentennial exhibition rather than art of the people; 2) the exhibition had only one painting by a woman and none by Black artists; 3) the Whitney needed to diversify and hire Black curators. I tried to keep the meeting friendly and cue Armstrong to say the appropriate things.

After the meeting, the three petitioners and I retired to the Whitney basement restaurant. Baranik, Lippard, and Andrews assured me that they knew I fully supported them and their demands for a diverse staff. Rudolf and his wife, May Stevens, had already become good friends. The four of us often engaged in spirited political discussions over dinner.

The AMCC had a picket line at the opening, and I regrettably crossed it. (Contradictions! Contradictions!) Inside, I charmed the Rockefellers in their tuxes and formal designer dresses. But I was aware of the flyer the AMCC had distributed: "Boycott This Museum!" The text reiterated the complaints:

The Whitney Museum is a privately owned institution, but through federal grants and a permanent tax-exemption, you pay for it. In return for your investment, the Whitney is obligated by law to be a politically neutral educational institution. What you actually get are the private interests and values of the ruling class ...

The fact that this show, with one exception, contains only the work of white male artists, clearly demonstrates the racial and sexist politics of the ruling class and their institutions. They would have us believe that our country is a product of personal initiative and foresight, but, the fact is, this country was built by waves of immigrants of many nationalities and races who were used as cheap labor ... [The] myth of America ... presents the views of the ruling class as the only correct ones. We protest the fact that museums are being used to exclude all but the ruling class from active participation in the development of culture. The museum removes art from its social context thereby forcing a separation between people and their history.

It was a forceful statement, and the Whitney eventually made some needed changes.

Today, museums strive to be diverse, by hiring staff from all backgrounds and ethnicities, and inclusive, by mounting major exhibitions of women, People of Color, Indigenous People, and artists outside the network of galleries, auction houses, and museums. Sadly, in 2025 such museum goals of diversity and inclusion have come under attack.

This incident exemplifies the contractions I then lived: rubbing elbows with the rich while sympathizing with the radical positions of my friends. It was risky business.

Protesters later published the 80-page *an anti-catalog,* written collectively by 17 artists/art historians with separate essays by Jimmy Durham and Gerald Honre. *An anti-catalog* elaborated on the points printed in the flyer. My art history buddy Alan Wallach was one of the most active in the group.

The same year as the Rockefeller show, I pitched the idea for an exhibition at the Whitney to open in 1977 that would showcase the decades before and after 1900. It would include both "high" art and popular art. I didn't mention that my catalogue would embrace a critical assessment of the 1890-1910 art world in line with the mission of the New Art Association.

I found inspiration in Barbara Tuchman's *The Proud Tower*, a history with separate chapters that ranged over issues of class and race during that turn-of-the-century period. Originally, I wanted to include sculpture and costumes, but finally nixed that idea because it would be both too complicated and an installation nightmare. My plan then focused on paintings, graphics, and photographs and, like Tuchman, I created discreet chapters for the catalogue, including documentary photographs, 1890s posters, portraits of the social elite, etc.

As I began selecting works in the exhibition, I dove into the history of photography, and my in-depth study opened up another world to me. Naomi Rosenblum, my colleague at York College who taught the history of photography, guided me to collections in three areas: Pictorial Photography (e.g. Alice Boughton, F. Holland Day, Edward Steichen, Alfred Stieglitz); Portrait Photography (e.g. Gertrude Käsebier, Clarence H. White, James Van Der Zee, Addison Scurlock); and Social Photography (e.g. Louis Hine, Jacob Riis, Alice Austin). Following her recommendations, I visited the collections of Sam Wagstaff, his ex-boyfriend Robert Mapplethorp, the Museum of the City of New York, and the Library of Congress, to name a few.

I spent much research time studying turn-of-the-century illustrations and included works reproduced in the political magazines of the era, such as *Puck* and *Judge*. Posters were also new subjects for me to master. I found a superb collection at the Mount Holyoke College Museum of Art. What I already knew were the paintings: the impressionist painters of the late 19th century and the young realists of the early 20th century. The ensemble of different media and different generations of artists at the turn of the century made for a lively exhibition.

In the catalogue essay I emphasized the contradictions. For example, I discussed turn-of-the-century writers who focused on the aesthetic issue of "beauty versus truth." I quoted from critic Samuel Isham's *The History of American Painting* (1905), where he observed many artists had to adjust their style and subjects to suit a buying public dazzled by beauty removed from urban realities. I brought in Thorstein Veblen's concept of conspicuous consumption. I devoted one chapter to The City, which combined both the impressionists and the realists. Along the way, I determined to include a generous number of women artists in each category/chapter, and as many Black artists and their art as I could find. The show hung four paintings by the Black artist Henry Tanner. Tom Armstrong liked the show. No one gave it a bad review.

I was thrilled when New York Black photographer James Van Der Zee (born in 1886) came to the opening, as well as Robert Scurlock, grandson of Washington, D.C. African American photographer Addison Scurlock, whose photographic portrait hung in the show. At the opening, Robert Scurlock took a photograph of my mom, Kevin and me, which I cherish.

In late Winter 1977-78, the exhibition traveled to the Seattle Art Museum. Kevin and I traveled to the opening in February. Getting to Seattle was tough, the whole East Coast had suffered a blizzard. Our plane was delayed a day. It was a bumpy flight all the way, which made my then pregnant self woozy and sick. The JC Penney people, sponsors of the exhibition, funded the travel and cheerfully came along.

Although one day late, we were nevertheless treated like Very Important Persons in Seattle. Charles Cowells, the Seattle curator, shook my hand vigorously and commented, "You will see that I hung the show aesthetically!" Puzzled, I looked for myself. Indeed, he had hung the Social Photography and the Ash Can Artists way in the back by the exit signs. That went against the purpose of the show: to give equal value to all the work, whether a grand portrait by John

Singer Sargent or a small photograph of a child laborer by Louis Hine. That's the problem with traveling exhibitions; the curator from the originating museum rarely has control as to what happens to the art in the subsequent venues.

I realized I needed a change. Morale hit a low at York College when City officials threatened to close York or to reduce it to a two-year college. Students began to flee, and I began to apply for jobs: University of Texas/Austin, Harvard, and Boston University. All responded and invited me to interviews. At the Harvard job interview, the professor in charge assured me that I would never, NEVER, get tenure at Harvard. Their Americanist position was a five-year-and-out situation that they had set up. While they hired tenured senior faculty with books galore and international reputations, their transient assistant professors were expected to be grateful for the opportunity to teach at Harvard. Those job conditions did not satisfy me, and I told them how disgraceful was their policy.

I flew to Texas for the Austin interview. The faculty gave me a cordial reception. All went well until we had the conversation about sabbaticals and salaries. The Texas legislature would not approve faculty sabbatical leaves—period! And their salary range was way below CUNY's scale. Not for me, I told them. We parted amicably.

Boston University (one of three doctoral programs in New England, along with Yale and Harvard) offered many perks. I had already taught grad students at CUNY, the Institute of Fine Arts (NYU) and Columbia. This would be my chance to forge relationships with art history grad students and participate in the robust American and New England Studies Program (AMNESP). They were both communities of scholarship I had sought. Moreover, BU made funds available for research and course release, and I would be able to teach classes in my field of American art.

In March I flew to Boston—a city still reeling from that

'78 blizzard. At my campus visit I gave a lecture on John Sloan's working-class women. I wore a Stetson hat and carried a leather briefcase. It amused me that possibly no one would notice my pregnant self in such an attire. I received mixed responses from the art history faculty, who couldn't understand why I focused on a socialist artist, but the AMNESP faculty were enthusiastic. They hired me as a non-tenured associate professor with a salary of about $21,000 a year [$105,000 in 2025] and with the tacit promise of tenure in three years.

On April 16, Kevin drove to Boston to look for housing. That night my bag of waters broke, and I frantically waited for his call. When we connected at 5 a.m., I pleaded for him to return immediately. Alone and unable to get a taxi on that rainy morning, I walked eight blocks to the bus stop and boarded the crosstown bus to Mt. Sinai Hospital on Fifth Avenue. The baby was one month premature, and we worried about his survival. The doctor waited for three days before inducing labor. They explained the delay as medically necessary because the baby might have respiratory distress syndrome (then called Hyaline membrane disease), a condition that had brought about the death of Jacqueline and Jack Kennedy's premature son in August 1963. The three-day delay would give his lungs time to mature before birth.

Andy jumped all the hurdles. He was born a healthy robust baby on April 20, with a weight of over six pounds. He was born during a time that saw family discord and teenage Sturm und Drang. The other adults handled the situation, but I focused on finishing up at York College, packing to move to Boston, and making a new life for our blended family and new baby.

We loved New York City and had mixed feelings about leaving. But the city had been crime-ridden and tough for the children in the late 1970s. Although Christina, our oldest, enjoyed the perks of the city, including three years of training at the school of the New York City Ballet, courses at the Art Students League, and enrollment at the High School of Music and Art, the public school system had become woefully underfunded, and many great teachers jumped ship. Brad had been attending a middle school in our neighborhood but was the target of racism as he was the only white kid in his class. His coping skills from the experience, however, shaped him into a street-savvy young man. Brad's situation was about to change for the better when admitted to the Bronx HS of Science. Emily and Mary had been attending Princeton schools where their mother held a prestigious fellowship, and Emily was also eager to join us. Mary stayed behind in New York to finish high school.

So ... Goodbye New York! But I'll be back!

11

Boston Ups & Downs, 1978-81

The spring of 1978 in New York was hectic—one might even say traumatic—for our family. Teenagers were rebelling, family therapists provided massive family meetings to improve the situation, Boston University had offered me a dream job, and I was 42 with a new baby. Outside in the streets crime had skyrocketed and New York City was going broke. Even as the movers were loading our furniture onto their truck at 104th Street, a hooligan stole one of our bicycles. Getting away to Boston would be our rescue plan.

We found a house to rent in Brookline, a suburb of Boston, that seemed to meet our needs. It was the left side of a two-family house facing the Brookline High football field. It had three stories with a basement, six bedrooms, an average-sized kitchen, dining room, and living room. The backyard held a small, charming garden. The friendly landlady who lived on the right side was unprepared for the sight of us moving in, as we poured out of our Buick station wagon—Kevin and me, three teenagers, a baby, my mother, and two dogs.

Why Brookline? Because Brookline High had been recommended by my friend John Walsh, a curator at the Boston Museum of Fine Arts. He considered the high school one of the best in Massachusetts. It promised a robust curriculum and seemed a perfect fit for Christina, Brad, and Emily.

Christina, an independent type, enrolled in the School within a School—an experimental "open class" situation with overstuffed sofas in classes instead of desks. Brad went for athletics, rode his skateboard everywhere, and signed up for the numerous weekend ski trips the high school sponsored.

Emily took up the flute and participated in the school's marching band. The early 1980s fashion style that Christina and Emily adopted was what I call "Boston grunge," which meant putting together mix-and-match ensembles of vests, scarfs, shirts, skirts, and pants purchased at consignment shops. Sometimes, combat boots were added.

Thankfully, no one adopted the "Goth" sartorial style—made popular by the *Rocky Horror Show* and the *Adams Family* TV programs. No one got tattoos, and no one dyed their hair purple. Kevin cooked Chinese dinners, while Emily, Christina, Brad, baby Andy and I (and sometimes my mother) sat at the kitchen table watching *Mork and Mindy* or *Get Smart*.

Our political friends would show up for a visit at 6 p.m. and were promptly invited to dinner. Nice memories of family life.

&

Little did I know when I arrived at BU that some of my new colleagues would initially snub me and continue to be antagonistic—sometimes creating petty complaints about me. For example, when one colleague noticed my tardiness in keeping office hours, she urged one student to complain to the Dean. I did not reveal the reason for my delay. I had slipped down the stairs from my office to meet Kevin outside in our parked car. He had brought baby Andy for me to breast feed. Of course, I would never mention that to my colleagues or the Dean. Tending to hungry babies would be considered unforgivingly unprofessional.

Why the resentment toward me? I was a mother with a baby and teenagers, the students seemed to like me, I published regularly, and I took students on bus trips to New York museums to see art. Perhaps it was because I was a feminist and a leftist. Or that my area of study was American art—a field some colleagues deemed an insignificant area of study.

Some colleagues knew exactly what my contribution would be to the Department. The chair, Carl Chiarenza, aware of my politics, shielded me from a newspaper photographer when I marched and held a placard at a faculty sidewalk protest against BU administration policies. He knew that if I had been photographed and identified as an activist, I would lose any chance for tenure. When the BU staff later went on strike, I invited our department secretary to come to my classes and explain the staff's demands. My invitation turned out to be risky. About two days later, the then Acting Chair (not Chiarenza) called me into his office and scolded me for bringing issues into my classroom that were outside my field. I was at first puzzled by his remarks, but quickly concluded my crime had been giving the department secretary a voice about labor issues in my class.

&

Even with the move to Boston, I maintained my position as Adjunct Curator at the Whitney, not wanting to give up the job I loved.

One day in spring 1979, during one of my frequent New York visits, then director Tom Armstrong called me into his office. He wanted to mount a large exhibition of figurative art from the Whitney's collection. He had in mind Linda Nochlin as the curator. I responded, "No, let me curate the show," and I pitched my qualifications. He agreed. I added that I wanted a co-curator to address the sculpture.

Armstrong suggested a male scholar who had bold-face font recognition as an art historian but no real knowledge of sculpture. I countered with the suggestion of Roberta Tarbell, a young scholar trained at Delaware who knew more about early 20th-century American sculpture than anyone else I knew. Armstrong gave me the go-ahead. Tarbell and I proved to be a great team.

The family spent the summer of 1979 on the Jersey Shore. For about five weeks I commuted to the Whitney every day to look at every single figurative painting in the basement storeroom. (Back in the old days, all art storage resided on pull-out racks in museum basements.) With an art handler's help I recall sliding out the racks and closely studying each work, with an open mind to the possibilities of each. Because many had been purchased from Whitney Biennials, these works served as messages from former directors and curators of their tastes in past years.

It was a great learning experience to see all the paintings, especially those from the 1920s unfamiliar to us all. I made a point to include as many women and Black artists as I could find, but in those days, the Whitney primarily had artworks by white men. I did, however, select my friend Audrey Flack's *Lady Madonna* (1972) to be reproduced in color. Back in Boston in the fall, I wrote my essay and conferred with Tarbell. The following summer she and I installed the show on a hot summer day. Exhausted but exhilarated when we finished in midafternoon, we went down to MoMA to see the large Picasso show then on view. I recall our taking off our high heeled shoes and walking barefoot through the exhibition ignoring the chronological order set up by the curators. And giggling all the way.

The Figurative Tradition and the Whitney Museum of American Art opened in the summer of 1980. Again, Hilton Kramer slammed my show. As an old Cold War Warrior, he objected to the inclusion of Ben Shahn, who had been considered politically subversive in the 1950s. True to form, Kramer lied about what I said and then attacked me for what he said I said. For amusement, Director Armstrong had campaign-like buttons made that said, "Hilton who?"

The exhibition was timely. Not only did it give a good survey of forgotten artists from the period of 1900-1960, it also came at a time when more and more 1970s artists were exploring the figure as an expressive vehicle for ideas. They included, Audrey Flack, Alice Neel, Peter Saul, Alex Katz, Duane Hanson, Robert Arneson, and Mary Frank. Moreover, the show included the work of those 1950s artists who had been eclipsed by the triumph of abstract expressionism: Stephen Greene, Peter Blume, Philip Evergood, Jack Levine, Karl Zerbe, Hyman Bloom, and Ben Shahn.

I made a point to include the many California artists in the Whitney's collection, such as David Park, Richard Diebenkorn, Elmer Bischoff, and Nathan Oliviera. The Abstract Expressionist artists who incorporated the figure in their work, such as Willem de Kooning, Lee Krasner, Grace Hartigan, Eugenie Baizerman, Abraham Rattner, and Herbert Katzman were welcomed participants in the exhibition. Chicago artists such as Jim Nutt, Christina Ramberg, and Roger Brown were also highlighted.

&

My department back at BU assigned me many committee tasks. In those years many women academics shouldered responsibilities not demanded of the men, who were considered the more serious scholars. If women hoped to get a place at the table, we knew we had to work harder, volunteer more, and publish more than our male colleagues.

Not only did I teach my full load of three courses per semester, I was also charged with overseeing the Museum Studies Program then being set up as a special four-course certificate program for MA graduate students.

I crafted a program that piggy-backed on BU's regular MA program. I did not use the word "museology," a term I intensely disliked. It seemed to represent a field in which one learned technical details about registering works and selecting frames, but not the special character of subject, style, and the individual media (e.g. painting, textiles) and their place in time.

To embrace that larger history, students needed a thorough study of art history. They needed also to become connoisseurs—knowing which artworks in an artist's oeuvre were the best examples for a particular theme. Hence, the program for the Museum Studies Certificate required students to take at least six graduate courses in academic art history, take the regular written MA exam, and write the MA thesis. Plus four extra courses, which included ones on the history of/introduction to museums, and approaches to collections management, as well as one or two internships in a commercial gallery or a museum.

As director of the program, I hired adjunct faculty to teach the curatorial courses, and I shepherded the students when they went off to work for 150 hours per semester in a museum or art gallery.

When, in the fall of 1979, the upper administration decided to pull the Boston University Art Gallery (BUAG) out of the studio program at the College of Fine Arts, they handed it over to the Department of Art History. The department chair selected me, since I had extensive experience working at the Whitney, to be the "faculty supervisor and advisor." I oversaw the schedule of exhibitions and staffing of the new BUAG with grad student helpers, one of whom functioned as student manager. My department chair considered my new duties trivial—since the students would be running the show.

Meanwhile, I was submitting my documents in

preparation for my bid for tenure, including syllabi of my courses and a statement on my philosophy of teaching. The department gathered student evaluations and letters from outside scholars and the Dean's office sent in colleagues from other departments to observe my teaching. I wanted tenure, because it meant a secure teaching position for the rest of my career with the benefit of exercising my academic freedom to continue researching and writing about the intersection of art and politics.

My tenure dossier elicited controversy from the start. At the Department meeting the vote split: four in favor and three negatives. My non-supporters acknowledged my service to the university and that I was a prolific writer, but they seized on the fact that I had primarily written for museum catalogues. Back in the early 1980s academic deans were looking for peer-reviewed books. They had not yet accepted scholarly, foot-noted essays in catalogues as a form of legitimate scholarship.

There was some justification to their opinions, since most museum catalogue essays in the 1970s were non-critical celebrations of the artists being shown. My peers in art were not yet recognized as the generation bringing scholarship to museum writings.

The non-supporters also declared my undergraduate teaching as subpar. They acknowledged, however, that I had gained a reputation as a popular and effective teacher of graduate students.

Disappointed, I knew I had to fight the decision. My history department friend David Hall gave me good advice: "Show no rancor to your colleagues." I became outwardly cheerful to them while gritting my teeth.

At the College level APT—Appointments, Promotion, and Tenure Committee— there were two votes against me and 10 in favor. (One of the negative votes came from an art history colleague who had also voted negatively in the department vote.) Then the dossier went to the University APT Committee. Their report declared a 100% endorsement with the statement, "Comments from her chairperson [not Carl Chiarenza] and Dean indicating that Professor Hills's undergraduate teaching ability was deficient did not appear to be well substantiated: the evidence was lacking, based on few undergraduate evaluations (n = 3)."

As a teacher of graduate students, the committee considered me "outstanding." As to my scholarship, the University APT nailed it when they said: "Her published work has emphasized her interest and expertise in historical, cultural and political influences inherent in American art." The recommendation concluded: "Her scholarly efforts and professional contributions, coupled with praise from some of the most highly acclaimed American art historians and museum directors, strongly outweigh the comments."

An associate provost then called me to his office for an interview. He was very cautious in his comments—subtly alluding to the fact that I had quoted Karl Marx in a footnote to my John Sloan article. At the next level the Provost himself balked, turning me down because of the negative reports of my undergraduate teaching and declaring that to him my scholarship could be described as "mid-range." I believe he had become aware of my Marx quotation. This is an example of how my politics affected my career. They knew a radical when they saw her—a persona non grata at Boston University. However, I would not back down. My feminism and radicalism were defining me.

The case stalled. Since the Provost had overturned the positive recommendations and votes of the College and University APTs, he appointed an ad hoc committee of outside art historians to review the case—the protocol for controversial tenure cases. Then the dossier went off to three scholars to review: John Wilmerding, Professor at Dartmouth, Joshua Taylor, Director of the National

Collection of American Art [now Smithsonian American Art Museum], and a third person.

I later felt comfortable enough to talk with both Wilmerding and Taylor about their assessment of the review committee, and they vouched for their enthusiasm for my case. As I sat by Wilmerding's desk, he searched his office for the report but could not find it. Taylor went so far as to say he planned to nominate me for membership to the prestigious Grolier Club. (I did not follow up on the nomination, having no interest in belonging to a mostly all-white, predominantly male, elite club.) The report never saw the light of day because BU President John Silber had another idea.

As a sidebar to this narrative, I admit that I was not successful with all my undergraduate students, and I got some scathing teacher evaluations during the 1980s focused on my jamming too much history into a 50-minute class. Having taken art appreciation classes, most students were not familiar with my historical and cultural approach. Some were antagonistic. One student asked me the week before a mid-term exam, "Do we have to know the little history lessons that go along with the art?" My reply, "You should know whatever is relevant."

On the other hand, many students in their teacher evaluations commented that I was the best teacher they ever had at Boston University, and I had a strong following of repeat students. I never felt I was imposing my left politics on the students, but I did insist on introducing the cultural and political sources and/or ramifications of the art's surround. However, great satisfaction came to me later, when in 2011 the College Art Association gave me an award as Distinguished Teacher of Art History for that year.

With my tenure case on hold, I went on with my life. Right after classes ended in early May 1981, I received a telephone call from President John Silber at the very moment when Kevin had finished packing the Buick so that he, toddler Andy, and I could leave on the first leg of a motor trip to Wyoming. We were headed toward Cody, where I had agreed to teach a Western art history course in the summer program of the University of Wyoming.

Silber had called to tell me he was setting aside any decision on my tenure at that time. Instead, he wanted to offer me a five-year contract as the Director of the Boston University Art Gallery. Heretofore, that had not been my title. What did all this mean? I asked. Silber said it meant that the University would take me off the tenure track but that I would get all the medical insurance, retirement funds, and sabbatical leave benefits as other faculty, and free tuition for my children. In the future I could go back onto the tenure track. All this he promised.

He had liked the shows I had organized for the Art Gallery. He praised me for my entrepreneurial skills and said, "You are just the kind of person we want at Boston University." I thought, *If he feels that way, then why is he not giving me tenure?* Instead, I asked, "Does this mean I will get released time from teaching?" He snapped back, "Released time is an invention of the 60s!" To me the offer meant a bigger commitment than I had had the previous year when only supervising the work of the student gallery manager. I would be stepping into a major job—plus all my teaching duties.

I told Silber I would think it over. I hung up, grabbed my purse, and joined Kevin and Andy in the car. Driving across the country to Wyoming, I stopped at various points and called sympathetic BU colleagues for advice. The faculty union head persuaded me to accept the offer. "Look, Pat, better to have five years to find a new job than just one." I finally called Silber back when we stopped for an overnight in Chicago (still on the way to Wyoming) and accepted his offer. I dared not refuse such an offer as Silber had proffered.

Back in Boston in the fall of 1981, I was faced with the new challenges President Silber had offered me—teaching, mentoring grad students, running the Museum Studies Program—and being the hands-on director who would organize exhibitions and develop programs that would bring national artists to Boston and help create community among the New England artists. This would be a whole new, albeit time consuming, adventure for me. I held the job until 1989.

The older children in high school took on after-school and summer jobs to augment their pitiful allowances. We argued about money and whether Kevin should drive a taxi, which he did for a brief period. To cut expenses, we bought powdered milk instead of regular milk, but had a family insurrection over that practice. For several months we took in a "gap year" boarder from England to help make ends meet.

To bring in even more necessary cash, I traveled the country giving lectures at museums and universities and wrote essays for encyclopedias (very low paying!) and exhibition catalogues.

Family vacations became possible when I could get grants to fund my research, housing, and travel. The rest of the family could then piggy-back on that situation, and we camped out on our long-distance trips. But we thought of those times as adventures.

I began to look for other academic jobs because the BU tenure situation was not being solved. I was invited to apply to the University of Pennsylvania, UC/Berkeley, and UCLA. The Penn and UC/Berkeley faculty seemed not interested in my critical and feminist social art history—except for Peter Selz at UC/Berkeley. Penn really wanted Elizabeth Johns for the job. In both places I gave a feminist reading on Mary Cassatt and the ways her relationship with Degas influenced the style and subject matter of her art— probably too unconventional for either school.

Invited to UCLA in spring 1983, which was then known as a hot-bed of radicals and Marxists, I gave my job talk on Philip Evergood and his politics. The faculty loved it and offered me the job. The Dean called me and talked about mortgage loans. However, a colleague, thinking she would help me, wrote a recommendation letter enthusiastically praising my Marxist approach. I never saw the letter, but two UCLA faculty admitted that the letter turned out to be the kiss of death.

At the Chancellor's level I was turned down. Meanwhile, faculty friends at BU went to speak with President Silber, warning that I—who contributed so much to BU and had won a Guggenheim Fellowship—might leave Art History, the American Studies program, and the BU Art Gallery. My colleagues were effective, and I was finally awarded tenure by Silber.

Our situation changed dramatically in 1988 when Kevin began a full-time job as a tech writer at Wang, a computer company, and inherited money from his bachelor uncle. Then, the art market saved us when I sold the Roy Lichtenstein drawing at Sotheby's.

12

BU Art Gallery, 1980-89

Back-stepping a few years: In spring 1980 the Chair of the Art History Department assigned me to be the faculty advisor for a student-run art gallery that had been closed but was going to be transferred from the College of Fine Arts to the College of Arts and Sciences Art History Department. Located on the ground floor of the CFA building on Massachusetts Avenue, the gallery was a windowless space measuring 2,500 square feet with ten-foot-wide moveable walls.

As my first project I called in a consultant to advise me on security issues, alarm systems, floor coverings, and light levels. I saw this as an opportunity not only to professionalize the gallery's operation and enhance the department's museum studies curriculum, but to make an impact on the art scene in Boston.

I listed our name in the Association of Art Museum's official Directory and began to attend meetings and conferences frequented by other university art gallery directors. I insisted on obtaining Library of Congress ISBN numbers for our exhibition catalogues. I saw my tasks as overseeing the planning of future exhibitions, raising funds from the penny-pinching BU administration, producing exhibition catalogues, and designing installations—. activities I was already doing for the Whitney Museum as an adjunct curator.

For Fall 1980 the Art History Department hired Amy Lighthill, a dynamic art history grad student to join me as Gallery Manager for the academic year. She was in charge of exhibition projects, as well assigning tasks to those six to eight grad students assigned to work in the art gallery (for 15 hours per week as part of their tuition free package). She worked a full-time job. I then estimated that I was working about 10-20+ hours per week on Gallery matters on top of my full-time teaching and curating shows for the Whitney.

Fortunately, the first exhibition that September 1980 was already on the schedule. *Victorian and Edwardian Photographs* had been organized by the Photographic Resource Center, a dynamic artist-run organization for Boston photographers. Amy, the students, and I had to scramble to bring in another show. I looked to my artist friends. The New York artist Alice Neel, whose work I knew and with whom I had conducted hours of interviews would be easy, since all the works I would need were stored in her apartment.

When the show opened in October 1980, the studio faculty at BU ignored the exhibition. The chair even advised students not to bother seeing the work. An exception was John Wilson, a Black BU studio teacher who brought his students to participate in a walk-through with Neel.

The critics were enthusiastic.

Other shows followed in the 1980-81 season, such as *9 Boston Painters* and *Pacita Abad,* both curated by Lighthill, and a tapestry exhibition that traveled to us from Pratt Institute. Lighthill liked to make studio visits to Boston artists, and her friendships with them helped to secure the BUAG's standing in the art community. At the end of the academic year, the School of the Visual Arts of the College of Fine Arts showcased art by its graduating BFA and MFA studio students, as they have every year since.

During the summer of 1981, without the 10/hour student

assistants, we closed the Gallery and took deep breaths. With the respite I could devote myself to my research and writing, and students could finish courses, write theses and dissertations, and graduate. What a feat!

By the second year, 1981-82, I had been promoted to Gallery Director by BU president John Silber. This promotion was his alternative to denying me tenure. Lighthill remained the Gallery Manager.

That academic year also saw another packed schedule. Lighthill organized a juried Massachusetts Quilt show, and with Robert Workman (who had joined the student staff) they co-curated *Boston Artists Works on Paper*. We also hosted three photography shows—two organized by the Photographic Resource Center.

Workman also curated an historic show, *To Promote and Preserve: A Century of the Bostonian Society*, with a sharp scholarly essay for the catalogue. He brought into the Art Gallery furniture, paintings and sculpture. I finished up the season with a show of the work of Philadelphia artist Sydney Goodman. Almost all the shows had catalogues, ready for sale on opening night.

My third year, 1982-83, I was on a Guggenheim leave. Daniel Ranalli, a photographer/conceptual artist, stepped in as acting director, with Robert Workman managing the gallery. A variety of exhibitions followed under their watch. Later in 1989, when teaching a course on curatorial studies, Ranalli stepped in to curate *Terra Ferma*, described recently by him as "mostly site works. There was a strong installation/conceptual flavor. A small catalog. One of the pieces had a live bird that escaped its cage, driving some folks a little crazy. CFA apparently hated the show."

But even when on leave, I was thinking about future innovative and politically inflected exhibitions. I am most proud of *Social Concern and Urban Realism: American Painting of the 1930s,* an exhibition that came out of my involvement with the labor movement. The show offered a new look at politically engaged artists of the 1930s, and provided me the opportunity to bring an exhibition on class politics to the BUAG.

The back story: Moe Foner, executive secretary of 1199SEIU, the Hospital Workers' Union headquartered on West 43rd Street in New York, had successfully won grants from the National Endowment for the Humanities, the New York State Council on the Arts, and the New York Council for the Humanities for his Bread and Roses Project that aimed at bringing art, music and theater to working people.

Foner knew me from an 1199 traveling exhibition project, *The Working American* (1979) that had been curated by Abigail Gerdts and for which I wrote the catalogue's lead essay. Following that he asked me to join his consultants for other activities. I was thrilled to go to meetings that strategized efforts to bring art to a working-class audience and to meet the actors and labor supporters Danny Glover and Ruby Dee, who were also on board. I volunteered to organize an exhibition for the Bread and Roses project on 1930s socially conscious artists to open at the 1199 Gallery and then travel to Boston University.

We explained the name Bread and Roses in the catalogue foreword: "During the strike of Lawrence, Massachusetts, textile workers, most of them women and children, and many of them immigrants, a coup of mill hands carried a banner proclaiming, 'We Want Bread and Roses, Too.' That slogan, which expresses the reaction of working people to the Biblical admonition, 'Man does not live by bread alone,' has been adopted as the theme."

To enlist the help and enrich the experiences of BU students, in the spring of 1981 I taught a Museum Studies seminar on socially conscious artists of the 1930s. Four seminar students took the course, researching, visiting artist studios with me, narrowing down the checklist and writing drafts of essays. The students were a smart and curious bunch who threw themselves into the project.

Social Concern opened in early 1983 at 1199's headquarters, installed with the assistance of then BU gallery manager Robert Workman. After the BUAG venue, the show moved on to four other museums across the nation, sponsored by the American Federation of the Arts. It was one of the first reassessments of 1930s paintings that stressed the social and political issues of the period.

In fall 1983 Patricia Johnston, a brilliant BU doctoral student with a background in museum work and who had prodded me into co-founding the Boston Chapter of the Women's Caucus, joined the BUAG as gallery manager. In 1984-85, when I was on leave to organize a John Singer Sargent exhibition for the Whitney, she was promoted to acting director. She brought to the job her skills in writing grants, in facilitating the traveling of shows to other venues, and media outreach. With her steering the projects and their traveling schedule we gained more visibility in Boston and across the country.

In late 1983, Cooper Union—the New York art, architecture, and engineering school—commissioned me to pull together an exhibition of the work of Raphael Soyer, who had once been on their faculty. I agreed as long as I could bring the show to the BUAG. The catalogue included Soyer's own reflections of a life in art, as well as my own essay. Whereas the BU studio faculty sneered at the painterly directness of Alice Neel's expressionist portraits, they loved Soyer and the technical ways he built up layers of paint. Soyer's working-class subject matter, however, did not enter their conversation.

In February 1984 the gallery mounted a companion to the 1930s show: *Social Concern in the 1980s: A New England Perspective.* Like the 1930s show, the 1980s exhibition involved Museum Studies students taking a fall

1983 seminar with me. For this juried exhibition we put out a call to artists in issues of *Art New England,* which was picked up by artists' newsletters. We also sent notices to individual artists. We reviewed slides by over one hundred New England artists and visited many of their studios.

Johnston secured a grant from the Massachusetts Endowment for the Humanities, which gave us the resources to produce a 32-page catalogue with individual essays by all 27 artists. I explained the narrative for the show and selection of artworks in the Preface, titled *The Mechanics of Selection*: "To a large extent, all of the art submitted determined the range of subject matter and the variety of styles ... [However], we made a conscious decision to limit the subject matter included in the exhibition to that which dealt with overt social concerns or the relationship between the artist and society ... In the end, we tried to incorporate as much stylistic and thematic pluralism as we could."

The participating artists came from a variety of backgrounds, races, and ethnic groups, including recent immigrants to the US. I made it a point to familiarize myself with Black artists who were part of the African American Master-in-Residence Program (AAMRP), housed in a Northeastern University building. Dana Chandler Jr., who founded the residency program in 1977, and Bryan McFarlane were included in the exhibition.

These juried exhibitions, then fairly rare for the Boston area, accomplished what Johnston and I wanted: to present the BUAG as a welcoming venue for local artists. We became a crucial part of an artistic community that included Karla Munsat, editor of *Art New England,* and the writers/critics who wrote for the journal: Charles Guiliano, Lois Tarlow, and art historians from the Women's Caucus for Art. Other critics enthusiastic about the BUAG programs included Nancy Stapen of *The Boston Globe*, David Bonetti of the *Boston Phoenix,* and later Christine Temin. Shows like ours give a sense of the energy for the arts during the 1980s.

However, this timely show meant another trip to the Provost's office to explain why I had introduced politics into the exhibition by including Arnold Trachtman's portrait of Ronald Reagan conferring with other contemporary war hawks. But with great reviews in the press, the Provost was grudgingly satisfied.

Left politics were certainly not what the University administration wanted to encourage in public art exhibitions. One year I received a zero raise. With all the work I had done for the university and all my publications, I was perplexed. I doggedly tracked down the decision-maker. Both the department chair and the Dean denied their roles: "It wasn't me who denied you the raise."

I made an appointment to see the Provost, Jon Westling, who clearly would have made the decision. We had a cordial chat, and then he raised the issue that I was bringing politics into the Art Gallery. He was referring to the fact that I had brought to the BUAG the traveling exhibition on the artists who did illustrations for the early 20th-century socialist magazine *The Masses*—a traveling exhibition that Rebecca Zurier had organized for the Yale University Art Gallery.

Without using the word "political" I reminded the Provost that "controversy is good" for a university.

He wondered aloud: "Why can't you bring a Dürer prints show to the gallery? "I replied that the low light levels such a show demanded would compromise the pleasure of seeing the Dürers. He accepted that. A few months later I received a letter from Westling that I was going to get a salary raise. He made it clear that the decision was based on the fact that I had just mounted a successful John Singer Sargent exhibition at the Whitney.

Arlette Klaric joined the BUAG as Associate Director in fall 1985. She seemed the perfect fit. She had been hired by BU for the 1984-85 year as a sabbatical replacement for me and to head up the museum studies program. Everyone liked her elegant touch to the presentations of exhibitions and her tactful relationships with administrators. In this year, I cut my working hours in the BUAG, because I was organizing a large John Singer Sargent exhibition for the Whitney Museum.

With Lighthill, Johnston and Klaric, the annual exhibitions presented in my nine years at the BUAG settled into a formula: One show would focus on a contemporary artist needing more art world attention. The Alice Neel show had set the tone.

Later solo shows focused on these artists: May Stevens, curated by me, a show of Rudolf Baranik's paintings sent from another university museum, Joyce Kozloff, curated by Johnston. A print show of the Uruguanian American Antonio Frasconi's series, *Desaparecidos* first opened at the art gallery of SUNY/Cortland University, with a catalogue essay by me, and then came to BU.

The essays for all these catalogues were thoroughly researched. For my Frasconi essay, Amnesty International sent me about 80 pages of their research notes on the disappeared of Uruguay—information I incorporated into my text.

A second category would be golden oldies, such as the Bostonian Society show, *Social Concern of the 1930s,* and a show of 1930s prints from the Boston Public Library. This category also included shows such as *Celestial Images,* an exhibition of 16th- to 18th-century astronomical charts selected from the collection of BU astronomy professor Michael Mendillo.

Mendillo recently recalled the origins of the show, which exemplifies how a casual look or conversation can spark a big exhibition project: "I was dean of the Gradutle School, and you came to my office for some budget issue. You saw two 17th-century astronomical framed prints on my wall and asked about them. You had a recent PhD student (Pat Burnham) who needed a job and so Celestial Images was created. Good memories."

After BU, the show traveled to four other venues from 1986 to 1997: The National Museum of American History in Washington, DC, Williams College, the Yale University Art Gallery, and the New England Science Center. The catalogue was revamped for another traveling show between 2000 and 2010 hosted by eight other prestigious museums, with the BUAG still listed as the sponsoring host. Thirteen venues was a record for the BUAG.

A third category of exhibition might focus on a group of artists or a media, for example, a show highlighting the BU studio faculty, or landscape artists in the Boston area, or photography shows. Klaric curated *The Human Presence in Sculpture: A Boston University Tradition* (1986), which focused on BU studio professors. She also brought to the BUAG the exhibition *Art in Fashion/Fashion in Art* (1988), then at the Fashion Institute of Technology. What spread our name abroad was *Contemporary Quilts* USA, curated by Klaric and organized by E. J. Montgomery as a traveling show under the auspices of USIA (United States Information Agency). It traveled throughout Europe for three years. As part of the programming Klaric went to Athens where she lectured on the show.

Some of Klaric's exhibitions focused on issues of social justice such as *Breath Taken: The Landscape and Biography of Asbestos: An Exhibition* (1991) that showcased the photography of Bill Ravanesi. When the BUAG mounted the traveling show *A Different War: Viet Nam in Art,* curated by Lucy Lippard of paintings done by Vietnamese artists and American soldiers caught up in that tumultuous war, Klaric insisted that the wall labels be written in Vietnamese as well as English.

We partnered with other BU organizations on

exhibitions, including the Photographic Resource Center. We also used the space to accommodate art history lectures and other groups needing meeting space, such as the Boston branch of the Women's Caucus for Art and the Empire Brass Quartet, which played noontime concerts. We even hosted parties and a wedding.

Tired of begging for funds, I finally quit the job in the summer of 1989. Klaric was ready to take over as Director.

As time passed, the BU administration became less nervous about the politically inflected exhibitions in the Art Gallery, since the University was getting inches of coverage in the Boston newspapers. During the years 1980-89 I continued showing the social and cultural dimensions of art movements and their participating artists. My modus operandi entailed getting to know contemporary artists and their thoughts on art making, working closely with the gallery managers, inviting feedback from students and administrators, and installing quality shows on a low budget.

During this time BU President John Silber grew to like me and my entrepreneurial skills. He liked the positive press reviews and raved about my Whitney Sargent exhibition while keeping mum about my politics. He came to all our openings, sometimes with deans in tow, and chatted with me. Whereas most BU faculty and upper administrators were intimidated by his rants, I was not. His quirky, sly jokes reminded me of my father. I laughed at those jokes, when other professors and staff froze up.

&

A university art gallery is not just a place to showcase works of art, but also a laboratory for students who want to learn about curatorial work. Although our department offered a Certificate in Museum Studies, the best BU education in curatorial work came when art history students were assigned to the BU Art Gallery as Research Assistants, putting theory into practice. Six to eight students, including at least one studio MFA student, worked for us each semester.

We held weekly meetings, and the gallery managers for the year—Lighthill, Johnston (later Acting Director) and Associate Director Klaric—and I made assignments. We also made the important decisions concerning upgrading the facilities, writing grants, providing copy for catalogue publications, negotiating traveling exhibitions, and overseeing art shipments.

I recall Johnston and I, and later, Klaric, spending many evenings in the back offices of the BUAG drinking leftover cheap red wine from past openings and eating takeout pizza, laughing, and strategizing. We were always scheming on ways to cut costs. We borrowed exhibition cases when we needed them. We enlisted my husband Kevin to help transport art in our Buick station wagon to the gallery to save money on commercial vendors. My son Brad sometimes ran errands, and my step-daughter Emily took a turn or two sitting as a receptionist at the front desk.

Our plan was always for the students to learn the protocols and take on many of the responsibilities. One student would be assigned to registration duties—examining and doing the paperwork for all art that came in and out of the BUAG. Another would take charge of getting out the press release, sending invitations, and doing media relations. Another would focus on education, making housing arrangements for out-of-town gallery lecturers and scheduling visits from the local public schools. Still another would make sure all the wall labels were written, edited and mounted. Others would take charge of assigning student guards, setting up tables of food and wine, and cleanup. They even took turns sitting at the desk at the entrance, relieving Evelyn Cohen, our beautifully dressed and coiffed senior receptionist who let us know of the VIPs who came to the Gallery.

Although Johnston and I were in charge of the exhibition installation, all of the students would join the installation crew by spackling, painting, moving the moveable walls, vacuuming, cleaning up spilled paint, and putting up the signage for the title of the exhibition. They learned to hang frames with a mid-line of 57 inches from the floor, to design a wall as it were a flat blank canvas with square and rectangular shapes on it, with including so many inches from a door and so many inches from the adjacent wall. We double-hung frames when necessary. That meant that students needed to engage in a final walk-through of the actual installation. They learned that exhibitions are an ensemble, not just a series of walls on which paintings are hung.

Which artworks introduced the exhibition? Were the spaces between works appropriate? What were the sight lines to pull the viewer from space to space? What were the imaginative pairings? What juxtapositions of different images would lead viewers to new interpretations? What would be the impact on the viewer if a series of images similar in size, subject matter or treatment would march across the horizontal space? Did the exhibition's conclusion encourage the viewer to experience take-away ideas?

The point is that installation pacing and design make a difference to visitor responses. As William Lieberman taught me at MoMA: *A curator makes art out of artists' artwork*. Every artwork should be memorable not only in what it shows, but in its context within a room or space.

As to the openings, all of us pitched in. We scraped carrots, sliced cheeses, and laid out shrimp when we could afford it. I even got a wholesale flowers license from the Boston Flower Mart to provide fresh flowers on the cheap for openings. The refreshment table in the hall outside the Gallery was popular with students and the public. MFA students would grab a handful of veggies and crackers and a plastic glass of wine on the way to their studios. One middle-aged man showed up regularly, shabby but still dapper, wearing a black opera cape and a wig more appropriate for a Halloween party. He probably lived on the snacks he consumed on his rounds of gallery openings.

Several times I would have an afterparty in our home for staff and the exhibiting artists. Students never complained about working overtime, for they knew they would get time-off for personal emergencies. These experiences provided us all with the sense of community and mission. They also trained BU students to qualify for jobs at museums.

As mentioned above, even after I had resigned as BUAG Director, I continued to have a hand in educating students in curatorial practices. Beginning about 2000, the gallerist Warren Adelson gave me funds to set up the Jan and Warren Adelson Fellowships in American Art for doctoral students. I crafted the requirements to include the students curating or co-curating an exhibition at the BUAG. I was very hands-on with the Warren fellows who organized their own exhibitions. I raised funds for their catalogues, discussed their checklists, reviewed their essays, helped solve shipping issues, and wrote Forewords.

I fondly look back at the years between 1980 and 1989, when I developed this laboratory community of enthusiastic nascent curators, and when I later served as a visiting curator and informal faculty consultant. I cherish my memories of the BU Art Gallery and having had the opportunity to train and educate students in curatorial practices, with an emphasis always on the quality of the art and its presentation—and maybe a little politics thrown in.

13

The Boston Women's Caucus for Art, 1983-89

Regarding feminism: it's not just espousing feminist critique to your friends, but also allowing queries and ideas to help shape your practice. I applied my new ways of thinking and goals for practice when curating exhibitions for the Whitney in 1972, teaching in 1974 and running the Boston University Art Gallery in 1980. In the 1980s I was ready to become an activist for women artists and art historians.

The idea of founding a Boston chapter of the Women's Caucus for Art was first broached to me in 1981 by my doctoral student Patricia Johnston. Before coming to BU for a doctoral degree, Pat Johnston had worked for a museum and was already a WCA member. When she suggested we start a chapter, I agreed enthusiastically. I would step in to become a public activist feminist. In February 1982, at the time of the annual CAA meetings, Pat and I met with the WCA national officers, who gave us guidance. Muriel Magenta, the president wrote to us:

We feel that it is extremely important the WCA be represented in your locale. The large number of women art professionals in the metropolitan Boston area will contribute significantly to the national status of our organization, which represents women in the visual arts throughout the United States.

We know from the networking experience of chapter members in the existing 23 affiliates, participation on the local level directly benefits the professional careers of each individual involved.

The national office sent us copies of the WCA Bylaws, a dues schedule, and guidelines for establishing a chapter. We submitted an ad to local newspapers—*The Boston Globe*, *Equal Times*, and the *Boston Phoenix*—inviting women to attend a meeting on June 22, 1982.

Another meeting of the fledgling Boston chapter took place in September 1982, with artists Susan Schwalb and Adria Arch, as well art historians Alicia Faxon, Liana Cheney, Diane Radycki, Melissa Dabakis, Johnston, and me. We were soon joined in subsequent meetings by artists Prilla Brackett, Leslie Sills, Sarah Sutro, and X Bonnie Woods. We realized that if the Boston WCA chapter were to grow, we needed to offer members a variety of programming along with regular monthly business meetings. We decided to have co-chairs—one artist and one art historian, resulting in Schwalb and I becoming co-chairs. Carla Munsat, who had started up the bi-monthly journal *Art New England*, hired the WCA art historians as critics and showcased WCA women artists at the BU Art Gallery, as well as other venues.

Many of our BWCA meetings and evening events took place at the spacious BU Art Gallery, to which I as director had a key to the front door. In those early years, I spoke about Alice Neel, whose paintings had been on display in the BUAG. Radycki and Maureen Giovannini, an anthropology professor, spoke on subjects such as "Images and Reality of Pregnancy." Jo Ann Rothschild presented her research on the sorry statistics of women's inclusion in area museum exhibitions. Johnston gave a talk on the different threads within feminist art criticism. Cheney and Faxon regularly talked about historical art issues pertaining to women. We had slide nights with artist-members showing their work, potluck suppers, and Christmas parties.

A challenge for our WCA chapter came when CAA scheduled its annual meeting for February 1987 in Boston, which meant that the WCA national conference would simultaneously be in Boston. The national WCA president Annie Shaver-Crandell came to Boston to give us a pep talk. Art historian Cheney was to oversee the WCA's annual conference, as well as overseeing regional and national exhibitions connected to the event. X Bonnie Woods served as treasurer and managed to secure venues without paying fees. The planning became very ambitious, but in spite of Cheney's diplomatic skills there were tensions and vocal disagreements among members. The conference was a success, but we were wrung out.

By then I had turned over my co-chair responsibilities of the Boston Women's Caucus for Art to others. My last event was a 1988 WCA Invitational exhibition of Boston area women artists to be shown at A.I.R. Gallery in New York. The jury consisted of Faxon, *Art New England* editor Carla Munsat, and me. We chose 30 works by twelve artists. Today, almost all twelve have attained national recognition. I felt my job had concluded. By 1989 I had resigned my position of BUAG Director and became less active in WCA activities. The indefatigable Pat Johnston stayed on with the BWCA as co-chair for a few years, as curator for another exhibition, and as an organizer for a two-day symposium on women's art supported by the Massachusetts Foundation for the Humanities.

What kept art historians connected to an organization clearly focused on the artwork and careers of women artists? Why did we spend so much time, energy, and frantic organizing to come up with highly successful programs? Simply, the moment had arrived when feminists felt optimistic about changing the world. Art historians wanted to connect with practicing artists and to find common ground. I made many friends among the Boston artists.

At that time—in the 1980s—I was also mounting political art exhibitions at the Boston University Art Gallery. I hoped to radicalize some of the Boston area women artists, many of whom lived suburban, nonpolitical lives, even while experiencing inequities because of their gender. In connection with these BUAG exhibitions and to stretch their minds, I brought in artists and critics to speak: Alice Neel, Lucy R. Lippard, Lawrence Alloway, Donald Kuspit, May Stevens, Lowery Stokes Sims, Cecilia Vicuñia, Elizabeth Hess, Deborah Bright, and others.

Although I never succeeded in radicalizing artists toward a political and economic critique who were not already radicalized, I did contribute to the effort of getting them connected to something larger—to the collective knowledge and belief that women and their art mattered. In turn, the artists helped me to feel connected to a community of people in the world working for social change. My experience was always one of practice, even if advancing the theory lagged somewhat.

As I moved into the 1990s, my friendship with artist-feminist-activist May Stevens flourished. She inspired my feminism in many ways by strongly voicing her opinions that class and socialist ideas were co-equal with feminist ideas.

When Stevens and her husband Rudolf Baranik moved to Santa Fe, Kevin and I visited them often. I became friends with the feminist women clustered in the Santa Fe area, many of whom had formerly been active in the WCA and the feminist publication *Heresies*. One of May's best friends, Lucy Lippard, lived in Galisteo along with her neighbors, artists Nancy Holt and Harmony Hammond. Their friend Sabra Moore lived nearby in Abiquiu, New Mexico. Lucy, among the top five American art critics of the late-20th century, continued to write her books; soon her concerns embraced Indigenous peoples, Latinx, and Black people. One of her major books on this subject was *Mixed Blessing: New Art in a Multicultural America* (1991). The Santa Fe/Galisteo/Abiquiu women clearly had ambitions to change the world. Like me, they had embraced the Women's Caucus for Art, but had moved on.

14

Blockbuster Exhibitions, 1986 & 2005

I organized the biggest blockbuster ever for the Whitney—*John Singer Sargent,* which opened in September 1986. The week before the show ended lines wrapped around the block. It brought in 450,000 visitors, plus another 450,000 visitors to the second venue, the Art Institute of Chicago. Press response soared. Several TV show hosts interviewed me. I was probably the first woman who had ever organized a retrospective exhibition of a major 19th-century American artist.

It was a smart career move, but it must have mystified some people that a lefty feminist—especially one charged by the likes of Hilton Kramer for ignoring aesthetics for social history—could pull off such a curatorial feat. I had some qualms, since I deplored the wealth and privilege Sargent's portraits projected. And I did not know how to come to terms with the many visitors who wanted to plunge themselves into that Gilded Age splendor while ignoring the history and social realities of the embattled labor movement in the late 19th century.

Mostly what drew me to Sargent were the aesthetics—his virtuoso application of paint to canvas, exercised brilliantly in *The Daughters of Edward D. Boit* (1882, Museum of Fine Arts Boston). I was also deeply intrigued by his process of drawing several versions of figures in movement, such as the sketches of dancers and nude men—highlighting their energy in a particular moment. But were the aesthetics enough to balance the representations of *a dolce vita*, a life of splendor, self-indulgence, and physical pleasure? To parry this question, I chose many subject paintings that represented French and Italian working women and men, as well as Middle Eastern people of color. The latter peaked Sargent's curiosity and he gave them the respect they deserved. In the end, I was pleased with my ensemble that, upon closer examination, tacitly challenged the usual cultural expectations of Sargent and his work.

Originally it was not my idea. In the early 1980s, Margaret L. Kaplan, the editor for acquisitions at Abrams Books, had been impressed with the progress of my book on Alice Neel. She invited me to lunch and asked whether I would consider writing a book on John Singer Sargent. I agreed, thinking about how I could catapult that project into a Whitney exhibition on Sargent. I asked Whitney Museum director Tom Armstrong whether he would be interested in such a Sargent show—one not done in decades in New York. As usual with my proposals, he agreed with enthusiasm. He scheduled the exhibition to open in 1983. That would be a tight schedule for research and writing— especially since I was still committed to finishing the Neel book and running the BU Art Gallery (along with my usual teaching).

The National Gallery of Art in Washington, D.C. showed an interest in a joint venture with the Whitney, but plans remained vague. With the NGA involved, other museums would likely commit themselves to lending. I had already made visits to the big museums that owned Sargent paintings and watercolors, including those in the UK. It was important to me—as it has been to other curators—to curry the favor of directors with the aim of securing loans.

Theodore E. Stebbins, Jr., Curator of American Painting at the MFA, with whom I had discussed my exhibition plans, brought my project to a halt. He admitted as much in his

May 20, 1981 letter to me: "I want to apologize for having unintentionally pulled at least part of the rug out from under your proposed exhibition on John Singer Sargent. I do not think that our minds have ever met very well on exactly what such an exhibition should be like ... I am not terribly optimistic about our being involved with a Sargent exhibition of the kind you are planning."

In his remarks, he was not dismissing me, we were simply approaching art in different ways. I viewed Harvard-trained art historians as mainly interested in issues of connoisseurship focused on masterpieces. As a former studio art student, I found connoisseurship less interesting than the processes of making art. I especially embraced unfinished drawings and oil sketches for their insights into an artist's mind at work. Moreover, having been trained at the Institute of Fine Arts (NYU), I felt that the study of any artist needed to include questions about iconography and the social and cultural issues surrounding the artist. I also wanted to examine the economic politics of the patrons in that era.

In any event, Stebbins had gone ahead with planning a major exhibition for 1983. *A New World: Masters of American Painting, 1760-1910,* would travel to Europe. Hence, the MFA's most major Sargents would not be available for my show. Moreover, both the Metropolitan Museum and the Corcoran curators reluctantly told me that they could not honor their previous commitment to lend their masterpieces to my Sargent show. To them the MFA had priority. The MFA was too powerful—a power based on the MFA's great collection of American 19th-century paintings, which those curators might one day want to borrow. That's how it works.

With the MFA's show on the calendar, I had no option but to reschedule my exhibition from 1983 to 1986. I later appreciated the extra time to do needed research and to travel across the country, the United Kingdom, and Paris to visit museum directors and Sargent family members. (So thank you Ted Stebbins!) I was aided by the gallerist Warren Adelson, who knew the Sargent family well. He sold many of their Sargent paintings, and put me in touch with private collectors abroad who owned Sargent's work.

My travels and research produced a strong object list that ranged from early to late, from oil paintings to watercolors and drawings—all of them stunning works. Under orders from Tom Armstrong, I went back to the National Gallery of Art to persuade the NGA director and curator that the Sargent show should go to Washington, DC. John Wilmerding, then the curator and always supportive of me, set up the meeting in a huge board room. The NGA men were skeptical at the very beginning. Gil Ravenau, the NGA installation designer who seemed to lead the meeting, criticized one aspect or another of my checklist, saying things like, "But this is just a wish list."

I pushed back, saying that I had been to the museums and homes of collectors who own the paintings, and they had made personal commitments to lend. The men in the room seemed incredulous at my response. John Wilmerding, the curator, was embarrassed by their rudeness.

Deeply dissatisfied by the NGA administration's trivializing my professionalism and their ambivalence towards the project, I returned to New York. My good luck came when Milo Naeve, the curator at the Art Institute of Chicago, entered the scene. He enthusiastically snapped up the Sargent show and helped facilitate loans from big museums. He was the perfect partner. And in the end, I got almost all the pictures I wanted to stage a stunning retrospective.

Moreover, I secured commitments by leading scholars to write essays on specific aspects of Sargent's life and art. Sargent biographer Stanley Olsen offered a succinct account of Sargent's life. Linda Ayres, Albert Boime, William H. Gerdts, Gary Reynolds, and Annette Blaugrund each contributed essays on different aspects of Sargent's art. The head of Whitney publications told me I had to write three essays to fill in the holes not covered by the others. Doing that was a pleasure. Pick any aspect of Sargent's art—they are all conducive to rich interpretive prose. Any hyperbole is well deserved.

With the help of BU's M.A. student Lisa Hilgeman, I did the whole show almost single-handedly. I would write the loan letters for Armstrong's signature and mail them to New York for him to sign. He would mail back the lenders' replies for me to respond using his name.

The Registrar leaned on me to solve logistical problems in the shipping of the paintings. For example, I wanted to include Sargent's grand portrait titled *Charles Stewart, Sixth Marquis of Londonderry, Carrying the Great Sword of State, at the Coronation of King Edward VII, August, 1902, and Mr. W. C. Beaumont, His Page on That Occasion,* (1904). It was owned by Henry Kravis, the billionaire who specialized in leveraged buyouts. His apartment was just west of 5th Avenue. The only way we could get the painting from a very high floor was through the window—which meant a tall crane. I campaigned for that solution, but the Registrar argued that expenses would be too high. That painting was not included in the New York venue of the show.

I wrote copy for the press releases, texts for the walls, and closely worked with the editor to see the catalogue through to press. Gratefully, I took a leave of absence from BU for that 1985-86 year, so I could accomplish what I needed.

More satisfying to me than the exhibition's success was that I had the opportunity to analyze Sargent as a product of his contemporary art world as it moved from the moralizing subjects of mid-century into (in the words of English critic Matthew Arnold) the "sweetness and light" of impressionism.

I was also intrigued by Sargent's experiences and those of other artists who lived in the Gilded Age—a time of rapid industrialization, predatory imperialism, and conspicuous consumption. Still, I admit to my own contradictions and will say it again: While I abhor the display of privileged wealth, I can also declare Sargent to be the best painter— one who puts paint on canvas—of the 19th century. No one comes close to his *alla prima* (wet-into-wet) fluid painting for his portraits and for his range of sparkling whites.

Armstrong was ecstatic over the attendance records and gave me a gift certificate for the Quilted Giraffe, a fancy New York restaurant. My husband and I were joined by our screenwriter friend Eleanor Bergman and poet Michael Goldman (Kevin's college buddy). The sample menu and wine engaged us for three glorious hours. Our restaurant trip reminded me that museum work could be glamorous and dazzling. Over dessert I did recall that while trying to advance to the public my thoughts on Gilded Age capitalism, I was enjoying the glamor and dazzle that museum perks can bestow on an underpaid curator.

The laudatory newspaper and magazine reviews stacked up on my desk, all positive. John Canaday reviewed the show three times in the *New York Times*, but never mentioned my name. I wrote him complaining about critics never mentioning women who were curators, where they always mentioned the men. I later wrote to other critics complaining about the same failure to recognize women curators.

&

BU President John Silber, a Sargent enthusiast, ordered copies of the catalogue for all the trustees. He also decided to have a big gala BU party staged at the Whitney, with trustees and BU patrons invited.

For the gala evening I gave a private tour of the

exhibition for Silber and his son, an actor then living in New York. I also gave a lecture in the Whitney auditorium to the BU patrons before we all retired to dinner. Silber rose to speak, his remarks focused on me. He narrated the time I had come up for tenure a few years earlier when he decided "to look into the mouth of the horse" for confirmation of my worthiness. Everyone in the room gasped at this remark and looked at me. But I burst into peals of laughter and told my table mates, "Well, he's from Texas, that's how they talk." Everyone relaxed after that.

As mentioned before, Silber liked me and always gave a warm smile when seeing me on campus. The university provided me with a suite for two nights at the upscale Carlyle Hotel. The two-night hotel bill totaled more than my previous year's raise. However, within a few months I received my full professorship and a small bump in salary.

&

Fast forward to 2005 and the exhibition *Syncopated Rhythms: 20th-Century African American Art from the George & Joyce Wein Collection,* which I curated for the BU Art Gallery.

The Wein show was a big leap from focusing on an international painter of the Gilded Age (as Sargent was) to one celebrating Black American artists who painted the everyday life of their working-class communities. These were women and men who struggled to make a place for themselves in the art world. They were not born with the privileges and access to patrons like Sargent. Many worked day jobs to maintain their studios. During the 1930s, the government's Federal Art Project (FAP) employed the most destitute of them so that they could continue painting.

This Wein exhibition also has a backstory. I had previously done research for my catalogue essay, *"Cultural*

Legacies and the Transformation of the Cubist Collage Aesthetic by Romare Bearden, Jacob Lawrence, and Other African American Artists," commissioned by the National Gallery of Art for a publication of essays on Romare Bearden. The George Wein collection housed a great comparison—Eldzier Cortor's award-winning painting, *Room No. 5* (1945). I needed to see it.

George Wein was a music impresario who founded the Newport Jazz Festival in 1954, the Newport Folk Festival in 1959, and the New Orleans Jazz and Heritage Festival in 1970. Everyone knew he and his wife Joyce collected African American art.

I reached out, and Wein invited me to his Manhattan apartment. I examined the Cortor painting, and then Wein walked me around his spacious apartment to show me their full collection of African American art. I was overwhelmed by the variety and the museum quality of the works. I jotted down notes of the works by 35 artists including: Charles Alston, Benny Andrews, Romare Bearden, John Biggers, Elizabeth Catlett, Miles Davis, William H. Johnson, Lois Mailou Jones, Jacob Lawrence, Hughie Lee-Smith, Faith Ringgold, Betty Saar, Augusta Savage, William T. Williams and the self-taught artists Minnie Evans and Sister Gertrude Morgan. And there were more!

I immediately asked if Wein would be willing to lend his paintings for a BU Art Gallery show. He and Joyce agreed. No curator had ever asked him to show the Wein works as a total collection. Although no longer director myself, the then director was enthusiastic.

I made the selection of artworks and invited my student Melissa Renn to co-author the catalogue. I also wrote the lead essay, *The Expressive Modernism of 20ᵗʰ-Century African American Art.* Renn and I divided the artists, and we each wrote biographical essays. The title—*Syncopated Rhythms*—seemed a natural. With their passion for music, Wein and his wife Joyce had gravitated to pictures by Black American artists that suggested the rhythms of songs. In my essay I commented on the many instances in which artists declared that music had been inspirational to their paintings. I then defined syncopation as the defining practice of ragtime, and offered up the Random House Dictionary definition: "A shifting of the normal accent, usually by stressing the normally unaccented beats." This characteristic defined many of the art works in the Wein collection. It seemed fitting that we include two paintings by Miles Davis.

Television journalist Ed Bradley of *60 Minutes* fame wrote a brief memoir of his friendship with George and Joyce which begins: "Going to dinner at Joyce and George Wein's apartment is like visiting a jewel of a museum that specializes in African American Art."

Bradley then explains that the first painting acquired by the Weins was Bearden's *New Orleans Farewell.* "It resonated with George because his life had been so involved with New Orleans, both the music and the politics. George and Joyce helped end segregation in that city through their first Jazz and Heritage Festival in 1970, which brought musicians and patrons, black and white, together in the same venue."

Our show was successful. The 104-page catalogue was superbly designed by a press in Vermont— and we received good reviews. I was even interviewed by a Chicago radio station whose audience consisted of serious jazz fans.

Sadly, Joyce Wein died of cancer on August 15, before the exhibition opened. Her memorial service, which I attended in New York, featured Wynton Marsalis playing a trumpet solo and Pete Seeger leading us in song.

The opening reception was held in November 2005 at the Boston University Castle—the best venue for a big event we could ever hope for at BU. Deans and provosts were all smiles, partly because they hoped BU alum George Wein, who had already provided partial funds for a named chair, would also fund the balance of that chair (or even fund a new building). On view for two months, our show, was successful in every way.

I gained from the experience by researching, recording, and writing about more Black artists just at the time when I was planning my year-long Jacob Lawrence research journey. I thought all the artists had important things to say through their art: the humanity of people, the colors of the world, and the day-to-day rhythms of the heart.

George Wein was pleased with the show and benefitted financially. Shortly after the show closed, the Boston Museum of Fine Arts bought a half dozen of his paintings and a sculpture—forming the core of MFA paintings by African American artists. The MFA purchases included Cortor's painting. No matter what ideals the curator has about kindling an appreciation of art and educating viewers about history, someone is always making money.

Which show did I enjoy curating the most? I do not want to choose. I do not want to be pigeon-holed. Both were challenging, and I learned a great deal about the Gilded Age of the 1880s and 1890s, as well as the Black Harlem Renaissance of the 1920s and 1930s. All the works chosen for both exhibitions were grounded in the aesthetics relevant to the dictates of their time and place. Studying those contrasts helps us define our own age.

15

The Daughter Track, 1989-91

Home life always involved complicated situations. When we moved to Cambridge in September 1989 my mother, Glennie, then almost 81, moved with us. I continued teaching but got a university badge for parking so I would be available to drive from class to home in an emergency.

It was years before one had the option to call a home health aide for regular help. Agencies had not yet been set up to accommodate working caregivers. Medicare would probably not solve our problems, since Glennie was not physically sick. But there were elderly day-care programs connected with hospitals and paid for by local government. So, we enrolled Glennie in one at St. Elizabeth's Hospital in Boston. I confided my worries to the Assistant Dean of my college at Boston University and proposed I take a leave of absence. She was adamant I should keep teaching and try to manage. She stressed the necessity of not abandoning my professional life while being mindful of my mental health. So I tried to do it all.

Glennie continued to live with us, except for one weekend each month during 1988, 1989 and 1990, when I drove her to a highway restaurant halfway between Boston and Durham, Connecticut, where my sister Gail lived. Gail would pick up Glennie from the rendezvous stop for a weekend stay at her home.

In the earlier 1980s, social workers had talked about

the phenomenon of "the sandwich generation," a situation described by Dorothy A. Miller, a professor of social work in 1981: "Adult children of the elderly, who are 'sandwiched' between their aging parents and their own naturing children … [They] are subjected to a great deal of stress. As the major resource and support for the elderly, this group has a need for services that is only beginning to be met by the healing professionals."

Social workers such as Miller were concerned about the stresses on the whole family—women and men—and the social resources not available to them. This was a new conversation for social workers in 1981, long before the Family and Medical Leave Act was passed in Congress and signed into law by President Clinton in 1993. The act provided that both men and women would be covered for 12 weeks of unpaid leave with job security to care for a family member.

I was aware of the sandwich generation concept in 1989, but "daughter track" was new to me. This was a new phrasing that joined the "mommy track" conceptualization that had already gained traction among feminists. The *Christian Science Monitor* (June 20, 1989) ran a brief story about this new phrase by Marilyn Gardner, who observed: "The latest catch phrase describes women whose careers may be threatened because of the time they spend caring for elderly relatives." It seems that those who used the phrase wanted to emphasize women and the trajectory of their careers.

I was not theorizing or historicizing the concept, it was my lived experience. To me, the Mommy + the Daughter + the Career Woman tracks became one heavy package that I, like so many others, bore on my back without complaining, as if the situation was a natural condition for women in the modern world.

But this also included men caregivers, like my husband Kevin, who was the guardian for his uncle in Florida in the late 1980s, and who participated in the caring of our children. He had no ambitions for building a career. However, the feminists focused on women because it was women who historically were considered the primary caregivers, and it was women who had difficulty juggling their familial and career responsibilities.

In 1989 someone at Channel 4 in Boston somehow heard about my situation. Suzanne Bates, the moderator of the show *Live on Four*, called the current situation of many women as "holding down three jobs." And I, she thought, would be an articulate spokeswoman for the "daughter track."

Thus, in September 1989, Bates's TV crew came to film me on location immersed as I was with the three duties: caring for my mother and my son and working as a professor of art history. The TV crew began with shots of Glennie, Andy, and me at breakfast in Cambridge, then my getting them ready to go to school and to the day care center at St. Elizabeth's hospital. The crew then followed me to BU as I went to class and taught, with additional camera time in my office, where I sorted slides to prepare for the next day's lecture and meditated on challenges of my situation.

I emphasized to the TV crew that I was most grateful to Kevin for soldiering on with the household responsibilities and for having benevolent feelings toward his mother-in-law. These remarks were edited out of the 2.47-minute segment. They did include my remarks that I was exhausted but still needed to keep up with my research and scholarship, as that's what was expected of me.

That TV episode was probably one of the first times American media focused on caregivers and told their stories. Some of my comments on the segment are as follows:

"I'm worried and tense … Always misjudging the amount of time [I have]." "My own research has been curtailed … It's publish or perish."

I answered their question as to whether or not women feel they can bring their burdens to the workplace. I responded: "It seems unprofessional. There's this atmosphere that if you raise these domestic issues, that you are using this as an excuse. What you try to be [is] super mom or super daughter."

None of my friends mentioned that they had seen the *Live on Four* episode. However the day after the episode aired, one of the guards who stood inside a kiosk outside the gates of a BU parking lot paused my car as I entered and complimented me on the broadcast. He shared that he was a vet suffering from PTSD and would really like to talk with me. I nodded ambiguously and drove in to find a parking spot. I never went to that parking lot again. Perhaps that was cowardly, or maybe it indicated my inability to have compassion for a man who had, no doubt, wrenching experiences and great psychological pain. But at that time, I did not want to get involved in another person's misery. I had enough on my plate.

&

Glennie died in March 1991, a few months after my sister and I had placed her in a Cambridge nursing home near Mt. Auburn Cemetery. I had finally admitted to myself that it was difficult to continue as a full-time caregiver and that she was safer in the nursing home. I would not have to worry that she might wander outside, fall down the stairs, or set the house on fire when she lit her cigarette on the flame from the gas stove.

She did not yet have a full-blown case of dementia, but since the early 1980s her fantasies had increasingly defined her manufactured reality, most of it focused on her boyfriend "Howard Hughes." She would regale our friends at parties about his clandestine visits. When my friends caught on to the craziness of her conversation, they would stare over at me. I just shrugged my shoulders. She was who she was. At the nursing home she did the same, but the staff realized it was just an old person's babbling.

After Glennie died, I turned my energy to spending time with my Uncle Arnold, frail in body but intellectually present. A nice man. Cautious man. Good man. I called him every Sunday morning at his home in Alexandria, Virginia. He had spent a lifetime working for the Food and Drug Administration looking for microbes in canned food to keep the public safe. He came out to me as a gay man when he was over 80—a secret he had buried for decades and truly wanted to share.

In December 1996 we looked forward to his usual Christmas visit. I had also planned to discuss the possibility of his moving into an apartment near us in Cambridge, since I was ready to pick up my daughter duties again. But he died in his sleep the morning before his plane was set to depart from Washington, D.C. He was 83 years old. My daughter Christina speculated that Uncle Arnold willed himself to die because of his anxiety about moving out of his longtime home in Virginia and starting a new life in Cambridge. Perhaps she was right.

16

Leda and the Swan, 1989

In 1989 we were still renting in Brookline, Massachusetts, close to Boston University. When Kevin's uncle died, we were left some money, which allowed us to pay off our many credit card bills. At that time, Kevin also had a full-time job. Now debt-free and with two incomes, Kevin suggested we buy our own home. I resisted. I had never owned a home, and I did not look forward to the ordeal of packing and unpacking. Moreover, we lacked funds for a down payment.

Meanwhile, earlier that spring I had wandered into a Sotheby's sale of contemporary prints and drawings. I could not believe the high prices for prints by Andy Warhol and other Pop artists. I came home and told Kevin that if we sold the Lichtenstein drawing *Leda and the Swan*, we might have enough funds for a down payment on a house.

Sotheby's accepted the work with an estimate of $40,000 to $60,000 [$104,000-$156,000 in 2025]. They would also give me a discount on their cut since I was always on hand to render opinions about Eastman Johnson paintings for their auction house. I then borrowed money from my mother and my Uncle Arnold for a down payment on the speculation that we could return the money after the Lichtenstein sale. In September 1989, we went ahead and bought our house in Cambridge.

Kevin, 11-year old Andy (dressed in a blazer), and I went to the sale that November. We felt like peasants out of our element. The bidding took off for *Leda*. Within seconds, it was sold. Hammer price: $210,000 [$538,000 in 2025]. Wow! I was sitting near the young, stylishly dressed woman whose paddle kept rising long after other bids had ceased. I leaned forward to say that I was an art historian and that the drawing was in perfect condition. She brushed off my remarks with a knowing, but somewhat anxious smile. "I bought this for my boyfriend," she said.

In thirty days, we were supposed to get the payment, minus the auction cut. Thirty days went by, and then thirty-one and thirty-two. I called my dealer friend Jay Maroney to ask what I should do. He said that if the bidders decided not to pay, there was nothing I could do about it. The drawing would be "burned" in terms of a near future sale. He went on to advise me to put on my best "Mrs. Got Rocks" voice and call Sotheby's to demand to know why I had not received the funds. I did. The strategy worked. The clerks at the other end of the phone apologized profusely and said the wired money would soon be in my account. In the meantime, I somehow learned that Larry Gogosian had bought my *Leda*; the elegant young woman was probably his employee. Or maybe the girlfriend?

As to the windfall: We netted $120,000 [$307,500 in 2025] after auction house fees and the IRS took their cut. We paid back my uncle and my mother, bought a new car with cash, and took a three-week trip to some German cities and the Venice Biennale, always staying in fancy hotels. We gave Christina, Mary, Brad, and Emily $5,000 each [$12,800 in 2025]; bought Andy a computer; and purchased a set of rattan living room furniture for the New Jersey house. The money evaporated, but the windfall had been unreal to me as I had not ever lived such a plush life.

We now owned a wooden, Mansard roof, Victorian home that we loved within a few blocks of Harvard Yard. It sat on a 40 by 60-foot plot with a back patio garden that with great pleasure I tended. The house was especially welcoming to our friends and my grad students, whom I invited for big sit-down dinners at the end of each semester.

As homeowners—and finally with roots—Kevin and I became involved in neighborhood politics. We helped to create the Riverside Neighborhood Association (RNA), which included an integrated group of homeowners—just east of the Harvard campus, below Massachusetts Avenue and above Memorial Drive, and west of River Street where the Cambridgeport neighborhood began. I co-wrote the constitution and functioned as the recording secretary— keeping minutes and distributing flyers about meetings on the neighbors' doorsteps.

Our meetings mostly focused on Harvard's buying up real estate in the neighborhood, the need for affordable housing, and zoning to slow down the developers. Police relations and a mega-church that wanted to establish a meeting house and gym in one of the old Cambridge buildings across the street from where we lived were also the Association's concerns. The mega-church backed down when they discovered that the interior brick columns could not be engineered to support their mega-plans. The RNA was going strong for about three years, then it fizzled out when the charismatic chair was offered an out-of-state job. No one wanted to take on his responsibilities. However, the City of Cambridge gave me a fancy document lauding me for my contributions to the community.

That made me proud.

17

A Combative Feminist, 1980s-90s

During the 1980s I began to take on the role of combative feminist as I turned my attention to theory-mania—the explosion of theories, many coming from France and Britain. By and large, these theories originated in departments of literary studies, and some made their way into art history departments, although rarely into museum exhibition catalogues. How do theories do their cultural work in terms of the interpretation of history?

Before I dive in, I first want to distinguish between methods and theories—concepts often confused when applied to art history. Methods are the pathways one chooses to grapple with and explicate art, artists' biographies, and art movements. Methods can include visual analysis, archival research, interviews, the study of the critical reception, marketing, patronage, and the distribution of reproductions. Maybe the art interpreter employs all of these for a book-length study. Perhaps only one or two for an essay.

Theory, as relevant to art, can be formalist or based on philosophical and psychoanalytical theories, but it aims to encourage a bigger explanation for the ways human behavior affects culture. More specifically critical theory (as used today) probes deeper into history. It includes the anthropological, sociological, and political forces that shaped the production of the artwork in its contemporary time. "No theory" means simply describing artworks (often with flare and sophistication) or verbalizing an artist's purported intentions (through guessing or research). Much of art writing is "no theory."

David Macey, author of *The Penguin Dictionary of Critical Theory* (London, 2000) admits to the fuzziness of the term *theory*. He begins his Preface to the book by stating:

To be advised that one should "go and read some theory" or, worse still, "do some theory" can be an intimidating experience. This is in part quite simply because there is so much theory. Academic bookshops are full of it; journals abound in it. Yet there is no real consensus as to just what constitutes theory. Louis Althusser repeatedly insisted that there could be no revolutionary practice without revolutionary theory. Paul de Man wrote dismissively of the resistance to theory. Homi K. Bhabha writes of his commitment to theory and urges us to emulate it. They are, of course all speaking of very different things and theories.

When we add the theorists of the last forty years, it becomes even scarier to the novice academic art historian and curator.

I suggested to my students that they read all the theorists that offered them insight. They should be able to recognize a complex set of ideas behind a word or phrase.

For example: When Pierre Bourdeiu speaks of "cultural capital," students should be able to deduce that he is speaking of situations in which money counts less than being familiar with the arts and serving as a patron of culture (the reason why capitalists join museum boards).

When W. E. B. Du Bois refers to "double consciousness" he is giving words to the phenomenon of Blacks having always to be aware of their blackness while also being conscious of themselves as American citizens.

When Henry Louis Gates, Jr. points to the tradition of "the signifying monkey" he is talking about the ways that Blacks historically have played the role of "trickster" to their own advantage.

When Clifford Geertz encourages "thick description" he is advocating a study of the smallest details when analyzing culture, such as a "wink."

When Laura Mulvey uses the term "male gaze," she refers to the fact that traditionally art has been created to satisfy the desires (and even lusts) of male viewers.

When Fredric Jameson admonishes his readers to "historicize, historicize, historicize" he is emphasizing the need to always find historical evidence before declaring a new interpretation.

When Gayatri Spivak asks "Can the subaltern speak?" she is encouraging scholars to find ways to discover how the "lower" classes or indigenous peoples have been able to express their own history through rituals and material culture.

All of these deductive concepts suggest the possibility for rich, evidence-based, interpretations.

I became especially concerned about the Deconstructionists. To them an artist's conscious intentions had no traction with these scholars. Nor were they interested in social history.

They approached the meaning of a work by rejecting those elements that at first seem obvious. The real meaning lay in the details. For literary academics, it was the mutability of words that needed to be unpacked. For art historians it was images and their details. Hence, close examination of an artwork (or close reading of a literary text) was needed to ferret out potential signs of meaning.

Once these deconstructionists pointed out those bits of seemingly unimportant details in a literary text or artwork, they were obliged to offer an interpretation. Many argued that all interpretations had equal validity—a concept especially promulgated by De Man. To my leftist outlook, there was a sense of anarchistic thinking in their "anything goes" thought processes.

The concept that there is no one meaning—no "master narrative"—gave scholars and their students permission to interpret a work anyway they wanted, without necessarily connecting the set of mini-interpretations to the evidence of history.

In my classes I would argue against the deconstructionists and their obsession with giving all details equal import. To me there were primary interpretations (drawing evidence from history and the ways ideologies work), but also secondary interpretations, sometimes focused on an artist's private life, and even tertiary interpretations, which could be trivial, amusing, or way off the mark. Primary interpretations compatible with historical evidence had explanatory power and paralleled our experience within a changing world.

A group of young Yale scholars, focused on the analyses of American painting, broke onto the scene in the 1980s with their embrace of a deconstructionist approach akin to that of Jacques Derrida and Paul De Man, both associated with the Comparative Literature Department at Yale. Many of these Yale art historians were influenced by the psychoanalytical theories of Sigmund Freud and Jacques Lacan. They were Bryan Jay Wolf, David Lubin, and Jules Prown, joined by Johns Hopkins Professor Michael Fried. A sample of their interpretations are as follows.

In Bryan Jay Wolf, *Romantic Re-Vision: Culture and Consciousness in Nineteenth-Century American Painting and Literature* (1982) the author reads the mountains, mist, and valleys in the paintings of Thomas Cole as theater stages wherein Cole sublimates his own Oedipal impulses. To Wolf, Cole's painting Sunrise *in the Catskills* (1826) reveals Cole's "homosexual love of the child for the father."

To his credit, by plunging deeply into psychoanalysis, Wolf was working toward a larger interpretation of culture:

> To trace the oedipal underpinnings of Cole's sublime canvases, therefore, is to pursue psychoanalysis as a system of tropes leading to larger cultural generalizations. Our concern lies not so much within the province of Cole's private life as with those larger patterns of mental operations that together constitute a recognizable moment in the history of the sublime—a moment known to us today as Romantic.

I concede that Wolf's mission was bold, but it did not speak to me and my cohort of feminist art historians.

Michael Fried, in his article "Realism, Writing, and Disfiguration in Thomas Eakins's *Gross Clinic*, with a Postscript on Stephen Crane's Upturned Faces"(1985), turns to Thomas Eakins's *The Gross Clinic* (1875). The painting is a group portrait focused on Dr. Samuel Gross, a professor of surgery, who stands by a patient lying on an operating table in the amphitheater of Jefferson Medical School in Philadelphia. Attended by five medical students, he pauses in his surgery to make a point to the medical students in the surrounding seats.

Fried gives the painting a Freudian interpretation and concludes that "it is inevitable that the *Gross Clinic* be construed, sooner or later, in Freudian terms. With Gross's bloody scalpel before our eyes, it should be unnecessary to add that among those terms will be the problematic of castration." Elsewhere in his article Fried equates Dr. Gross with Eakins's father and maintains they had a psychologically fraught relationship.

David Lubin, in his book *Act of Portrayal: Eakins,*

Sargent, James (1985), suggests an interpretation of the central figure standing among the group of medical students in the surgical amphitheater in Thomas Eakins's *The Agnew Clinic* (1889). In this commissioned painting Dr. David Hayes Agnew, a surgeon at the University of Pennsylvania Medical School, also stands to make a point to his medical students as he performs a mastectomy. Lubin spots a student with hands in his trouser pockets standing in the middle of the composition and interprets this student as indulging in masturbation. Lubin impishly asks: "could that therefore be a covered but erect penis touched lightly, lingeringly, by his pocketed hands?"

But I will tip my hat to David Lubin, who is playful with language and adept at delivering clever turns of phrase. He constantly hedges his bets on statements he seems obliged to defend. At one point he states: "there is something preposterous about my interpretation." Then he shows his hand when he states: "It is not out of perversity, a penchant for parlor tricks, or a desire to outrage that such interpretive possibilities are proposed, but because the best way to read a portrait is to coax from it as many viable interpretations as it will yield." He also admits that what he offers is a "narrative of male sexuality," "a perspective that is phallocentric" and "a penis-eye view of the world." The interpretation of art has become a game for him.

Jules David Prown published his article "William Homer in His Art" in the inaugural 1987 issue of *Smithsonian Studies in American Art* (now called *American Art)*. Prown begins with a statement that conforms to art historians' usual practices: "A work of art is a historical event. It is something that happened in the past. But unlike other historical events, a work of art continues to exist in the present." He then argues for interpretation based on what today's observer can bring "by adhering to a close analytical reading of the image, moving from objective description to deductions derived from empathetic engagement with the object, to creative speculation and interpretation in which our late twentieth-century perspective can become a scholarly advantage, permitting insights without distorting the objective data."

Prown chooses Winslow Homer's *Life Line* (1884), a work depicting a rescue at sea with a sailor and a young woman from a foundering ship sharing a life buoy hanging from a cable pulley that is attached to a rope moving from ship to shore. Prown sees interdependence in the couple's relationship. "[D]espite their isolation, despite their limited perceptions, the clasped couple exudes an unexpected aura of sensuality and perhaps even a sense of physical pleasure as they rock to and fro together on their dangerous passage."

He adds: "In *Life Line* Homer seems to indulge in a schoolboy's fantasy that conflates heroism, damsel-saving, and sex, a fantasy marked by a large measure of frustration." As to the woman: "Despite her apparent swoon, she is not completely unconscious, she is grasping the rope, even suggestively, with her left hand. Her supine pose is compositionally suggestive of postcoital exhaustion."

At the end of the article Prown circles back to the rationale for its writing, stating that "these are only suggestions, not proofs." While he maintains that "Homer's paintings are informed by a deep investment of the artist's own psychological makeup in the creation of imagery," Prown never really addresses the "psychoanalytical" in the style of Wolf and Fried.

To me, these sorts of presentist interpretations based *only* on a contemporary response get us nowhere.

Maybe I was not hip. In contrast to the psychoanalytical bent of these male scholars, I was not concerned with male fears of castration or their claims of female passivity and submission. What engaged me during the mid-1980s were my problems with patriarchy and sexism in social life and at the workplace.

Lubin's book was published in 1985. The year before I was part of a four-woman team that attended the Sixth Berkshire Conference on the History of Women: Margaret [Peggy] Supplee Smith, Diana Long, Eugenia Kaladan and I. We geared our conference talks toward an analysis of the history behind Eakins's *Agnew Clinic*.

I gave the introduction, later published in *Prospects*: "Our goal was to peel away [*The Agnew Clinic's*] explicit and implicit layered meanings —what it meant to the artist, to the doctors involved, and to what was seen as the world of modern medicine—in order to reveal the values and ideology operating among the elite of later-nineteenth-century Philadelphia." To us women, we were doing the best kind of art history. Through archival research we could relate images to specific historical markers. There were no mentions of sexuality, penises, castration, or erotic desire.

Sadly, there was little attention paid to our seminal essays after they were published in the American studies annual *Prospects*. Perhaps our essays were just not sexy.

&

In 1990 Professor William Homer, University of Delaware, asked me to chair a panel discussion sponsored by the Association of Historians of American Art (AHAA) caucus at the next annual CAA meeting. I proposed the topic "Deconstruction: Its Uses and Abuses." It would be an opportunity for me to clarify the ramifications of Deconstruction and articulate my criticism. When Homer agreed, he was, in a way, asking the wolf to guard the hen house.

I started to line up the panelists. My friend Alan Wallach, then teaching at William and Mary, was on board. I asked

Michael Fried of Johns Hopkins and Bryan Wolf of Yale. They both agreed. I also asked Moira Roth of Mills College in California. She asked if there would be any people of color on the panel; she never joined panels that did not have at least one person of color. In any event she could not join us because of a previous commitment. Her determination not to join non-diverse panels made a big impression on me. I then persuaded Leslie King-Hammond to join us.

Not surprisingly, my session, held on February 22, 1991, was packed. I tried to lay out as objectively as I could the parameters of Deconstruction. A sample of my introductory remarks follows—and I quote myself extensively because *no one* else at the time was *publicly* critical of the deconstructionist tilt in art history. Hardly anyone was being a "combative feminist" in the intellectual field of American art history theory.

> There are many aspects to the project called Deconstruction, a movement originating in literary criticism that has been around for a couple of decades although recently under attack and perhaps about to be supplanted by the 'new historicism.' Its attraction is that it attempts to recapture the 'force' of the text—be it literary or pictorial. Geoffrey Hartman asks, "What does that force consist in, how does it show itself? Can a theory be developed that is descriptive and explanatory enough to illuminate rather than pester works of art?"
>
> Deconstruction quite properly has warned us against the intentional fallacy, reductionist explanations, and, moreover, would seem to accommodate itself to feminist interpretations ... My task today is to moderate a panel of scholars at the forefront of defining [this] new art history and the role that deconstruction may or may not play.

The other panelists stated their views and either elaborated or disagreed with my synopsis. Fried scolded me because I referred to Derrida as a literary critic, when he was actually a philosopher. (I believe his main followers have been literary people.) Bryan Wolf declared that "Deconstruction was the greatest theory since the Enlightenment." I ended the panelists' talks section with my own appraisal:

Some of us (with critical approaches influenced by Marx, Foucault, Raymond Williams, critical feminist [discourse], and the newer scholarship of black studies) reject the word Deconstruction when characterizing our work since Deconstruction as a developed theory, is, first, associated with the subordination, or even denial, of historical reference and, secondly, also associated with the elevation of the view that all interpretation is ... a form of play—and, at base, arbitrary ... While we may want to recapture the original power of a picture, we think of that power not just in aesthetic terms but also in terms of its instrumentality, that is, its social and political potency. We cannot help but see many of those pictures as part of the arsenal of dominant cultures to sustain a view of society useful to themselves.

The analysis that engages us goes beyond stylistic analysis (à la Wolfflin) and beyond iconography (à la Panofsky) and beyond even social history (à la Arnold Hauser) to engage in a close textual reading bonded to pertinent historical references (not just literary or autobiographical references, although they can include these). In such a reading, we view the pictorial choices of the artist as strategies intimately connected to cultural agencies in the process of formation, culmination, or dissolution and which, consciously or not, service old ideologies struggling to maintain their cultural hegemony or newer ones attempting to subvert and/or gain dominance.

I then turned to specific readings of earlier art: paintings which showed women and Black people at the margins of the pictures, or women in interiors as decorative objects with the same moral weight as Chinese vases, exotic flowers, and silk curtains. And I concluded: "This kind of analysis (a critical social history) opens up the discourse to historical social change. It encourages further discovery. It is materialist and dialectical and sees art, art making, patronage, criticism, and canon formation as a process that empowers some at the expense of others."

At the end I concluded by critically placing the timing of the psychoanalytic tilt by these art history deconstructionists: "I wonder whether directing the discourse toward a reading of pictures as revelations of male latent desire (not as critique but as fetishistic celebration) isn't, in fact, a latent ploy to seize back the territory of art history from the inroads of the Marxists, critical feminists, and black studies people."

The fireworks began with the Q&A. One older respected scholar got up from her chair in the audience and started pacing and complaining about the deconstructionists and, essentially, defending her own brand of art history. But mostly, the men in the audience dominated the conversation. Until King-Hammond finally barked into the microphone: "Where are all you women?" King-Hammond also pointed out the sorry state of art history, a state in which she, as a Black person, had been the last to be asked to join such a panel.

Soon the panelists heated up as they responded to the barbed questions from the audience. Michael Fried stood up and marched out, declaring as he left that he was not going to subject himself to "these low-grade terrorists." As more pandemonium ensued, the session ended.

At that time I had figured it out—phallo-centric Deconstruction had come along in the 1980s just as a large cohort of women scholars and artists were challenging traditionally-held beliefs about gender. Some women artists, such as Miriam Shapiro, Judy Chicago, and Audrey Flack were responding by making artwork that celebrated women, their bodies, and/or their art/craft traditions. Others, such as May Stevens and Kiki Smith emphasized women's experiences under patriarchal power structures.

Many women scholars were on board. They acknowledged the truth and subtleties of the phrase "gender is socially constructed." And they looked to writers such as Lucy Lippard, Laura Mulvey, Julia Kristeva and others who recognized that women had to confront male dominated discourses. Freedom meant embracing the premise that women's critical voices needed to be heard. Activists, such as the Guerrilla Girls through their wryly witty posters, also established a backup for feminist thinkers.

And here were the males holding onto their professional status and powers (and getting all the big grants), bringing attention back to their own interpretations of mountains seen as playing out "homoerotic desires," of scalpels as instruments of castration, of medical students masturbating when viewing a mastectomy, and of women experiencing "post-coital exhaustion" during a shipwreck rescue.

Deconstruction was a trend that happened decades ago, but its legacy continues to haunt us.

&

In 1997, *Time* magazine art critic Robert Hughes published *American Visions: The Epic History of Art in America*. It was an outrageous book, and I published a scathing review, titled "Half the Story," for the *Los Angeles Times Book Review*. In my review I took Hughes to task for flagrantly borrowing scholars' unique research without citation, emphasizing the Jewishness and/or gayness of critics and artists, making fun of lesbians, and including only four Black artists. A paragraph from my essay gives readers today a look inside Hughes's tome:

A telling symptom of Hughes' macho approach is his use of dismissive epithets guaranteed to raise the hackles of some readers and pander to the prejudices of others. For example, art patron and salon hostess Mable Dodge Luhan is the "Miss Piggy of the early American avant-garde," and later, "an intolerable bitch." Even so, Hughes prefers Luhan's Taos of the 1920s to the Taos of today, which he sees overrun with its "wannabe witches, ethnic kitsch dealers and matched blond lesbians in Jeep Cherokees." He explains the ambiguity in Grant Wood's paintings by outing him to a mass audience, reading such work as American Gothic in the context of Wood's "timid and deeply closeted homosexuality." In the same way, he gratuitously refers to Marsden Hartley as "an aging queen with a crush on Adolf Hitler."

This is really his language. I'm not making it up. I concluded my review:

Hughes's agenda for a centrist vision of America (neither 'politically correct' nor 'politically patriotic') is premised on the old melting pot mythology of an America that absorbs all ethnic groups willing to be assimilated. Hence, when he calls Bernard Berenson a "29-year-old Boston jew, [sic]" he quickly adds, "who would rise to become the feared and waspish pontifex of I Tatti [and] the world's ultimate authority of Italian Renaissance painting and sculpture." But Hughes's version of the melting pot disregards such ethnic and cultural groups as Latinos, Asian Americans and Native Americans, as well as blacks and women unwilling to be assimilated on the old terms. Hughes' refusal to confront these resistances and take them seriously when manifested in art explains why of the 365 illustrations, only 22 pictures represent works by women, only four by African Americans and only one by a Latino. *American Visions* thus turns out to be a seriously blinkered vision of art in these United States.

The review caught Hughes's attention and, in his rebuke published in *USA Today,* he brimmed over with sarcasm, first toward the *Los Angeles Times* art critic Christopher Knight, and then me. The *USA Today* article sets up Hughes's response: "Hughes is still smarting from the *Times* pan by Boston University professor Patricia Hills." The article continues by quoting Hughes: "It seems entirely appropriate ... given the *Los Angeles Time'*s predilection for the more sentimental forms of P.C. [a reference to Knight's art criticism] that they would have sent the book to a black feminist deconstructionist academic for review. But I'm surprised at the poor intellectual level. It was just a piece of bean-counting, interspersed with half-witted attempts to imply that there was some racist or sexist agenda there."

But read the book and you see the racist and sexist agenda revealed in many more instances than I have offered above.

A few days after the *USA Today* article, I received a phone call from a Black colleague and friend, who said, "Welcome to the club." Great praise indeed!

18

West as America, 1991

The museum culture of the 1970s began to change with the hiring of fulltime fundraisers. Government grants and corporation money brought issues about taboo subject matter and content, as well as forms of censorship and self-censorship. This is noticeable in the unexpected removal of artworks from museum walls to basement storage, or when whole exhibitions are canceled.

The culture police—whether right-wing conservatives or culturally sensitive centrist liberals—are always adding new categories to the hit list of what needs to be censured and censored. For right-wing conservatives today, taboo subjects include unflattering images of rulers, revisionist history, overt and implicit sexuality, and climate change.

Art historian Amy Werbel, who wrote *Lust on Trial: Censorship and the Rise of American Obscenity in the Age of Anthony Comstock* (2018), summed it up to me in an email. Whoever the censor, "They all share … the goal of not only removing art from the public sphere, but also doing so in a highly visible way intended to silence artists and others who might courageously defy existent power structures."

While true, the eras are distinct. During the 18[th-] and 19th centuries, conservative censorship targeted art critical of or satirizing establishment institutions, including government leaders (kings, dictators), the church (popes), the system of capitalist inequities (millionaires), and imperialist wars. One thinks of Goya. Or Daumier, when he and other contrarian artists spent time in prison.

Today established governments still retaliate against artists poking fun at religion or the government and its symbols. Think of the members of Pussy Riot (a Russian women's rock group) jailed by President Vladimir Putin for their critique of the dictatorship and alleged disrespect of the Russian Orthodox Church. Or Ai Weiwei, the self-exiled Chinese artist who has produced art critical of China's politics and government. Or Dread Scott, who was accused of desecrating the American flag when he showed his mixed media installation *What Is the Proper Way to Display a U. S. Flag?* at the gallery of the School of the Art Institute of Chicago in 1989. Scott's piece created an uproar from conservative politicians.

Sexually explicit themes—another area of art where conservatives direct their censorship. This includes artists performing with their own bodies—such as Yoko Ono, Carolee Schneemann, Hannah Wilke, and Ana Mendieta. With President George H. W. Bush in office, the National Endowment for the Arts (NEA) sought to placate conservative politicians, such as Senator Jesse Helms (R-NC), who demanded "decency" in the arts. The House and Senate introduced a bill that required grant recipients to sign a pledge not to use NEA funds to create obscene art. In spring 1990 NEA director decided to overturn grants pending for Karen Finley, Tim Miller, John Fleck, and Holly Hughes—all artists who used their bodies in their art. They became known as the NEA Four.

Photographers were also prime targets for censoring, such as Sally Mann, who photographed her children in the nude. Nan Goldin and Robert Mapplethorpe chose to photograph nudity with a homoerotic content. When some museums nevertheless showed Mapplethorpe's work, there was often a placard set up at the entrance to the exhibition space—a "disclaimer" in which the museum apologized that the sexually explicit content might be disturbing to some museum goers.

Then there's the censorship and censuring that targets revisionist history—a history that explores both progressive actions and retrogressive responses. In the US, this revisionist history includes researching and writing about the attempts of oppressed people to rise up and claim their rights to an equitable life. This history also unveils the atrocities of slavery, attacks on the working classes, the inequalities imposed on women, genocide of Native Americans and the suppression of their culture, and the exploitation of immigrants. These were the ideas making their way into exhibitions—specifically *The West as America.*

&

The most controversial exhibition of the decade—because of its presentation of a revisionist history—was *The West as America—Reinterpreting Images of the Frontier, 1820-1920,* mounted in spring 1991 by the National Museum of American Art (now the Smithsonian American Art Museum—SAAM). In his selection of works to hang on the walls and in the accompanying catalogue essays, curator William Truettner incorporated a critical history of the territorial expansion, land grabs, settler colonialism and genocide by European-Americans usurping the lands of the western Indigenous Peoples.

A few years earlier Truettner had decided to organize this exhibition on American artists who had painted scenes of the frontier and the West. He was working toward a thesis and realized the messages conveyed by many of the pictures needed to be unpacked. He told me that he had been inspired by my 1973 Whitney exhibition *The American Frontier: Images and Myths,* and asked me to be one of the six contributing authors to the catalogue. The other writers were Nancy Anderson, Elizabeth Johns, Howard Lamar, Alex Nemerov, and Julie Schimmel. Truettner later convened a meeting with all of us in Washington to discuss the exhibition and to solicit our suggestions for artworks that would serve as examples for our essay themes. My essay, for which I drew on new research as well as relying on material in my already extensive research files, was "Picturing Progress in the Era of Westward Expansion."

All was going fine with the pace of the overall organizing and my own essay. At some point Bill asked us contributors to write a series of wall labels providing synopses for the various themes in our respective sections. He set the tone with his own introductory label:

Images from Christopher Columbus to Kit Carson show the discovery and settlement of the West as a heroic undertaking.

Nineteenth-century artists and the public believed that these images represented a faithful account of civilization advancing westward. Grand compositions filled with light, color, and factual detail persuaded viewers that western scenes were literally true.

A more recent approach argues that these images are carefully staged fictions, constructed from both supposition and fact. Their role was to justify the hardship and conflict of nation building.

This exhibition advocates the latter view. It assumes that all history is unconsciously edited by those who make it. Western scenes, therefore, extolled progress but rarely noted damaging social and environmental change. Looking beneath the surface of these images gives us a better understanding of why national problems created during the era of westward expansion still affect us today.

We might take issue with Truettner's phrase "unconsciously edited," when the evidence points to a celebratory history that was always the explicit agenda advancing ruling-class ideology.

Following Truettner's lead, in my wall labels I pointed to the ways so many pictures served as propaganda for "Manifest Destiny" and for what we now call settler colonialism. Many of these pictures advanced the assumption of the "dying Indian"—a necessary ideology to justify denying the rights of Indigenous Peoples.

But Truettner, who had recently embraced critical art history, wanted me to ratchet up my wall label synopses even further. "It was a land grab," he said on the telephone, and I needed to tell that to the viewer. "Bill, one person's Contra, is another person's *Freedom Fighter*," I cautioned him.

My message was that we need to be measured in our approach to be effective in encouraging others to consider our viewpoints. I knew from my curatorial experience that one should not bash the viewer over the head with wall labels. That doesn't enlighten anyone. To my political friends, what Bill was doing would be called "left-wing adventurism." I made some revisions, but Bill was not satisfied. He tweaked many of my labels.

My above reference to "*Contra*" was apt. This was at a time (1991) when the US military was launching Operation Desert Storm, also known as the Gulf War. Meanwhile, right-wing Contra forces in Nicaragua (backed by the US government) were still fighting to overthrow the (then) left-wing Sandinistas led by Daniel Ortega. The US government through the media encouraged Americans to support US efforts to control Middle East oil and to reject any nation's reformist legislation in Central and South America considered contrary to US interests.

Not surprisingly, influential critics objected to the exhibition's history lessons when the show opened in

March 1991. Charles Krauthammer, a conservative political columnist, was rising to media power and influence at the time. He slammed the exhibition in his May 31, 1991 review for the Washington Post called, "Westward Hokum." New York critic Hilton Kramer did not specifically review the exhibition, but could not miss an opportunity to point to "The West as America," as an example of what was wrong with the museum world. He wrote a long essay for *The New Criterion* (September 1991) titled, "Has Success Spoiled the Art Museum: On the De-aestheticization of the Art Museum":

> While militant Marxists remain a small minority among museum professionals, the Marxist notion of relegating art to the so-called "superstructure," where it is seen to be an embodiment of social and economic forces more profound than itself, has now become part of the conventional intellectual wisdom of a great many curators who have never read a line [of Marx].

Undoubtably few curators have read Marx, but the insights and ideas of Marxists were already in the air.

Kramer then singled out *The West as America*, which he called—perhaps quite consciously—"The West as Art" [sic]. With his title, perhaps he meant that a focus on geography was supplementing aesthetic considerations.

Many public viewers who contributed to the comments book were also critical of the exhibition. Alan Wallach, in his timely article "The Battle Over 'The West as America'," discussed the newspaper reviews of the exhibition, as well as the comments written in the museum booklet by establishment historians and politicians, which were mostly negative and dismissive of the premises of Truettner's exhibition.

It was not only the political wall labels that riled some critics. They also took issue with labels that sexualized the subjects. For example, Alex Nemerov, a Yale doctoral student and one of the authors, penned the description of the painting *The Captive* by Irving Couse and gave it a Freudian reading. His wall label draws from his catalogue essay, from which I am now quoting:

> Depicting the seventeen-year-old Lorinda Bewly as captive of the Cayuse Chief Five Crows, Couse's lurid treatment of a historical event (set in 1847) unconsciously expresses his culture's fears of miscegenation. This is evident first in the network of intimations that thinly repress an actual sexual encounter.
> Bewly's skewed and foreshortened body ... suggests as much as the blood on her wrist a violent physical confrontation with Five Crows. The array of phallic objects pointing in her direction, together with the tepee's open entry, further imply a sexual encounter, as does the picture's one instance of cross-cultural 'touching'—the nudging, in two dimensions of Five Crows's right foot against Bewly's body.

The wall label was removed, rewritten, and a new version posted. In fact, many of the wall labels were rewritten under orders from the Director. A sidebar question: What would today's scholars of Indigenous Peoples say about Nemerov's Freudian analyses? I don't think they would be pleased. The *West as America exhibition* was not cancelled. It was censured.

Wait, there's more. And that is the issue of erasure.

One academically serious review stands out, written by Yale Professor Alan Trachtenberg, "Contesting the West," for the September 1991 issue of *Art in America*.

He faults Truettner's effort because it lacked how "meaning [for 19th-century viewers] … got established in the first place, how interpretations were put into circulation, how paintings communicated their messages and whether those messages were always taken to be universal." Then Trachtenberg hits a Marxist chord when he points out that there is little "about modes of production and distribution of art works, and no analyses of patterns of reception and response to other contextual specifics about the art itself … "

As to wall labels, I agree with Trachtenberg, who was critical of "their tendentious and didactive tone, their outright gaffes, and, in a few egregious instances, their painfully obvious misreadings." Trachtenberg then comments on the essays of Yale Professor Howard Lamar and wryly notes the "deconstructive hermeneutical gymnastics" of Yale graduate student Alex Nemerov.

Where were the women scholars? I penned a Letter to the Editor of *Art in America,* published in their February 1992 issue. Julie Schimmel signed it with me, but the other women scholars declined. Our letter stated: "And while Trachtenberg does discuss … Truettner's persistent thesis that the paintings functioned as a gloss to the social and economic history of expansion, Nancy Anderson, Patricia Hills, Elizabeth Johns, and Julie Schimmel, don't even rate a mention in his essay. We were left out, we suppose, because our way of analyzing historical contents and artistic form is not the Yale way … We are distressed, however, that the women essayists who contributed to the catalogue stepped into anonymity behind the Yale males."

To his credit, Trachtenberg apologized in the same issue: "I am indeed sorry that so many names went unmentioned. The fact that all the [unmentioned] names were those of women certainly seems suspicious, which makes me all the more sorry, embarrassed and regretful."

Trachtenberg's remarks imply that he acknowledges

erasure as a form of censorship. We women are still here.

&

Fast forward to 2025. The new administration in Washington, D.C., continues to fire not only science researchers, but also cultural and parks workers and to cut funds for educational institutions such as museums and federal parks. Universities are also being destabilized. With the firings comes censorship of content.

Censorship of content was clear when President Trump signed an Executive Order–*Restoring Truth and Sanity to American History*. This EO ratchets up the culture wars. President Trump now demands that curators working in government-funded museums and national parks can no longer incorporate a critical historical context to the display of pictures and sculpture. Only texts celebrating history will be acceptable. Educational programs must follow the same marching orders.

Museums are aware of these government pressures and attempting to craft position papers that will advocate their positions on censorship, diversity and inclusion. On March 13, 2025, the College Art Association sponsored a Zoom session on "Censorship and Self-censorship in Museums." The description of the session, which I attended, reads as follows:

> As political, social, and security pressures mount, museums face increasing challenges in curating exhibitions, developing educational programs, and presenting content. From controversial artwork removals to the subtle self-censorship of complex histories, how are museums navigating these tensions? Drawing on an analysis of a recent survey about museum censorship co-produced

by PEN America and Artists at Risks Connection, this conversation will examine recent incidents of censorship and self-censorship, the forces driving these decisions, and the implications for artistic and curatorial freedom. Presenters will discuss strategies for upholding museums as spaces for open dialogue while managing institutional risks.

Good luck on that! We still have much work ahead.

19

The Boston Massacre, 1999

The late-1980s and early 90s saw a trend towards top-down control by many museum directors emulating the corporate model and moving away from the collaborative approach when directors allowed their curators to make curatorial decisions. Because of the challenges of government and corporate censorship, directors anxious about the cuts in funding sought to appease the politicians by diminishing the independence of curators.

At the same time, museum trustees began looking for a new kind of director. Instead of art history people rising through the curatorial ranks, the new directors often had MBAs and were fully in step with the corporate models. Directors were now called Chief Executive Officers (CEOs) assisted by the Chief Financial Officers (CFOs). Of course, some directors relished the tactics of total corporate control because of their need to be on top. However, powerful insiders on the boards of trustees, marketing departments, and CFOs were increasingly writing the script.

One example of what I call governance overreach occurred in the summer of 1999 when 18 professionals—including many top-level curators and administrators respected in their fields—were laid off at the Museum of Fine Arts, Boston.

The MFA also hired 20 new staff, which tells us that the MFA trustees ordered the firings not just for financial exigencies, but because of their need to replicate the corporate model—a model not adverse to mass layoffs to boost efficiency and maintain profits. Lay-offs were then in the news. Indeed, from 1999 to 2000 industry layoffs had affected 1.2 million American workers.

Museum colleagues across the country were shocked at the MFA's swift firings. They had all taken for granted that they belonged to a profession with secure jobs because of their expertise, their smarts, their imaginative projects, and their connections to networks of artists, academics, and patrons. Moreover, museum professionals were willing to work long hours for pathetic pay checks. They compared themselves to academics with written tenure contracts, even though tenure was not an actual perk in museum work. Museum staff members working for government-sponsored museums felt especially secure because they had their government jobs.

In retrospect, this 1999 change at the MFA towards a top-down corporate model of mass firings of knowledge workers presaged the early months of 2025. That was when workers in the knowledge field—the arts and the sciences— were indiscriminately fired with no acknowledgment of the special skills they have to make us safe, well fed, healthy, housed, educated, and enriched by the arts.

In 1999 the MFA layoffs in Boston seemed to me (and others) to be based on Director Malcolm Rogers's personal need for control. Moreover, he seemed to be indifferent to how much the top-level curators had brought to the MFA in terms of raising money, cultivating patrons, and overseeing cutting-edge scholarly research. I found myself leading the protests against the layoffs.

So, let me tell my side of the story.

Rogers, formerly Deputy Director at The National Portrait Gallery in London in the mid-1990s, accepted the MFA's offer of the directorship after (it is rumored) he had lost his bid to become the director of the Portrait Gallery. To Bostonians, he was urbane without being stuffy, seemed responsive to the community, and had a lovely, resonate British accent. According to *Boston Globe* reporter Patty Hartigan, Rogers was enthusiastic about re-opening the Huntington Avenue entrance that faced a Black and working class neighborhood. The entrance had been closed for years.

Because of his stand, many believed Rogers would be a progressive leader and community advocate. Instead, he took his marching orders from MFA trustees, such as Edward Johnson, head of the successful Fidelity Investments.

Charles Giuliano, who has made a detailed study of the MFA, succinctly states the situation leading up to the hiring of Rogers. "During an economic downturn the museum had fallen on hard times under prior director Alan Shestack, who served from 1987 to 1993. [The director] was given a broad mandate to kick-start what had become a moribund institution." In 1991, there were broad layoffs to "trim $1.7 million off a projected $4.7 million deficit [$11 million in 2025]. Forty-two positions were affected, and 21 people were laid off. The MFA had borrowed an estimated $6-10 million from its endowment, which had decreased to $145 million More cuts and shakeups would follow." Indeed, they did.

Fast forward from 1991 to 1999: The financial situation still remained a problem for Rogers—solved by a further reorganization, likely dictated by the trustees. Rogers, probably in collaboration with Johnson, advanced the "one museum" slogan, which meant that the director would actively focus his energies on all aspects of scheduling, curating, and managing exhibitions and loans, with little input from curators other than their writing wall labels and entries for exhibition catalogues. Curators were becoming "content providers" rather than true curators.

On Friday, June 25, 1999, the 18 fired employees included Jonathan Fairbanks, the Katharine Lane Weems

Curator of American Decorative Arts and Sculpture, and Anne Poulet, the Russell B. and André Beauchamp Stearns Curator of European Decorative Arts. Rogers also fired other high-level administrators. Most of the staff and many outside academics with connections to the MFA interpreted his actions as a way to humiliate the professionals and instill fear in the minds of other museum staff.

That summer day, Rogers called the individuals into his office, fired them, and told them they had to clear out their offices, turn in their keys and badges, and vacate the museum before the end of the day. Although there had been rumors earlier in the week that Rogers was up to something, the targeted staff were blindsided. They had not been previously consulted about such a "reorganization," and there had been no indication that firings would happen. Those fired were escorted back to their desks by security guards. Fairbanks, a 28-year veteran of the MFA, told Rogers, "I don't need the guards. I know where my office is." When Fairbanks returned to his office, his computer had been disabled—which also had personal emails and private papers. Museums, usually genteel institutions, had never treated high-level staff so outrageously.

Rogers was no doubt charged to act by the Trustees. Although he justified the purpose of the firings as the restructuring of the MFA, most of us in the field believed that Rogers resented the independence of long-term curators like Fairbanks, who raised his own funds to purchase artworks. Fairbanks's special group of collector/patrons, "the Seminarians," remained loyal to him. Known internationally, his department had long been considered the flagship for the study of American decorative arts.

Rogers merged the American Decorative Arts and Sculpture with American Painting to create one department. Curator Theodore Stebbins' job was expanded as he took on new responsibilities as the Acting Director of

American Painting and Decorative Arts. Stebbins tendered his resignation in November in protest of Rogers's clear intentions to control all aspects of the planning, curating, and managing of the upcoming new "American Wing." When curator Anne Poulet was fired, her European Decorative Arts department merged with European Painting. Poulet went on to become the director of the Frick Art Museum.

The Boston press ran articles and editorials deploring the events of 1999. Christine Temin wrote a lengthy article for the *Boston Globe* on July 26 in which she quotes me saying the following:

> I see two issues here. One is Malcolm Rogers firing a curator like Jonathan Fairbanks, who built a department and has been collecting extremely knowledgeably. [Rogers's] treatment of him has been outrageous. The second issue is policy making at the top and proletarianizing your professionals. The independent voice of the curator disappears. Museum directors now are micromanaging, making decisions based on advice from financial officers and marketing departments. The trend among directors like Malcolm Rogers is to be in complete control.

Besides my words here, I also wrote a sharp, short piece, "The Boston Massacre," published in *Art New England.*

In addition to raising my voice to the press, I participated in agitation. On July 15, I sent the news about Rogers' handling of the firings to the American Art list-serve [Amart-L], which served hundreds of art historians across the country. I urged the listserve readers to write letters to both the MFA Chairman of the Board of Trustees, as well as its President, whose addresses I supplied.

Not surprisingly there were counterattacks from the Rogers forces. A Rogers defender wrote to Jon Westling, the former Provost and then President of Boston University, and enclosed a printout of the two pages of my July 15 listserv email. Excerpts from the letter follow:

> I am writing to you in response to an E-mail that I received last week regarding the restructuring and layoffs of the Museum of Fine Arts … that originated from one of your staff members, Patricia Hills … I felt that I had to comment on her lack of judgement [sic] … I am both appalled and surprised that Boston University, a public institution, would countenance the use of its email internet services for the purpose of criticizing and second guessing the policies of the Director of the Museum of Fine Arts … How the Museum of Fine Arts chooses to operate should not be the business of BU or its staff.

The writer continues: "At the time Malcolm Rogers was hired as Director, nearly five years ago, the place seemed to 'lack spirit' and was stagnating … There must have been some very good reasons for the decisions that he and his trustees made regarding the latest restructuring. Perhaps Ms. Hills should have found out what really happened before sending out her ill-advised and damaging memo." Her letter was cc'd to Malcolm Rogers.

President Westling replied on July 30, politely thanking the writer for the letter and adding:

> Please be advised that Patricia Hills is not one of my staff members but a professor of art history. Boston University is not, as you put it, 'a public institution,' but a private university. We do not censor our faculty members' mail or attempt to control their expressions of opinion. As far as I can tell, Professor Hills acted within the bounds of academic freedom

in writing to you and others about the recent dismissals at the Museum of Fine Arts.

You observe that Professor Hills sent her message via a list-serve and through her Boston University e-mail account. You are wrong, however, to infer from her use of her University e-mail account that Boston University endorses the substance of Professor Hill's [sic] statement. Boston University has taken no position on the MFA dismissals.

On the question of whether a university should 'countenance' a faculty member in art history expressing views ... about the policies of the Museum of Fine Arts, I must admit that your objection astonishes me. You may disagree with Professor Hills professional judgment, but to object to her right to express that judgment is surely counter to the spirit that ought to animate both Universities and art museums.

His letter was cc'd to both Rogers and me. Of course, Westling did not "fire" me.

Public response to Westling's letter was picked up by media people, who somehow obtained copies. Hilton Kramer, a critic who once slammed my Whitney exhibitions, wrote in praise of Westling for defending my academic freedom. A reporter for a Boston neighborhood newspaper, *The Beacon Hill / Back Bay Chronicle* went digging into who the writer was and what might be her motivations for writing a letter complaining about me. The reporter somehow unearthed the complainer's occupation: "an employee of Crosby Advisors, part of Fidelity Investments."

I switched into high gear. The incident became known as the "Boston Massacre," alluding to the Revolutionary War incident when British troops fired on Boston colonial protesters.

That summer was already busy. On May 1 Christina had married Shamus Brown, and the family flew to California to participate in the lovely ceremony on a hilltop in Marin. On the same day my friend May Stevens opened a show of her recent works at the MFA. The show was well received. While I was pleased with the museum's recognition of my friend May, I was still furious about the firings.

By July I was immersed in the protests against the MFA. I began collecting the copies of protest letters written by directors, curators, and university people connected to the museum world. These letters from Fairbanks' supporters had been sent to the Director and the President of the MFA, with carbon copies going to Fairbanks. I also received emails from my own colleagues in the field. One eminent curator responded to my email: "I am horrified by the MFA's action. As I immediately wrote Jonathan, he did exactly what curators were supposed to do and did it the best. I've known him since 1971. Among his other legacies is the series of North American Print Conferences which have spawned the best research and writing on American prints."

I took the copies of the protest letters and photocopied them into large stacks. Fairbanks' daughter mailed them in batches to all the members of the MFA's Board, since we were convinced that neither the Director nor the President were sharing their letters. A fourth batch we sent to the "overseers." There were more than a hundred letters, including an enthusiastic letter from television star and art presenter Sister Wendy.

For the cover letter to my second batch I pointed out the response of Ivor Nöel Hume, a leading colonial archaeologist. He wrote of the firings that had happened at other institutions and commented that such "manufactured attrition ... has left the surviving staff in a state of constant fear—none knowing whether next Friday may be their last day of employment. Therein lies the tragedy of such Draconian policies. They not only hew away at scholarship; but in the process destroy the morale of the survivors." Hume ends by saying: "Directors are appointed whose expertise goes no further than ledgers and turnstiles, and in consequence pandering staffers with P. T. Barnum mentalities stoop lower and lower in their attempts to reach new audiences. They are purveyors of what a cynical media calls edutainment, in whose cause truth all too often is slowly generalized away until only the glitter remains."

In my cover letter I followed Hume's comment with my own: "In my opinion (which I share with many of the letter writers), the firings, the method of the firings (eight hours' notice) and the direction that Mr. Malcolm Rogers seems to be taking the MFA are wrong. Museums are not 'corporations' in the sense that Fidelity is a corporation."

But before I duplicated the letters, I made it a point to telephone or email each of the letter-writers and get verbal permission to distribute their letters. Almost all agreed. Then came the interesting part. I took notes on the conversations and in the process gathered a lot of information about the MFA trustees. They were indeed an "inside" group—many of whom were members of the super exclusive Brookline Country Club—a golf and social club where the patrician elite gather. One woman told me that she sympathized with those fired curators, but she dared not voice her opinion in her social circle. I had a range of responses, including anecdotes about the museum's underside, its fakes and its scandals.

Fast forward: Patti Hartigan reported on Rogers's resignation in her August 25, 2015, *Boston Globe* article, "Malcolm Rogers Has Left the Building—Did He Save the MFA or Ruin It?" Hartigan: "Rogers's decisions seem controversial because he bucked the old-guard trend, but the modern world of museums has borne him out—the commercialization of art that once seemed so dramatic is now commonplace." Her conclusion reminds me of Shakespeare's line from *The Tempest* (Act 2). "What's past is prologue."

Today many museum directors have moved to a more collaborative model as we all become aware of the positive inroads that diversity, equity, inclusion and access initiatives are making in the field. Strong leadership is always needed, but that leadership does not have to come from one person. The spirit of diversity and inclusion will not easily be crushed.

20

Building Community, Expanding Boundaries, 1980s-90s

Looking back, I realize how engaged I was as an *advocate* focused on causes in and out of the University. Most of these causes promised to make teaching and learning experiences better for students, better for teachers. Behind it was my persistent need to create communities to which I could then contribute, but not try to dominate. Maybe it was my "mom impulse"—to give birth and early guidance, and then sit back while the child develops.

During these years I did not actively engage in political protests, as I was focused on earning enough to keep the family going. However, my husband Kevin carried out the political strategies of organizing protests opposing the Ku Klux Klan and other racist groups attempting to organize in New England. He installed an old mimeograph machine in our basement that turned out hundreds of leaflets. I occasionally went on marches and hosted meetings in our home.

As mentioned in earlier chapters, during the 1980s, I was involved with Boston artists in the Women's Caucus for Art and with shaping the BU Art Gallery as a place hospitable to contemporary artists. My impulse to expand my idea of community often relied on my published writings to achieve this.

Karla Munsat, editor of the *Art New England,* asked

me to write reviews of Boston area shows for her bimonthly journal. Charles Giuliano and Lois Tarlow wrote regular columns, and my art history colleagues and I—including Liana Cheney and Alicia Faxon, as well as many artists— wrote exhibition and book reviews. Although payments to *ANE* contributors were always minimal, we all rallied behind Karla's excellent journal.

I was soon writing lengthy articles about contemporary artists and the social and political issues that influenced their art. In ANE's March 1985 issue I wrote, "Where is the Women's Movement as It Affects Art Professionals Today: Some views by Linda Nochlin, Charlotte Rubinstein, May Stevens, Joyce Kozloff and Barbara Zucker."

In "Contemporary Art Criticism and the Role of History" (September 1987 issue), I spelled out my goals for my own criticism. I insisted that "the exigencies of our historical moment point toward an engaged critical response." In other words, history "plays a role in our understanding of art and its cultural place in our times." But this also means incorporating "the dual imperatives of non-judgmental description and of contextual interpretation." I wanted vivid, original description. However, I then cautioned about the pitfalls of descriptive criticism, such as "facile cleverness [or] bending to a select audience."

When Munsat asked me to be a regular ANE columnist in 1991, I created my "Art in Context" series. Since I was no longer running the BU Art Gallery, I thought I could manage a regular column for the journal. I was allowed to put into practice what I had theorized in the essay "Contemporary Art Criticism and the Role of History." I was done with *theory*—now was the time to do *practice*.

My first piece was published in the October/November 1991 issue, and I continued submitting essays until June/ July 1993. Totaling ten essays, I touched on a broad range of subjects, such as the Boston Museum of Art's collection, the Black artist William Johnston, Sargent's El Jaleo, N.E.A censorship, early montage in Russia and Germany, Fra Bartolommeo's drawings, border art, Alice Neel, Joseph Beuys and Andy Warhol. Years later, when I decided to end the series, I wrote one last long essay: "Sighting/Siting/Citing Women: Issues of Identity and Alterity in Contemporary Women's Art and Criticism" (February/March 1996).

My writing art criticism only enriched my offerings to students. One year, I taught a course in Art Criticism in which I gave students assignments to write local exhibition reviews. After editing the pieces, I sent them off to Munsat for publication in *ANE*. She liked what she read and published a few of them, paying the student authors and treating them like bona fide writing professionals.

&

In the mid-1900s, as a full professor, I was a logical person to be chair of something. One day, the Dean called me into his office and asked me to head up the American and New England Studies Program. I responded that I would rather be Chair of Art History. The current Chair, my colleague Keith Morgan, planned to go on leave and someone had to steer the ship. The Dean agreed and said, "Okay, for one year." I think he would not have been comfortable saying that to a male professor. I insisted on being called "Chair," not "Acting Chair." He agreed and offered me the Chair's full stipend. After several months on the job, we all concurred that I should continue for a second year. I was the first woman to chair Art History at BU.

In that meeting with the Dean, he asked me why one of our junior faculty members (a Medievalist) had not been recommended for renewal of her contract. "It was simply misogyny," I said. He gave me a puzzled look, as if he did not know the meaning of the word. I told him she was a good scholar, and had a promising career ahead. I had voted for her contract renewal, but the old guard would not budge from their negativity. These old-guard men and women in the department trivialized the younger faculty women (especially if they were pretty) and refused to acknowledge them as serious scholars.

I mentored these untenured women. Told them to keep their mouths shut on trivial issues, so as not to appear "uppity." Many of them got my infamous kicks under the faculty meeting table that signaled the message that Pat, who had tenure, would finesse the issue at hand.

As Chair, I learned how to write and stick with a budget, how to soft talk the Dean into doing something I wanted, how to keep the staff happy, and how to be persuasive with the faculty. University staffers were fully transitioned into the electronic age under my watch. All the faculty got computers, and they were all set up for email. The technology mystified them, however, and I had to nag them to get on board. Mostly, I saw my chairperson role as an advocate, championing the faculty and students and pushing through new programs.

I introduced other changes. I once commandeered an office left empty when a colleague moved on to another job and I gave the space (along with the keys) to the graduate students to serve as a student lounge. A few months later, when the administration sent in contractors for renovations for another department's use of the room, they discovered the student-occupied lounge. Advising the students not to budge, I persuaded the administration that this was needed. That the graduate students needed to have their own space. That was not easy, but I prevailed. Today, graduate students still have their own lounge.

But it was not always smooth sailing. My administrator and the secretary did not get along. Every day it was petty squabbling and stubborn standoffs in the Art History office that measured about 12 x 12 feet. It drove me crazy, so I scheduled a staff meeting with both every morning. They both eventually found other jobs.

In the 1990s, BU Students—those not married to successful doctors, lawyers, and businessmen—desperately needed financial support. My first success at fundraising came in the early 1980s when I persuaded Edward Johnson, the founder of Fidelity, to contribute to museum interns' stipends.

This was the situation: area art institutions would welcome art history interns who would work free for about 10 hours a week for 15 weeks. The students would get course credit. However, some institutions were located some traveling distance outside Boston. I thought the students should at least be reimbursed for travel expenses. Then I cold-called for an appointment with Johnson.

His secretary reserved a table at the Ritz for breakfast. When I had finished my eggs benedict, I made my pitch. He took out his checkbook and promptly wrote a check for $14,000 [$46,000 in 2025], while insisting I approach other patrons to give. Johnson's check helped subsidize many students, but I never succeeded in persuading his colleagues and rivals in finance to make similar contributions.

I did succeed in persuading the Henry Luce Foundation to include BU in its new program that funded a select number of graduate programs (at BU, Delaware, Yale, et. al.). Such institutions would re-grant to doctoral students studying American art. The Luce Fellowships lasted for years. Eventually, grants were open to applicants from any university's doctoral program. Along the way, I also organized two symposia for the Luce—one with co-organizer Wanda Corn held at the Institute of Fine Arts in New York with scholars giving talks, and a second, working solo, at the Metropolitan Museum, where one student selected by their faculty from each of ten graduate programs gave a scholarly talk. These were good conferences to show the academic and museum world that American art was scholarly—important and exciting!

As chair, I could fund-raise again. I started a Graduate Art History Alumni Association. It had three purposes. One was to encourage community among alums by organizing annual receptions held during the College Art Association February meetings. Another was to keep alums in touch with news through an annual newsletter, which we mailed out as a paper copy. It conveyed news from the graduates, current news of the Department, and a long article focused on a former MA or PhD graduate. We featured many graduates over the years, including Robert Workman, who had gone on to direct the Crystal Bridges Museum, Warren Adelson, a successful gallerist in Boston (now in New York and Palm Beach), and Patricia Johnston, who was teaching at Salem State and organizing large NEH-funded conferences on art of the early Federal period.

The third purpose for the Alumni Association was to collect needed contributions from the alums so that the Department could give financial travel assistance to current grad students presenting papers at conferences. The Dean approved of this fundraising effort and offered a modest stipend for a student assistant to work with me.

A big boost for funding the study of American art at BU came in the form of large checks from Warren Adelson, a former BU art history MA graduate. When he proffered the first check in the late 1990s, he asked what I would do with the money. I said I would put it in an endowment fund that would generate income for student travel grants. Previously I had set up small traveling awards funded by Alumni $5 and $10 gifts. The new grant, named in honor of Adelson's parents, would be a lump sum of about $1500- $2000 [$3000-$4000 in 2025] awarded annually to just one Americanist student for their research expenses.

Another year, Adelson wrote me an even bigger check, so I could then create two-year stipends for each new Americanist doctoral student, supplemented by tuition funds provided by the Dean of the Graduate School. I thus launched the Jan and Warren Adelson Fellowship program and was adamant that the Adelson students learn curatorial skills by working at the BU Art Gallery. Hence, even when taking courses, awardees spent one or two semesters curating or co-curating an exhibition for the BUAG.

Between 2001 and when I retired in 2014, about a dozen students were aided by these fellowships, several of them Black students that I had recruited. I managed yet another fund for five years, also facilitated by Warren Adelson, the Mr. and Mrs. Raymond Horowitz Dissertation Grants, which fully funded (tuition, fees, and a generous stipend) five Americanist doctoral students for one year each while they did dissertation research.

My success flagged the attention of the President's and Dean's offices. The Dean was so enthusiastic about Adelson's largesse, that she forbade me to talk to him at all, and especially not about money. She and the Development Office had suddenly realized my success in working independently on my own and decided to dismiss me and set higher stakes. Robert Brown, the then current BU President wanted to engage Adelson personally, with the aim that Adelson or the Horowitz Foundation (of which Adelson was president), would provide funds for an endowed teaching chair.

Of course, I continued to talk with Adelson. He was my friend, and his son Adam was an art history major and one of my undergraduate advisees. After I retired in 2014, a large check for the endowed chair was indeed granted by the Horowitz Foundation. BU now has a permanent chair for a Visiting Scholar of American Art.

The department and its programs continued to grow during these years. Thanks to former chairs Fred Kleiner and Keith Morgan, BU was also becoming an increasingly prestigious university. During two years as Chair, I made three hires for scholars/professors to expand the art history offerings. Through all of this, I was greatly helped by the administrative assistants and younger colleagues who applauded the new changes.

&

In the early 1990s, I became a vocal advocate for expanding the boundaries of art history to other aspects of the visual. I was doing this myself, and I hoped others would join me.

To me, visual culture includes anything that you can carry as an image in your mind or make decisions about from reproductions circulating in the culture by way of books, newspapers, and outdoor posters. It differs from material culture, in that visual culture involves optics and not the materiality of objects. The topics of visual culture include not only painting and sculpture publicly available to influence people, but also illustrations, comics, ritual performances, parades, photographs, and films that circulated in public forums and mass media.

The editor for Cambridge University Press and I got together and discussed visual culture as a project for a Cambridge Series. We came up with a title: "Cambridge Studies in American Visual Culture." I pulled together an Advisory Board and commissioned scholars who probed the public contexts of art making. The statement I wrote about the series was concise:

Cambridge Studies in American Visual Culture provides a forum for works on aspects of American art that implement methods drawn from related disciplines in the humanities, including literature, post-modern cultural studies, gender studies, and 'new history.' The series includes studies that focus on a specific set of creative circumstances and critical responses to works of art, and that situate the art and artists within a historical context of changing systems of taste, strategies for self-promotion, and ideological, social, and political tensions.

I published four authors: David Bjelejac, Melissa Dabakis, Jonathan Harris, and Cécile Whiting. Other manuscripts were in the works, but then the press decided to cancel the series.

Wanting to spread the word and form a new community of colleagues in the mid-1990s, I also founded the Visual Culture Caucus within the American Studies Association (ASA). I had previously been elected to the ASA Council for a three-year term in 1995, which meant attending the annual board meetings at the ASA Conference. The scholars dominating ASA were mainly affiliated with only two disciplines: history or literature. This had been the situation since ASA was first organized in the 1950s. Meanwhile, a group of art historians who worked on craft, design, textiles, pottery, furniture, and jewelry had formed the Material Culture Caucus. The MCC's mission was to open up the ASA to new ways of looking at American studies.

I wanted visual culture studies to get the same attention. The executive who ran ASA said to me, "Pat, if you want your group to be heard, you should form a caucus like the Material Culture Caucus." I then circulated a petition among my art historian friends to see if they were interested in such a caucus. The following year, our group met with the Material Culture Caucus to decide whether we should join the MCC or have our own caucus. Overwhelmingly, both groups agreed there should be two caucuses (two were better than one), although we would have joint receptions. In 1997, we formalized ourselves and I was elected chair. In

1999, we worked on a constitution, but I turned down the opportunity to continue as chair. By then we had a robust roster of academics who headed up committees, such as Miles Orvell, Patricia Johnston, David Brody, Susan Kilgore, Sarah Burns, and Janice Simon.

We made a difference. We were able to persuade the ASA board to allow us to sponsor at least one official conference session on visual culture—on the paintings, photographs, posters, book illustrations, bank note engravings, playgrounds, city designs, department store displays, advertisements, parades, ceremonies, and vernacular architecture (such as prisons and gas stations)—almost anything that visually impacted the culture of the United States. The Visual Culture Caucus is still a vital part of ASA—organizing meetings and holding a joint reception with the Material Culture Caucus. Both the Material Culture and the Visual Culture people now felt we had found a scholarly home in ASA—a home more welcoming than the College Art Association.

By then I had received some name recognition within the organization. The ASA executive director came back and recruited me to run for ASA president in 2001. At first I declined, but then dutifully agreed. Somebody needed to run against the highly favored and well-known ASA activist Amy Kaplan. She had already agreed to be on the ballot and was sure to win. She did indeed win. I was grateful. My ego, however, felt some satisfaction when I garnered 43% of the vote. That meant many colleagues were paying attention to visual culture. However, I did not want to commit myself to running any organizations. Again, my *modus operandi* was to help start a needed organization, develop leadership, and then step back. At last, I could devote myself to teaching, writing, and curating.

Like all organizations, the ASA eventually adapted to the needs of scholars studying new areas. Ethnic studies became a much-welcomed addition, which soon eclipsed history and literature in terms of sessions, members on the council, and jurors for the annual awards. This change was for the better.

By the early 2000s, American visual culture had also been accepted as a valid area of study by the College Art Association, mostly through the efforts of the Association of Historians of American Art (AHAA). Americanist art historians began to drift back to CAA. The days of CAA doing the old art history of connoisseurship and formal analysis had gone out with the 20th century as new methods and subjects (often with political agendas) emerged.

21

Older & Wiser, 1990s–2014

By 1996, with kids on their own, no more elderly people to care for, no more directing of the BU Art Gallery, no more advocacy groups to distract me, and fewer committee assignments, I could focus more fully on my teaching and research. As I taught, I also learned from recent academic books discussed in class, from research my students shared in their presentations and papers, and from the classroom experience itself.

I learned how to build community within the classroom. For the first five or ten minutes before the hour, I would ask students if they had seen the previous night's episode of *The Daily Show* hosted by Jon Stewart. As we talked, I would fix my eyes on an individual student for around 10-15 seconds, then, move on to another. In this way I established a real connection with every student in the class.

One year, my teaching assistant David Brody started striding up and down the aisles when he was teaching a lesson. I adopted that, too, making the students shut down whatever extra-curricular program was on their computer. These tricks made a difference.

Besides the general surveys of American art and architecture, my most challenging undergraduate course was "Art and Politics," in which students worked on teams to make an artistic presentation of social and political issues and events, such as the Columbine Killings, Exxon Oil Spill, sexual assaults on campus, workers in meat packing plants, the real estate market, etc. They presented their 20-minute presentations the last week of classes and we all voted on the best project, with me casting five votes.

Graduate seminars on the "Visual Culture of the Civil War" and "African American Art" were also favorites of mine and eye-openers for students. When I taught the Civil War to undergraduates, I handed out pages from George L. Aiken's 1852 playbook of *Uncle Tom's Cabin.* The students then playacted the characters in the classroom. When I taught 20th-Century American Art to the graduate students, they had to playact leading critics as if those critics were performing at a MoMA speakers' event. In this way the students had to dig into the personas of historical figures—like method acting.

I attended lectures given by colleagues at seminars and symposia, and audited semester-long courses taught by professors in other departments. These included Shakespeare in the English Literature Department, Intellectual History in African American Studies, The Black Film in Film Studies, and Hegel in the Philosophy Department. I actively participated in the New England and American Studies Program and the Afro American Studies Program. Teaching and learning merged in my head and at my podium.

Inspired by my students' needs, I decided to share what I had learned by writing a reader pitched to undergraduates. The book would offer an overview of American artistic life, the machinations of the art market, the workings of patronage, the idealism, social consciousness, and the artistic choices of artists and the critics who wrote about them. With the go-ahead from a Prentice-Hall editor, I gathered copies of the photocopies I had handed out to students and augmented those readings with new research. The anthology included introductions from me, as well as 120 entries by other writers, artists, poets, gallerists, art historians—and even one US President. I wanted these writings to incorporate a variety of opinions, including writings by and about Black artists and critics, Asian Americans, Latin Americans, and Indigenous People.

The anthology, *Modern Art in the USA: Issues and Controversies of the 20th Century,* became a teaching aid and a reference book for names, dates, and bibliography. It was also an interpretation that much American art could be potentially radical once we understand its cultural and political surround. I wanted no retrospective assessments by people of a later generation, just art writing in its contemporary context. Through all the stages, I was helped by BU student Stephanie Taylor , who deftly tracked down obscure readings and addresses of the authors.

That textbook later got a Macedonian language edition. Why Macedonia? When I first received a telephone call from Macedonia, I thought it was a joke and referred the caller to my publisher. About nine months later I was surprised when the translated book arrived in the mail. I queried the original contact person. Apparently, the Macedonian minister of culture had decided that some key books in English needed to be translated, and my book was among them. Do you speak Macedonian?

&

My greatest concern for my students was their writing. Are they developing critical and dialectical views of art and events? Can they write with fluency, passion, and insight? Can they maintain their sense of balance and sense of humor? Looking back, I am proud of my accomplishments as a mentor reading MA theses and PhD dissertations for graduate students.

Teaching gave me identity and community. It was challenging, rewarding, and a good balance to my curatorial work. It was a privilege to have known such brilliant and curious students, many of whom are still in touch.

&

When I left teaching in 2014, my graduate students Charlotte and Will Moore threw me the best good-bye party by organizing a symposium, "American Visual Culture in Context," in late April—an afternoon of scholarly talks by my former students and colleagues. I was pleased that all our children came to the event. During the reception after the talks, one of my former grad students, Aaron Lecklider, reminisced about his memories of my office hour pep talks. He said that the phrase I would always use when considering the students' new ways of viewing art was, "Why not?"

The summer was spent filling out forms for retirement and planning what Kevin and I would be doing in the coming years. At the end of August, Andy got married to Jason Flegel. Both of them had been living together in San Francisco—Andy as an opera conductor and chorus master and Jason in the tech industry. It was a lovely wedding. The reception was held at the top of the DeYoung Museum, where we all toasted with Moscow mules in copper cups.

Why not, indeed?

22

Travels with My Art, 1981-2006

While I was curating, teaching, mentoring, chairing, and writing, my husband Kevin was also teaching, working for computer companies, engaging in left politics, coaching our youngest Andy on the violin, and sharing other household and childcare tasks with me. We had a great partnership and many laughs together.

We also traveled—to my conferences and to visit friends and family. Christina, by then an animator for Hollywood films, her husband Shamus Brown, a hi-tech engineer, and my adorable granddaughter Magenta were living in Nevada City and then San Diego, California. Bradford, then working in market research, lived in Santa Monica. Andy, a conductor and chorus master, lived in San Francisco, and my stepdaughter Mary, a community college chemistry teacher lived in Seattle. I was grateful that my stepdaughter Emily, a media relations director, and her family still lived in New York. In Seattle we also visited artists Gwendolyn and Jacob Lawrence and May Stevens and Rudolf Baranik in New York and Santa Fe.

We took short vacations, sometimes with children and relatives, sometimes by ourselves. These included traveling abroad to Monaco, London, Paris, Berlin, Munich, Budapest, Vienna, Venice, Rome, Barcelona, Guernica, Madrid, the Netherlands, Jamaica, Puerto Rico, Cuba, and Montenegro. My son Brad and I took a week's motor trip in 2012 to view the exhibitions strung out across Southern California associated with *"Pacific Standard Time: Art in L.A., 1945-1980,"* funded by the Getty. In 2017, Kevin and I took a Viking River Cruise along the Rhine with family. A year later, we took a ten-day tour of Sicily and Rome. Finally, in 2019, we went to a family wedding in Montenegro on the Adriatic.

Travel meant more experiences with the natural landscape, as well as the architecture and public spaces of towns, cities, and museums where the art and culture of local areas would be on view. I could bring such experiences to my teaching. Such travel went beyond just seeing, it meant absorbing the panoramas, feeling the weather, walking on the streets and pathways, catching the mood of the inhabitants—all things familiar to those artists past and present who called such destinations home.

What follows are memorable travel to places where we lived or spent extensive time: Cody, Wyoming in 1981, where I taught a summer course on artists of the American West; Germany and Venice for three weeks in 1990; Monaco, where I taught in June 1991; Santa Fe, where I held a three-month fellowship in 2006.

&

The Buffalo Bill Historical Center in Cody, Wyoming hired me as the C. V. Whitney Lecturer, in 1981, where I taught a three-week course on the art of the West at the Summer Institute of Western American Studies. The six-week absence from our teenagers would be the first long sojourn we ever took away from them. Three-year-old Andy came with us as we set out from our home in Brookline, Massachusetts to spend the next ten days traveling to Cody.

We camped on our way, stopping for a night with friends in Chicago before pushing on. We marveled at the utter horizontality of the Great Plains, the modern wind farms spread out across the landscape, and the mile-long freight trains sweeping through the expanse. These long vistas with their train cars reminded me of the many 19th-century paintings and book illustrations that attempted to portray the vastness of the West as a site not just for tourists, but for development and industry.

We sought out regional museums to visit, where I took slides of the works of Western artists about whom I would be lecturing at Cody. Driving along Interstate 90, we camped along the Missouri River outside Des Moines, Iowa, and in the Badlands National Park of South Dakota. We took a detour through the Pine Ridge Reservation to the site of the Wounded Knee Massacre, South Dakota, where almost 300 Lakota men, women, and children were massacred on December 29, 1890.

The Army claimed the massacre was justified to suppress The Ghost Dance—a religious movement that fostered the traditional cultures and rights of Indigenous peoples.

I wanted to see, experience, and take slides of this historic battlefield, the surrounding hills, and the plot of land that was the site of the infamous mass grave where the white militia threw the dead bodies of the Lakota. A 19th-century photograph, available on Wikipedia, depicts the bodies in the open grave with the unapologetic soldiers standing around the periphery. I tried to get close to that historic spot, but the grave itself was surrounded by a chain-link fence. I still photographed it, because I wanted to share the site with my students back in Boston through slides and narratives of first-hand experience.

I took photographs not only of the Pine Ridge sites, but also of Kevin negotiating with an Oglala Lakota highway patrolman and patrolwoman. He had been driving fast on a deserted two-lane highway, which had sneaky speed traps. The officers said we had a choice: we could get the speeding ticket issued from the State of South Dakota or from the

Oglala Lakota Nation. We asked for an explanation. The patrolwoman answered that if we accepted the Oglala Lakota ticket our names and the car would not be entered into a national registry. That was a no-brainer. We drove into the town of Wounded Knee to pay our ticket. The town looked ramshackle and the buildings in need of repair. Then we drove on to Cody.

The three-week sojourn in Cody, Wyoming, proved to be an exciting adventure for Andy, Kevin, and me. The two other professors teaching courses that summer on the American West included William Goetzman, the well-known University of Texas historian of the American West, and Alvin Josephy, a former Hollywood film writer, war correspondent, and historian of the Nez Perce.

During the week we bunked at a dude ranch outside Cody. Every morning, I would drive into town and spend three hours teaching the history and culture of artists who went West to paint. Back at the ranch, late every afternoon, one of the hands would take us horseback riding through the magnificent hills. Andy would sit in the saddle in front of Kevin, while I rode solo. Once, the ranch hand spied a rattlesnake. He leapt off his horse, picked up the snake, crushed its head and skinned the snake, all in less than five minutes. Who else in the world would put on such a display of rugged machismo (except perhaps the Australians)? I later picked up a sun-bleached horse's skull, which reminded me of Georgia O'Keeffe paintings of steer skulls.

Andy, who had graduated from the "terrible twos" and was now in the "terrible threes," thrived as he learned about the world. When staying overnight in Chicago on the way to Cody, our hostess (another academic) peppered her conversation with words such as "F---," "Motherf-----," and "Sh--." Andy picked up on that and started using those words. I told him it was okay to use the words, but he must never, *NEVER* use the word *"Fiddlesticks."* In Wyoming,

Andy would sidle up to a stranger, look that person in the eye, and then say: *"Fiddlesticks!"* I would fake a cringe and immediately apologize for Andy's behavior; the stranger would look either puzzled or bemused. After a week or so, Andy gave up on his dirty language.

I now had about 500 slides with me to use in teaching my course. The students came from all over—most of them to study with Goetzmann. On weekends we made excursions led by Goetzmann and Josephy. The students and faculty spent nights in individual tents, even during a heavy rain squall. I learned a great deal about the history, sociology, and current circumstances of South Dakota on those field trips.

On our trip back to Boston we stopped off at Mount Rushmore National Park in South Dakota to view the 60-foot-high portraits of Washington, Jefferson, Roosevelt and Lincoln. One cannot conceptualize how large they are without seeing them in person. Again, we stopped over in cities with museums. Our red Buick station wagon was never the same after driving over the various terrains of dirt and rocks. But the experience of the West—its landscapes, powerful rivers, constant wind, and its past and living history—made a deep impression on me.

&

In the summer of 1990 Kevin and I wanted to experience the new undivided Germany and to visit the Venice Biennale. Caregiving tasks were solved by enrolling my live-in mother Glennie in the St. Elizabeth's Hospital "respite program" (my respite, not hers), while graduate students Will and Charlotte Moore stayed with Andy in Cambridge. I had no specific research project in mind, I just wanted to immerse myself in the art, architecture, and landscape of Europe, to probe the rapid changes in Berlin and Germany since the

1989 Fall of the Wall, to practice the German language, to see my old home in Heidelberg where I lived in 1948-49, to take a train over the alps, and to visit the Venice Biennale. Vivid memories!

We planned Berlin for our first stop, as we were eager to see The Wall. The two Germanys had not yet merged their currencies, which meant exchanging West marks for East marks after walking from our hotel to Checkpoint Charlie, still guarded by US Military Police. We showed our passports and walked through a four-foot passage from the former West Berlin to the former East Berlin.

The Berlin Wall had not been destroyed—only small parts of it had been removed, and the remainder snaking through the city was covered with graffiti. We hiked across the landscape to get familiar with the empty strips of spaces of the formerly militarized zones where escapees who attempted to climb over the wall were shot dead by East German sentries from lookout towers. Besides us, many tourists were chipping away pieces of the Berlin Wall for souvenirs. The scene reminded me of a surreal De Chirico painting, but the idea of the wall reminded me of the architectural ruins of Greece, where fortresses were built to be impenetrable—but never were. We grabbed a few small pieces of the wall to take home as souvenirs.

In East Berlin we saw no shops that appealed to us. We strolled over to Alexanderplatz—a place made famous to me after reading (in German) Alfred Döblin's massive 1929 novel *Berlin Alexanderplatz*. The plaza was a dismal space surrounded by office buildings, whose architecture might be called "Budget Brutalist"—slabs of concrete thrown up, punctuated by windows, with no interesting details or flourishes.

We took the elevator up the Berlin Television Tower, at 368-meters high the tallest structure in Europe in the early 1960s, and had lunch in the revolving restaurant at the top. All the table booths seated six people. We sat in one and were soon joined by a pack of obviously East German tourists, shoved by the waiter into our booth. Their dress and demeanor could not have been more different from the well-dressed and class-conscious Germans we encountered in the surrounds of our hotel in the western sector. This revolving restaurant with a panoramic view over all of Berlin did not cater to private tête-à-têtes. In East Berlin eating food and seeing panoramas were communal experiences shared with strangers, and so we adjusted.

We became increasingly aware of the actual economic differences between the former East Germany (Deutsche Demokratische Republic/German Democratic Republic) and West Germany (Bundesrepublic Deutscheland/Federal Republic of Germany). Each night, after retiring to our hotel room, we watched CNN, the only English-language television station available. The news constantly focused on the overwhelming migration of East Germans into West Germany as the result of unification. The message from CNN was that the West German government was performing a heroic task by feeding the recent arrivals, housing them, giving them medical care, finding them jobs and schools, and keeping up their spirits. The message was propaganda, of course, for an industrialized West Germany beginning to need more workers, but still our hearts went out to the migrants.

When traveling by train from Berlin through a stretch of farmland formerly part of East Germany and then through West German farmland before arriving in Cologne, we were struck by the visual contrasts. In the fields of the former we saw farmers (men and women) bent over and harvesting crops using large baskets; in the western part we saw machinery doing the tasks. The differences in economic development were vivid.

In Cologne we stayed in a hotel facing the square where

the large, magnificent cathedral stood. We had visited and appreciated the museums of Berlin for their old masters, but here in Cologne contemporary American Pop Art was on view at the fabulous Ludwig Museum.

From Cologne we rented a car and made a trip to Düsseldorf, where Eastman Johnson had studied with the German American painter Emanuel Leutze in the 1850s, and where the 20th-century artist Josef Beuys had taught at the Academy in the post-war years. We then drove our rented car down the Autobahn to Heidelberg, where I paid a sentimental visit to the house where my military family had lived during 1948-49. Next was a train ride over the Alps to Munich in time to feast upon *spargel*, the spring white asparagus that Germans fondly prepare in various recipes. Munich is a large rambling city with parks, beer inns, and a lively street life.

We took a serious side trip from Munich to the Dachau concentration camp—a sober contrast to the bacchanalian spirit of Munich. Dachau, like other death camps, exterminated not only Jews but also Communists, resistance fighters, Catholic radical priests, gays, lesbians, and Roma. It was chilling to see the crowded bunks where prisoners spent the nights, the rooms where they were gassed, and the grounds surrounded by barbed wire and lookout towers that prevented escape. Our mood that day as we confronted the emptiness and silence echoed the weather: an elegiac gray. So many starved and murdered because of the fascists. I made slides to later show my students.

The final stop of our trip was Venice, where I wanted to see not only the museums, canals, piazzas, bridges, and architecture, but the 1990 Venice Biennale. Karla Munsat, editor of *Art New England,* who regularly commissioned me to write art criticism, had given me a press pass for the opening days in mid-May. We thus had a chance to see the highlights of the Biennale in a leisurely way before the crowds arrived. It was exciting to be at the biggest of the international art fairs (at the time) funded by different international governments.

The artists and their works were memorable. Anish Kapoor represented Britain. Jenny Holzer's wittily ironic sayings lit up the American Pavilion with moving neon lights. At one point we rode on the same gondola with Holzer and her party—a large gondola cruising up and down the canals that functioned like a public street bus. The Bad Boy of the Americans was Jeff Koons, who had (with assistants) fabricated a life-size sculpture of himself thrashing about in bed with his naked girlfriend, the porn star (and later politician) Cicciolina. Koons and girlfriend may not have been fully naked in the sculpture but the love-making storyline was evident. We even saw the real Jeff Koons charging through the galleries, loudly slamming the art of other artists, with a gaggle of acolytes in his wake. The Biennale was great fun.

Venice's Piazza San Marco was filled with a thin layer of water from spring rains, but that did not prevent the overabundance of tourists strolling toward St. Mark's Basilica. If you want to see everyone you ever knew, then sit for a while in a San Marco outdoor café, and they will all walk by. We flew home exhausted but invigorated.

&

The next year, June 1991, I had the opportunity to teach a museum studies course in Monaco set up by Boston University's International program. The course would focus on the contemporary art world—museums, patrons, exhibitions, auctions—and be filled with American students, whom I would teach in English. However, I was embarrassed by my miserable grasp of the French language. I got some Pimsler tapes and dutifully studied each lesson in the three weeks before I left Boston. My French eventually became adequate for grocery shopping and eating in restaurants, but not for discussions about the weather, much less intellectual matters.

Fortunately, BU hired a chic French woman, fluent in English, and the wife of a BU adjunct professor who taught in BU's Paris program. We called her "Madame." Her job entailed taking care of the students' housing with Monaco families, arranging trips to Nice and museums close to Monaco, and coordinating receptions for the whole class. I had ten students, all enthusiastic and adventurous, their needs deftly handled by Madame.

BU had secured for me a tiny apartment at the east end of Monaco. I walked to the west end to teach my classes at a local preparatory school. The walk could not have been more than a mile, since Monaco is a tiny (but rich) principality with an area of .81 square miles—just a dot on the French Riviera slightly east of Nice. Monte Carlo, the swank gambling establishment dominates the principality and is Monaco's main source of income.

Family joined me. After the first week, Christina (fluent in Italian) came, then Kevin and Andy a few days later. I met an American expatriate whose boyfriend drove us to tiny towns in the hills of Southern France. From him I learned that most residents of Monaco were of Italian heritage even though French served as the official language. Moreover, all citizens received a yearly stipend from the government. The economy rested on the Casino, which we never visited. When Brad, Emily, and Mary arrived, we had to get another equally tiny apartment—fortunately, located in the same apartment building.

Madame also organized trips to the nearby Picasso and Miro museums and a Christie's auction in Monaco. But the highlight for the students was a private reception/party with Prince Albert, Monaco's heir apparent. The party offered us a great time, as everyone in our family mingled with the students and Monaco royalty! One of the perks of being an art historian is meeting rich celebrities who rule countries, even though I deplore monarchy and, in general, any autocracy, plutocracy, or kleptocracy. *Contradictions, contradictions!*

When the course ended, Kevin and I took Christina, Brad, and Andy on a motor trip up through Provence to Paris. We usually stayed in one big room in a cheap hotel, each with morning complaints about the collective snoring. I relished seeing the old Roman cities, the somewhat arid landscape with lavender blooming everywhere, the Saturday market at Arles, where Van Gogh had painted, and the mountains painted by Cézanne.

One of our unforgettable stops was the Pont du Gard, a 1st-century Roman aqueduct, measuring about 1,224 feet-long as it straddles the Tyne River. As a reminder, I keep a postcard of the aqueduct taped to my study wall, reminding me of our risky walk across the top. In 1991 the public was allowed to walk on the top. No guard rails anywhere. We were on our own. It was the scariest walk ever, as the width of the flat top going over the arches was no more than twelve feet across, with a pocked surface of missing stones and many gaps waiting for a tourist to plunge down 160 feet into the river.

Kevin and I walked cautiously, Christina got down on her hands and knees and crawled, Brad walked briskly, and Andy skipped along with untied shoelaces flapping in the wind and a big grin on his face. To sum up: Kevin and I were prudent; Christina was super-cautious; Brad was self-possessed; and Andy was reckless. I thought, *Oh my God, we will lose him!*

Another highlight was our visit to Les Baux de Provence, where we climbed the rocky fortress and enjoyed the cool of the castle and the rugged landscape. My friend Lisa Peters visited Les Baux many years ago and recently recalled, "The landscape around it is often described as Dante's Inferno—nature's desolation in all directions." Like the Pont du Gard, the castle had no guardrails or cautionary rules—perhaps because the French are less litigious. Hence, nothing to keep little kids from falling off precipices—so different from the United States. Kevin laughed about the lack of guardrails. "That's because the French want to enhance their gene pool."

Near the village we visited a winery and, in a musky cellar, was regaled by the owner, a stout woman who spoke fairly good English. We drank wonderful samples of her wine and bought some. She told us of the centuries-old villa where she lived and the history of her family. She verified the veracity of her tale by adding, "The stones, they do not lie." I always remembered that.

A third highlight was Vézelay, in Burgundy. Art history people like me would know of the Romanesque "Abbey" church in Vézelay for which the 19th-century architect Violet-le-Duc had made major (and sometimes inappropriate) restorations, but we would not necessarily have known of the three-star restaurant *L'Esperance* on the outskirts of town. My French-savvy friend David Hall had recommended it, and we made reservations for lunch. We showed up at the restaurant sweaty and hot from the drive, then dashed into the restrooms, splashed water on our faces, and switched into more suitable attire. It was, after all, a three-star restaurant that deserved respect. The amazing lunch placed before us had many courses, with waiters hovering over us as they anticipated and attended to our every wish. To us, the ambience and food equaled a thousand restaurant stars.

Finally, we arrived in Paris to see the museums, the cathedrals, Versailles, and eat exquisite food in little cafes. At the Louvre, I made a beeline to my favorite Louvre painting—Gericault's *Raft of the Medusa* (1818-1819), which represents the survivors of an actual shipwreck and their determination to survive. Even at the time, the shipwreck was seen as the outcome of a corrupt government that allowed unfit ships to sail. The composition, handling of paint, and slivers of light are perfect. After a few days of museums and a trip to Versailles—the palace of autocratic pompous kings, silly queens, and idle sycophantic courtiers—we left for home.

&

My sojourn in Santa Fe in 2006 as a Fellow at the Georgia O'Keeffe Museum Research Center deserves some words. At the culmination of my cross-country trip hunting down places where Jacob Lawrence's footsteps may have been, Kevin and I arrived in Santa Fe in mid-March, where I settled down with a research residency to complete my research and begin writing on Lawrence.

Everyone should visit Santa Fe. The city, capital of New Mexico, offers art museums, ethnographic and contemporary galleries, an historic square and 17th-century church, and a mix of Anglo, Black, Mexican and Native American peoples. Some of the adobe architecture is very old, but most of it is recent. The newer buildings imitate the older pueblo style because Santa Fe's pro-tourist construction codes dictate that. Hence, when driving north from Albuquerque (the nearest large airport) ones sees at a distance a remarkably homogeneous site—anticipating for viewers a picturesque tourist city.

The Research Center gave me a great office, where I quickly made friends with the half-dozen or so other fellows. Lois Rudnick, a rock star in American Studies, became a great mentor directing me to background reading on African American culture. My great friend May Stevens lived just outside the town, as did Lucy Lippard, who still lives in Galisteo. Through them I got to know the other "Galisteo gals"—Harmony Hammond and Nancy Holt, plus Sabra

Moore who lives in Abiquiu, a small hamlet where Georgia O'Keeffe once lived.

During our three-months stay in Santa Fe I made it a point to see the art sites in the West that are under-visited by East Coast people, including Marfa, Texas, sixty miles from the Mexican border. I flew from Santa Fe to El Paso, where I met Stephanie Taylor, my ex-BU student then teaching at the University of New Mexico/Las Cruces. We drove in her car to Marfa where a former Army post had been purchased by Donald Judd, who transformed the post's barracks into a series of buildings showcasing his own art and that of other minimalist artists. Sculpture was outdoors and everywhere. The Chinati Foundation presently runs the complex. We stayed two nights in a motel, which gave us one long day to explore all the art. At night, we half-heartedly looked for the famous "Marfa lights" but never found them.

We left Marfa and sped down the highway until we stopped in our tracks. There in the middle of the desert was Prada Marfa. It was a small building, maybe 12 by 16 feet, with a glass front and no visible door. Behind the glass windows was a display of Prada shoes and handbags. No one was there. Weird, but brilliant marketing.

With Barbara Buhler Lynes, Director of the O'Keeffe Museum, I flew to Salt Lake City on the summer solstice. We rented a car and drove to see *Spiral Jetty*, the earth project created in 1970 by Robert Smithson—a spiral road of man-made land, constructed by dump trucks, that thrusts into the Great Salt Lake. The visibility changes as the *Jetty* rises and falls depending upon the annual rainfall.

As I recall, when we were there, it was almost all submerged. Nevertheless, to see *Spiral Jetty* in person is overwhelming. Photographs do not capture its beauty and audaciousness. It's not just the *Jetty,* it's the *Jetty* in context. Looking down from a small hill, one sees the manmade artifact, very small considering the sweep of the desolate, miles-wide, uninhabitable, moon-like landscape of Utah. It is as if the artist were imposing his graffiti signature in a place where such human-made disruptions seem insignificant. The sublime scene reminds viewers that we are on earth for but a fleeting moment. We realize nothing survives except the changing contours of the earth and oceans, and the earth itself exists only precariously in an endless solar system.

We drove on to Great Basin Desert to view Nancy Holt's installation, called *Sun Tunnels* (1973-76). We secured permission from Nancy to visit the site, since it was her own private property. Moreover, she provided us with a map with very specific instructions—totally necessary in that vast desert of Utah. *Sun Tunnels* consists of four large concrete tunnels, about twenty feet and perhaps 8 feet in diameter. Each tunnel faces the four directions of the compass. I wanted to catch the moment of the summer solstice sunset when the sun shines directly and perfectly through the two East-West tunnels. A bonus is looking through the large peep holes to see specific constellations of stars.

However, I made the mistake of scheduling our trip there too early. Barbara and I arrived in that corner of Great Basin Desert at about 4 p.m., and we would have to wait until dusk—some five or so hours away. I wanted to stay to experience what Holt had intended for us to experience, but Barbara was driving the car, and she insisted we leave. One did not argue with Barbara.

However, I did have time to scope out the scene. At least a dozen trailers and trucks were parked near the site, all filled with people and their kids who roamed the Western states picking up temp jobs and/or looking for new experiences. Perhaps hippies, but more likely outliers such as those people featured in the 2020 movie *Nomadland*. I talked with a couple of friendly guys who told me that they and their friends came every year on the day of the solstice to see Nancy's tunnels. I was impressed with their devotion.

I never told Nancy about folks partying all day and into the night with kids climbing and running through the tunnels.

Lois and her husband Steve, who were familiar with New Mexico, took us on local excursions to the archaeological sites of the Pueblo ancestors and the fully contemporary pueblos of the contemporary Indigenous Peoples. We experienced a long, ritual dance of Native Americans in tribal dress that was part of a festival. I was familiar with native artists' work such as Fred Kabotie's *Zuni Corn Dance* (1921). But seeing an actual dance in three dimensions, in motion, with sound chants, and performed on a warm sunny day, was thrilling.

During our three-month sojourn in Santa Fe our Boston friends visited, and we went again to the sites and museums. My sister Gail, her husband John and their daughter Molly came in early June. After they saw the sights of Santa Fe, we all drove to the Four Corners (the meeting point of Colorado, Utah, New Mexico, and Arizona). We then drove through a large Navajo reservation, saw groups of wild running horses, and reached our destination, the remnants of the ancient adobe canyon villages of Canyon de Chilly in Arizona. Our Navajo guide took us down into the valley. I shudder when I recall the images of those buildings poking out from the canyons where the ancestors of the Navajo once lived. From our distance, they looked like matchbook-sized buildings. How hard it must have been for those people to live like that—high on the cliffs, but isolated from their enemies.

At the end of June, all our children arrived for a big party we threw on the grounds surrounding our apartment complex. Brad and Andy drove our Subaru back to our family summer house in Ocean Grove, New Jersey, while Kevin and I flew back. I had succeeded in writing a prospectus for my Jacob Lawrence book, had drafted two chapters, and had secured a contract with a publisher. But the idyll was over. I had to go back to teaching. However, I was then maintaining a fellow's affiliation with the Du Bois Center at

Harvard, which kept me focused on the Lawrence project. It took me three more years of juggling teaching and attending conferences before finishing *Painting Harlem Modern: The Art of Jacob Lawrence*, published by the University of California Press in 2009.

I was pleased with the book.

23

Berlin Sojourn, 2013

Berlin drew me back. In December 2010, I had given a paper at a Freie Universität conference on the German American artist Winold Reiss. There I met the American visiting professor Katherine Manthorne, teaching in the Abt. Kultur department within FU's American studies program. The Terra Foundation, based in Chicago, financed these one-semester professorship visits. Other teachers in past semesters included Alan Wallach, David Lubin, and Vivien Fryd. I applied in 2012 and was tapped for the Terra Foundation Professorship for the 2013 spring/summer semester.

The spring of 2013 was especially busy. I was still recuperating from rotator cuff surgery I had had the previous September. In early March my old high school decided to give me an award so off we went to St. Louis, rented a car and drove to Muscoutah Community High School in Muscoutah, Illinois. My best friend in high school and her husband linked up with us.

Then in late March, Emily married Robert Fader. She was doing good work as a media relations director for non-profit organizations focused on social justice issues. Robert ran a chain of bookstores—in New York and later Atlanta, Pittsburgh, and Boston. The wedding was perfect. The site was the old Brooklyn docks, overlooking the Statue of Liberty. The *New York Times* gave it a write up.

Meanwhile, Kevin and I were negotiating our visas at the German consulate in Boston—not an easy task—but we finally got our documents together, flew out of Logan airport, and arrived in Berlin on April 4. David Lubin had recommended the two-floor apartment where he and his wife Libby had stayed in the Kreuzberg area of Berlin—close to Berlin Mitte (town center). We liked it, negotiated with the landlord, and moved in. The apartment was furnished in Ikea Modern, which meant the furniture was always breaking and collapsing, but the living room had a large open space, lots of windows and with the kitchen counters and appliances strung out along one wall.

The Kreuzberg location could not have been better. The subway stop was a block from us on a tree-lined boulevard, with shops, grocery stores, a small park, a multivendor market and great restaurants within three blocks. All the buildings except for ours were covered with graffiti—not unlike the other neighborhoods of Berlin. Many Berliners consider the graffiti to be art, and I was won over to that assessment. The air was somewhat nippy, and some snow still lay on the ground in that early April. Young and older Berliners sat at tables outside shops and pubs drinking their coffee and beer, huddled within lap blankets, and laughing. It was a good feeling.

Within a couple of days we had bought groceries, kitchen equipment not furnished by the landlord, and a printer. We secured a bank account, exchanged dollars for Euros, got in touch with old friends who lived in Berlin and went looking for a German tutor. By the end of the week I took the subway some 30 minutes from where we lived to the western edge of Berlin where the Freie Universität was located. I handled paperwork, presented myself to the police department to establish my identity, handled more paperwork and met my new colleagues in the "Abt. Kultur" department. These American Studies historians and literary scholars seemed to have a benign geniality toward those of us studying the visual arts. My schedule from early April to mid-July entailed teaching two seminars on American art: "The Visual Culture of the Civil War" to undergraduates and "African American Art" to graduate students. I only taught on Tuesdays, which permitted me to take trips outside Berlin.

A few days later I got a call from Vivien Fryd, who had also taught at Abt. Kultur for the Terra program the previous year. She liked Berlin so much that she decided to stay and work on her book project about her Jewish mother, a teenager in Nazi Berlin during the 1930s. Her mother's brother Henry Reiss (Vivien's uncle), who had already emigrated to the United States, desperately tried to get Vivien's mother out of Germany at a time when the US refused to welcome Jewish immigrants. He eventually succeeded, thanks to the Quaker organizations working on immigration cases. Her uncle later became a well-known photographer for his post-WWII photographs of Berliners struggling to clean up their city during 1945 and 1946, and of American military planes bringing supplies to West Berlin, known as the Berlin Airlift.

It was great fun having Vivien as a companion—exploring this magnificent city, its neighborhoods, and waterways. Bonnie Woods, an artist I had known from Boston, was also spending time in Berlin as an ex-pat (for six months of each year). Bonnie lived in a tiny apartment in the Kreuzberg area near the former East Berlin border. She guided us through our explorations of the many neighborhoods of Berlin. Other new friends made in Berlin were Betinna and Helveg Friedl, both German academics focused on American studies. They invited Kevin and me to their neighborhood in northwest Berlin and later visited us in the US.

Berliners know how to have fun. The Gay Pride Parade on June 22 was a hoot. People dressed in all kinds of attire, drinking wine from bottles they carried, throwing confetti, and plucking those on the sidelines into the parade, including

Kevin, his daughter Mary, then visiting, and me. Moreover, the few police standing by were also joking and generally enjoying themselves. It was the most festive parade I ever attended.

The subways ran on the honor system: no toll guards, no clerks selling tickets, and plenty of room in the cars for bicycles and large dogs. A rider would buy a ticket (from a vending machine or monthly passes at a special station), keep his/her ticket in a pocket and then show it only when a bunch of plainclothesmen swept into the cars demanding to see all tickets. To the Berliners, being caught without a ticket caused great humiliation. Being escorted to the local police station brought shame. This honor system is so unlike what we experience in New York.

During our four months in Berlin Kevin and I reveled in the cultural offerings: operas, ballets, symphony orchestras, museums, parks, parades, and tours on the Spree River and to government office buildings. One reason Berlin offers so much culture today is because for 45 years there were two Berlins. West Berliners wanted the same cultural institutions and municipal amenities as those in East Berlin. The Freie Universität was created in December 1948, because West Germany and the U.S. (with its own Cold War interests) felt that there should be a major university in West Berlin equivalent to the historically famous Humboldt University in the East section.

During our four-month stay we heard eight operas at three different Berlin opera houses, plus the Dresden opera house where Kevin, Andy, and I heard Wagner's *The Flying Dutchman*. We experienced Simon Ritter conducting Beethoven's Ninth Symphony in a park and the Berliner Ensemble, which featured the avant-garde plays *Lulu* by Alban Berg and *Peter Pan* by Robert Wilson. Kevin and I visited at least one hundred museums and large non-commercial art galleries. My favorite spaces were the Gemäldegalerie with its stunning old masters, Mies van der Rohe's Neues Galerie, the Hamburger Bahnhof Museum (where we viewed a mega-exhibition on Martin Knippenberger), the Five Museums on Museum Island (one of which has the famous sculpture bust of Nefertiti, another, the great Pergamon sculptures), the Holocaust Memorial, the Kathe Kollwitz Memorial, the Jewish Museum, and the Brandenburg Gates. Add to this list the Ethnological Museum in Dahlem, across from my office at Abt. Kultur, and the fabulous Berlin Zoological Garden, a zoo featuring more species than any other zoo in the world. Vivien often accompanied us on our excursions.

Winding through Berlin is the Spree River connecting to a multitude of canals (more than Amsterdam) that facilitated commerce in the old Berlin. Recommended are the flat river boats gliding under low bridges. Afterwards, one can enjoy the banks of the Spree where accommodating cafes provide beer, wine, Aperol Spritzers and Flammkuchen (pizza toppings on a brioche-like thin pastry). Friends introduced us to funky neighborhoods with cafes tucked into houseboats, Turkish food, and street art.

Reminders of the dark side of Germany's history—specifically Nazi history—aggressively asserted their messages in public places. This reckoning with their horrible past was not the Berlin we had seen in 1990. In our subway station were posters with photographs and texts reminding riders that attendance of Jewish children in public schools was curtailed in April 1933, three months after Adolf Hitler was declared chancellor of Germany. The Nazi-controlled German Student Union organized book burnings in May 1933. Some 25,000 books deemed dangerous to Nazi ideology went up in flames. Ten-feet tall round concrete pillars erected in Berlin's main square held poster portraits of those Germans, such as Marlene Dietrich, who had left Germany when the Nazis came to power.

Apartment buildings in our neighborhoods and all over Berlin had bronze plaques imbedded in the sidewalks in front of many residences—called *Stolpersteine*—alerting passersby of the Jewish people who had lived there, their names, birth dates and the dates they had been murdered. The plaques did not say "mort" (died) but "ermordet" (murdered).

A park near the Brandenburg Gate memorialized the Roma who died in the Nazi death camps. Another building— the *Schonebeger Rathaus*—open to the public, contains archives with index cards on all the Berliners taken off to the camps. An outdoor Memorial to the Murdered Jews of Europe, designed by architect Peter Eisenman, embraced a large area filled with large rectangular stone blocks. It stood next to the American Embassy. The Jewish Museum, brilliantly designed by Daniel Libeskind, dominates the architecture of its neighborhood. Their collections and exhibitions focus on German-Jewish history and culture, including the Holocaust. It is my favorite museum building.

My most chilling experience was viewing the photographs and artifacts and reading the wall labels at the "Topography of Terror Documentation Center," a large post-war building constructed on the site of the demolished Nazi headquarters of the Schutzstaffel (S.S.) and Gestapo. The exhibition documents in detail the history of Hitler's rise to power and the roles of Joseph Goebbels, Hermann Göring, Heinrich Himmler, and other murderous supporters. Across from the building is a large section of The Wall, which had been left to stand as a reminder of the repressive East Germany government in the years from war's end to 1989. Not surprisingly, there were no mentions of the capitalists' complicity, such as the steel manufacturing firm of Krupp AG, which financed the Nazis in their rise to power.

In late June, family came to visit. First Mary for about ten days, Emily and her husband Robert for a long weekend,

Andy for three weeks, and in early July, Christina with her pre-teen daughter Maggie for about two weeks. With them all we re-visited the museums we loved, walked extensively, and ate in wonderful ethnic restaurants. On July 9, with my classes over, Kevin, Andy, Christina, Maggie and I took a night train to Giverny, France to the estate and gardens of Claude Monet. The Terra Foundation had a summer program for pre-doc art historians, and I had been invited to give a seminar for the students.

The Terra accommodated the whole family with housing and delicious meals. We marveled at Monet's gardens and ponds, stayed two nights, and went on to Paris, where we stayed four nights in a small hotel near Notre Dame. Again, sightseeing and touring museums. Maggie, however, went shopping.

The only downside of our Berlin sojourn was my health problem. On April 28, I noticed strange heart palpitations, unlike the supra-ventricular tachycardia I had had in previous years. In this case, my heart seemed not to be doubling the beat, but rather, to be beating wildly. Late on the night of April 30, we went to the emergency room at the Charité Hospital—a university teaching hospital famous since the 19th century. The doctors told me that I had atrial fibrillation—A-Fib as it is known. A cardioversion was scheduled for six weeks later—the delay because a blood clot had already formed in my heart and needed to dissolve with the help of anti-clotting pills.

Those six weeks before the cardioversion were extremely difficult. I felt totally fatigued every waking moment. I had to climb 88 steps to our apartment. It took a long time to do that. Crossing the street was difficult. Rolling over in bed put me in agony. But I carried on and never missed the Tuesday classes at F.U. or my German lessons with my tutor. I also continued with my writing and editing reviews. Through all this Kevin was my rock—buying groceries, carrying my bags, and cheering me on. Finally, on June 9, I returned to Charité and had my cardioversion. My heart returned to its normal beats.

Living in Germany for four months prompted me to think about other countries to visit. What better way than a Viking River Cruise, where we could visit many countries, enjoy beautiful landscapes, and (in the cities) study great art, sculpture, architecture and plazas. On July 20, we flew to Munich, and the next day took a train to Passau and boarded one of Viking's long boats. The next day we joined a tour of Passau. The guide pointed out the recent floods in southern Germany which resulted in the Danube's overflow. Had we taken the boat ride a month earlier, the boat would not have been able to clear the low bridges.

On the third day, after traveling many miles and going through locks, the boat docked at Linz. No mention by the guides that Linz was Hitler's hometown—the city that Hitler wanted to elevate to the stature of Vienna, with grand boulevards, impressive neo-classical architecture, and museums brimming with the artworks stolen from Jewish collectors and European museums.

Instead of touring Linz, the Viking guides took us on an hour-and-a-half bus trip to Salzburg, Austria—famous for its musical tradition and the birthplace of Mozart. The long boat arrived in Vienna on Thursday, July 25. We had but one short afternoon to see museums, so I chose the Leopold Museum with its early 20th century Austrian artists, including Gustav Klimt, Egon Schiele, and Oscar Kokoschka, as well as the Jewish Museum.

Coming from Berlin, I had become obsessed with Jewish and Holocaust museums that featured photographs and artifacts, both pre-Nazi and post-Nazi. Vienna's Jüdisches Museum Wein (Jewish Museum) had mounted an intriguing exhibition of Jewish entertainers in Europe, especially those performing in the cabarets in Berlin and Vienna.

On Friday, July 26, 2013, we continued to Bratislava, capital of Slovakia and a part of the Soviet Union before its dissolution. Aside from the castle on the hill, Bratislava buildings are unadorned—typical of cities that never gained a long-lasting imperial status. The guide had some things to say about the former Communist regime that forbade citizens to communicate with the non-Communist world, even though Austria borders Bratislava.

Finally, we came to Budapest on Saturday morning, July 27. There is "Buda" and there is "Pest." The Buda part is the hilly area where the palace and cathedral are located; the Pest (pronounced "*pescht*") is the flat sweep of land on the other side of the Danube where the parliament is located, along with grand boulevards and a huge pedestrian square called the Square of the Heroes. The heroes are represented by larger-than-life statues, each of which depicts a leader of the seven tribes of original Hungarians. Another group of standing statues highlights Catholic history with St. Steven (Ishvan) followed by notable bishops.

On our first day, after lunch on the boat, Kevin and I, caught a cab to the *Szépmuvészeti Müzeum* (The Museum of Fine Arts). The museum's fabulous collection compares only with the Gemälde in Berlin. I especially liked the Lucas Cranach paintings: the two versions of *An Unlikely Pair* and a third, *Christ and the Woman Taken into Adultery*. The first shows a toothless old woman proffering money to an attractive young man, the second, a young woman reaching into an old man's purse. The Christ picture shows compassion toward the adulterous woman.

While there we also viewed a retrospective exhibition of Egon Schiele, a fascinating artist. There were many self-portraits, including one large painting, *The Hermits*, representing him and Klimt. The exhibition included portraits by Kokoshka and Max Oppenheimer. Schiele's portrait of Trude Engel, 1911, with her wild black hair is stunning. Schiele died of the flu pandemic of 1918, only 28-years-old, within weeks of his wife Edith's death.

The Mücsarnok (Museum of Contemporary Art) featured art of contemporary Hungarian artists. Our American curators' version of contemporary art is so grounded in the works produced in the US, the UK, and Germany, that it was refreshing to see the creative outputs of other countries' artists.

Bending to my obsession with art of the Holocaust, in Budapest we went to the Dohány Street Synagogue and Hungarian Jewish Museum. The synagogue is the largest in Europe, originally built in a 19th-century Moorish style. Bombed during World War II, it was restored in the 1990s. A young woman gave us a tour of the Museum, which is only about three or four rooms, filled with ritual artifacts plus a room of photographs relating to the Holocaust.

There were about 750,000 Jews in Hungary at the start of the war. The Nazis did not arrive until 1944 but quickly went about the extermination business. Jews were sent off to concentration camps, corralled into a ghetto, and shot on the banks of the Danube, their bodies thrown into the river. Six hundred thousand were murdered. A public sculpture that memorializes them consists of individual bronze shoes perched and strung out on a wall at the border of the pathway overlooking the river. Those shoes are a chilling sight. After seeing the shoes, we returned to our Viking boat, had lunch, and left for the Budapest Airport to return to Berlin.

After two days of packing and giving away household items Kevin and I no longer needed, we flew home to the States, but not before the airport agents at the gate insisted that we cull and rearrange our overweight bags. The last hour in Berlin was spent kneeling on the airport floor, repacking heavy items into smaller more manageable shopping bags, and throwing things out. Not a fitting exit after four months of glorious adventure.

Why had I become obsessed with the present-day campaigns to highlight the horrible Nazi past? It's because I identify with those who are targets of discrimination—whether because of their race, gender, religion, ethnicity, sexual identification, or politics. Because my ancestors hailed from Germany in the 1840s, I asked myself: *Had they lived in the 1930s, would they have condoned the extermination camps?* I hope not. Nevertheless, this pursuit of mine for anti-Nazi resistance found examples of—and solace in—the humanity and fortitude of those who fought back.

24

Alice Neel, 1973-Present

It was Jack Baur's idea. At a Whitney Wednesday morning staff meeting in 1973, Director Baur announced he planned to visit Alice Neel (1900-1984) at her studio. A hole existed in the Whitney's exhibition calendar, and he thought her work would make a good show. He asked if any of the curators would like to accompany him. Curious about the artist, I raised my hand.

Baur and I visited her studio on the Upper West Side about five blocks from my apartment. A 73-year old artist with bright blue eyes, grey-white hair pulled back into a bun, she lived by herself in a rambling apartment with paintings stacked everywhere. There was a small decrepit kitchen with a roach or two scampering along the walls and a large living room with various chairs and loveseats (seen in her many portraits). At the center of the room stood Alice's easel, where she perched on a chair to paint her portraits, an occasional still life, and the neighboring buildings she could see from her window. Lurking almost invisible in the room was her daughter-in-law Nancy, who served Alice as factotum, helping her set up her studio, arranging college lectures, organizing travel, shopping, etc.

At the first sight of Alice I was enchanted. But I soon discovered her looks were deceiving. Instead of a knitting-and-apple-pie-making grandma, she was smart, well read, and leftist in spirit. She had worked on the WPA Federal

Art Project during the Roosevelt administration and had associated herself with Communist Party politics during the 1930s and 1940s. A free-spirited Bohemian to the core, she had two sons out of wedlock with two boyfriends who minimally supported her. She lived for decades in poverty in Spanish Harlem. At this point she had moved to a larger rent-controlled apartment. With a twinkle in her eye, she sported one of the dirtiest mouths I had ever encountered. Jack and I chatted with her, and we left with an agreement for her exhibition. I volunteered to be the curator. Jack later sat for his own portrait (now at the Brooklyn Museum).

So, it was all set—until Marcia Tucker, one of the Whitney's contemporary curators—went into Baur's office a few days later to complain. She told him that because I held the title of curator of 19th-century art, I should not organize the show. Instead, she proposed one of her acolytes, Elke Morger Solomon, the curator for drawings. Marcia was a charismatic individual and had super-loyal admirers on the Whitney staff. Baur capitulated and called me in to break the news.

But I didn't let go. I thought Alice's life and art would make a great book. Several times I interviewed her during 1976. Two times I broached the subject to the publisher Abrams, and they rebuffed me. Finally, in November 1979, after discussing the Neel book project with the senior editor at Abrams, I received concrete encouragement to move forward.

Working with Alice would be fun, or so I assumed. The Women's Movement admired her for her tenacity. The artist May Stevens (by then a dear friend of mine) and Anne Coffin Hansen (well known as an outspoken feminist art historian) had frequently given lectures on her.

Alice was also accessible to me. Not only did she live near me in Manhattan, but she also had a summer house in Spring Lake on the Jersey Shore, about five miles from Ocean

Grove, where my family summered in my grandmother's house. Kevin and I would often visit Alice in Spring Lake and show off our new baby Andy (born in spring 1978). In 1980, before Alice got her cataracts surgery, she painted a double portrait of Kevin and two-year-old Andy, even though she complained about not seeing well. She proposed to sell the painting to us for $6,000 [$23,000 in 2025], but we lacked the money. She would not budge on the price and suggested that my "rich" mother buy it. My mother Glennie was not rich. Kevin said, "Alice should give it to you because of your friendship and for all the time you have spent with her." At the time none of us thought it really looked like Kevin and Andy, but in hindsight she did capture Andy's hyperactivity and Kevin's stolid patience.

She was especially fascinated by Andy's squirmy body and his frequent grabbing at his genitals beneath his little green shorts. Men's penises fascinated Alice, who had painted a full-length nude reclining figure of art critic John Perrault, as well as a naked and multi-penis-membered Joe Gould. But she was equally obsessed with female breasts and bellies swollen by pregnancy, as exemplified in *Pregnant Woman*, posed by daughter-in-law Nancy.

By 1980 I was teaching full time at Boston University, running the museum studies program, overseeing the running of the Boston University Art Gallery (BUAG) with a student staff, and regularly going to art openings. I needed a dynamic first show for the fall of 1980, so I decided to bring in Alice. That summer I taped interviews with Alice to have fresh material for my catalogue text. The show *Alice Neel: Paintings of Two Decades* opened on October 9, 1980. My three-page essay for the 20-page catalogue with 20 reproductions was called *Alice Neel: Art as a Form of History*.

In the last paragraph I wrote: "Thus, a Neel portrait becomes a dialogue between the sitter's social and intellectual stance as revealed in his/herself-created visage and Neel's critical and partisan response to what that sitter represents within history. In her words, 'Art is a form of history ... I want to get the specific person plus the Zeitgeist.'"

Shifting to the group family portraits—among the strongest in the exhibition—I concluded: "These family pictures blend the specific with the symbolic, the past with the present realities, the mother with the children. And they share with all her portraits a complexity of intentions and results. They are her response to experience as well as her challenge to future premonitions and hopes."

While the exhibition was a success by all measures, the BU studio faculty boycotted it. Perhaps they did not like her method of direct painting (which could look slapdash) as opposed to the careful building up of layers of paint they were teaching at the school. Studio Program Chair David Aronson's wife later confided in me that he told her not to bother seeing it.

However, John Wilson (the only Black BU studio professor) brought his class for a viewing followed by a Q&A with Alice. She also gave a funny, quirky lecture on campus about her work and her sitters, which had us all in stitches. As a performer, Alice did not disappoint.

Writing the BU catalogue essay on Alice served as prep for the book. More interviews followed, focusing on Alice's thoughts about her experiences growing up in the suburbs of Philadelphia, attending art school at a time when women were not considered real artists, marrying the Cuban artist Carlos Enriquez, living in Cuba, having children, witnessing a child die, being abandoned by Carlos, having her child Isabetta taken from her, experiencing a nervous breakdown, being institutionalized, struggling to be recognized as an artist, getting new boyfriends and raising their two sons, and interacting with other artists and neighborhood people whom she painted. I also probed her about the stories behind specific paintings hanging in New York and her studio in Spring Lake. Sometimes we would look at slides. Always on hand, Nancy helped and brought in drinks and sandwiches during our breaks.

I wrote a draft of the book, adding Alice's words from further interviews conducted in the summer of 1982. In the fall, I read my drafts back to her. During those readings I tape-recorded both my narrative and her comments about the draft—getting her approval regarding the wording, plus new comments on tape. I also incorporated a few of her writings to show she could be a writer as well as a reader and a talker.

The result was a narrative interspersed with my own clarifying comments and interjections contextualizing her life and art within the worlds of left politics and contemporary art. I also corrected dates and names of people. Different font designs made it clear which was Alice's voice and which was mine. The Abrams editor, Nora Beeson, referred to my task as "stitching it all together." Following the long narrative interview, I contributed an eight-page interpretive essay, "Alice Neel: The Work, the Words, the Woman."

What did not get into the book were Alice's snarky remarks about many, many people, especially women. Again and again, Alice's attitudes showed contempt toward those women whom she felt had prostrated themselves to patriarchy. She also disliked other assertive women who were in direct competition with her, such as Louise Nevelson. I asked her about the women's movement and pointed out that feminists had helped to advance her career. She didn't respond. I pressed her, "What do you have to say about the women's movement?" She shot back, "They can put their heads in a bucket!"

I told art historian Anne Coffin Hanson, who constantly promoted Alice in the early 1970s, that Alice had said nasty things about Anne behind her back. Anne's response, "But she's such a genius!" That's a most strange response—that being a "genius" allows one to be cruel to others. But history shows that genius male artists can be monsters. Think Bernini, Caravaggio, Picasso, and Jackson Pollock. However, since the "Me Too" movement of the 21st century, we tend to be less forgiving of people who belittle, dismiss, make passes, assault, and generally show no respect for women. We have yet to decide how to handle women who do similar bitchy things against other women.

In reading my edited words to Alice, she would comment to Nancy and me, "Yes, that is what I would have said." She rarely made corrections. But she wanted me to delete an anecdote about her affair with John Rothschild, a wealthy man who later lived in a room in her apartment. She explained the reason for the self-censorship: "My sons are prudes, you know!"

She also wanted me to tamp down the discussion of incidents of cruelty that Sam Brody, her lover and the father of her second son Hartley, directed toward her first son Richard. Phoebe Hoban learned the details of that abuse and published them in her 2010 book *Alice Neel: The Art of Not Sitting Pretty*. Hoban managed to get access to the unpublished journals of another male visitor attracted to Alice but appalled by her dysfunctional household. He was a person Alice never mentioned. Frankly, I could not read Hoban's book beyond the midpoint, as it recalled my own memories of hearing the many lurid details of child abuse from Nancy. I asked myself, *Why did Alice let Brody abuse her son?* Painting Brody as a monster (which she literally did) was not enough to absolve her from complicity in Brody's acts of cruelty.

She did not want me to say in my book that she had bought a house in Spring Lake in the 1930s. Even in the early 1980s, she still worried that the government might make her pay back her WPA/FAP salary because she in fact had not been dirt poor—a requirement for WPA/FAP employment. She had been a homeowner in a wealthy beach town during those hardscrabble years of the Depression.

I regret that I did not include in the book more about her role in the theater. She was friends with poet Kenneth Fearing, whose portrait she painted in 1935. Alice served as a model for the Bohemian woman painter in Fearing's 1948 novel *The Big Clock*.

The novel was later adapted as a movie starring Ray Milland, along with Maureen O'Sullivan, Charles Laughton, and Elsa Lancaster as Alice's character, an artist who lives in a tiny apartment with screaming babies and toddlers underfoot.

Alice became a movie star when Allen Ginsberg and his coterie of writer friends invited her to participate in the short film *Pull My Daisy* (1959). The story was written and narrated by Jack Kerouac and directed by Robert Frank and Alfred Leslie. The 26-minute film, shot primarily in an artist's studio-residence loft, focuses on Allen Ginsberg, Peter Orlovsky, and Gregory Corso as they clown around on the floor and the loft's overstuffed loveseat. Larry Rivers poses as Milo, a railroad brakeman getting ready for work, while his wife, played by French actress Delphine Seytig, nags him. Milo returns from work and a bishop shows up later in the evening along with his sister and elderly mother wearing a hat and gloves, played by Alice Neel.

The poets continue to riff on their own poetry interspersed with wordplay on the words "holy" and "cockroaches" and more clowning. Then Alice's character gets up to play an upright organ in the living area. More fretting by Milo's wife, then the bishop and his entourage leave, and Milo/Larry Rivers initiates a jam session. The film ends with Milo and the poets going off into the night, leaving the wife behind in tears.

When I showed the film in my BU classes I always

concluded with words like, "It is an anarchistic, anti-bourgeois, and *very male* story about the freedom of boys doing just what they want. The anonymous women in men's lives are not only saddled with chores and childcare but their creative and emotional selves are ignored."

Alice told me that playing the organ was not in the script, but that she got bored with all the fooling around, spotted the organ, got up, and went to play. That brief scene was the only bright one that shifted the narrative from word-play chaos to a concentration on jazz music performance.

Alice was capable of huge exaggerations, which I often let slide. For example, in my *Alice Neel* book Alice tells me: "In 1958, I was already getting rid of Sam [Brody]. People would come up and Sam would make a big fight. He drove some people out with a butcher knife once. They came to buy a picture and because they said to him,' You have more the attitude of an illustrator' he almost went crazy. He grabbed a knife and chased them out of the house." Nora Beeson, the book editor, told me she once visited Alice when Sam was there. Sam had read the above passage about the knife and, in the presence of Beeson, said, "Alice, I never did that." According to Beeson, Alice replied, "I know, but it makes a good story!" Both Alice and Sam giggled over that. Beeson asked me whether we should keep the quote. My response was a laugh and a "Why not?"

The manipulating Alice revealed herself fully that summer of 1982 when I discovered her full egomania. Her ego was so locked into the Abrams book that she went out of her way to trump the decisions that I, as author, had made. A few examples stand out. At one point I sent Alice a draft of the Acknowledgments page that read: "This book should rightly be dedicated to Nancy" to acknowledge Nancy's help to both Alice and me. When next I visited, before I had even crossed the threshold of her apartment, she shrieked at me, "How dare you dedicate my book to Nancy!" Nancy cringed in the corner, and I went about explaining that my words were not an actual dedication but a gesture of thanks. I wound up writing: "Nancy Neel should come first in any list of acknowledgments … "

Another instance shows her wild imagination as she tried to put me in my place. While visiting Alice one day, a woman art critic and historian from the Midwest came to call. We ended up chatting with each other more than with Alice, then flounced off together as if we had been best friends for years. The next time I visited Alice, she directed a volley of invectives at me for neglecting her. She said something like, "You both were flirting so much." Then in a few words she verbalized an image of sexual acts we might have done together. Classic Alice! I replied, "Alice, that is your fantasy, not mine!"

Then came the real troubles over the layout and contents of the book. I had shrewdly anticipated I would have troubles with Alice when I saw that Abrams had sent her an "author's contract" probably much like the copy they sent to me. The contract was lying open on her kitchen table. I didn't read it but saw the big letters "Author's Contract." That alerted me that trouble might be brewing. I insisted to Abrams that as the author I should be listed as such on the title page, my last name should be on the spine, and I should be the only author of the Acknowledgments. Abrams obliged, not knowing what had motivated me to make demands usually taken for granted.

Sure enough, Alice's egocentric self stepped forward. When all parts of the manuscript were finished and sent to Abrams, publisher Paul Gottlieb called me to say that Alice wanted to get rid of my interpretive essay—*and* my name off the book. I fought back. I called my ex-husband, Fred Hills, then a senior editor at Simon & Schuster, who told me to tell Gottlieb in no uncertain terms that my book would include my essay or there would be no book. Since I had taped the reading sessions with Alice and her responses, I owned the narrative. If my essay was scuttled, I would pull the whole manuscript. Gottlieb went to Alice's apartment, worked his charm, and told her that my essay would stay.

Alice retaliated. I discovered when the book was published that Abrams had capitulated to her and published a two-page Foreword written by William D. Paul Jr., a museum director from Athens, Georgia. As the author, I had been sideswiped.

The book debuted in October 1983. Gottlieb had a celebratory party at his Manhattan apartment in November. John Canaday of the *New York Times* included the book as one of the best art books of the year.

Alice was on a roll—loving every bit of her new celebrity. Now praised for her unexpected and humorous repartee, she brilliantly sparred with Johnny Carson when interviewed on NBC's *Tonight Show* in 1984. She came onto the stage decked out in a long, glittering and sequined dress. Carson barely got in a word himself, and she had both Carson and the audience in stitches.

In the summer of 1984, Kevin insisted that Alice and I reconcile. Our family went off to see her and Nancy in Spring Lake. It was all very amicable. At one point in our chatting, she looked at me full in the face and said, "After all, you won!"

Later, when doctors told her that there was no chance to reverse the progress of her cancer and she was going to die, Nancy confided to me that Alice cried for three days. Kevin and I visited her a week before her death. Our car was double-parked so I went in first. When I told her that Kevin was waiting in the car downstairs and would come after I left, she raised her voice to say, "Nancy! Get me my teeth!" For Kevin, a man she admired, she was vain enough not to want him to see her toothless.

The following Saturday, October 12, Kevin, Andy and I

went to the Fleming Museum in Burlington, Vermont, where I gave a slide lecture on Alice. Alice's son Hartley Neel and his wife Genny lived not far away and invited us to spend the night at their home. In the lecture I focused on her as a realist, expressionist, and nonconformist who painted brilliant portraits.

At breakfast the next day Hartley received a phone call that Alice had died during the night. It felt like someone had punched me in the stomach. We immediately left, knowing how much Ginny and Hartley would have to do to prepare for mourning.

Even with my mixed feelings, I still felt a responsibility to Alice after her death. I pressed her sons Richard and Hartley to publicize Alice's work. I argued that they should give key paintings to museums. My model was Georgia O'Keeffe, the widow who spent about two years placing Alfred Stieglitz's photographic portfolios in various museums around the country—an act that increased his audience and his fame. The brothers tried out my suggestion by hiring me to act as a liaison between the estate and museums. For two years I carried on correspondence with museum directors across the country and got some nibbles. At one point, the Smithsonian American Art Museum [then called the National Museum of American Art] bought the painting *Max White* (1935). It was a fine purchase: Alice at her best in delineating the psychological affects of a sitter's face.

However, it seemed clear to me that the Neels were more ambitious in spreading the news of Alice's genius and in selling. They apparently did not want to give away paintings and drawings but to market them. I severed myself from this part-time job— too much for me anyway as I was teaching, running the BU Art Gallery, and organizing a large Sargent retrospective for the Whitney. In 1986, the Neels hired another consultant to establish an international reputation for her. He was successful in this mission.

Tom Armstrong, Director of the Whitney, agreed to host a Memorial Service for Alice at the Whitney on February 7, 1985. He introduced the speakers. Mayor Edward Koch, whose portrait Alice had done, went first. Next came John I. H. Baur, who had considerably advanced her career by showing her work at the Whitney in 1974. Then I spoke. A Tribute by Raphael Soyer was read, followed by remarks from Allen Ginsberg. The Guarneri String Quartet provided music, and a reception followed.

In my archives, I have the written tribute from Raphael Soyer, which he gave me to keep for a good purpose or to publish. Soyer was about the same age as Alice, both lived in New York, and traveled in the same circles. They also shared the same friends, including Allen Ginsberg and his cohorts. Raphael Soyer on Alice:

It is sad that fame came to Alice Neel late. From the very beginning she was a fine painter but was unrecognized most of her painting life. The Patricia Hills monograph, *Alice Neel*, was published in 1983 … She enjoyed her monograph … but she believed in fame and immortality. "I want to be famous," she would say all her life … But where does Alice Neel really belong? Has there been any other painter, present or past, in American art, like her? The New York Times obituary calls her a portraitist, but to which other American portrait painter can she be likened? I could suggest the names of European painters—the early Kokoshka, Schiele, even Van Gogh and Soutine.

She is a unique figure in American art … The people she painted, the anonymous ones, the celebrities, the transvestites, the gays and the prostitutes, although they sit, stand or recline, are not static. They are convulsively alive; their limbs seem to be in motion. Their mouths, eyes grimace and contort. She depicts them clothed, often naked, emphasizing their constitutional inadequacies and their anatomical idiosyncrasies. She exposes their nakedness, vulnerability, mortality. Some of these figures seem to be in pain (*Carmen and Baby, Randall in Extremis*, the portrait of David Rosenberg dying of cancer).

Even children she painted as probingly, without sentimentality ... As for her naked female nudes, and the naked pregnant women, one has to go back to the medieval depictions of Eve to find something analogous ... At 81 she painted herself naked, full length, her flesh melting and hanging loose. One more self-portrait exists—only a skull. Would it be too much to say there was something Shakespearean in Alice Neel?

I would have added: "There was also something Rabelaisian about Alice—bawdy, prickly, bold, and finally humanistic."

In 2007 Alice's grandson Andrew made a documentary, *Alice Neel,* which premiered in Greenwich Village. I even had a brief talking-head appearance. Andrew did not shy away from the contradictions of Alice's life. In one segment Andrew focused on Alice's husband Carlos Enríquez Gómez, his family, and her daughter Isabetta who had been taken from her.

As a pre-teen Isabetta had visited Alice's home in Spring Lake at least once, but Alice subsequently lost touch with her. Later, Isabetta migrated to Florida with her family, as many wealthy families did after the Cuban Revolution. As I learned from Nancy's recollections and the documentary, the story turns tragic. Alice gave a talk, perhaps in 1978, when she had an exhibition in Miami Beach. Isabetta attended. Alice would not or could not recognize the woman in the audience as her daughter. I'm told they never spoke. Eventually, Isabetta committed suicide. Who will ever know the full story?

After seeing the film I staggered out to a nearby Washington Square eatery and wept unconsolably for 20 minutes. Despite everything, I still loved Alice, even when squarely facing the hurts she had imposed on so many people.

The Philadelphia Museum of Art organized a traveling retrospective, *Alice Neel*, that showed in five major museums during 2000-2001. The Metropolitan Museum in New York held an even larger retrospective, *Alice Neel: People Come First,* which traveled to the Guggenheim Museum in Bilbao, Spain, and to the de Young Museum in San Francisco during 2021-22. My favorite painting in the show was *Last Sickness* (1952), a portrait of her dying mother. Her face in its dual visage of resignation and alertness is one of Alice's most poignant and moving portraits; Alice took care of her mother when her mom was ailing, and something of Alice's deep empathy comes across in the portrait.

In 2023 there was yet another large Alice Neel exhibition at the Musée de Pompidou in Paris, which moved on to a London venue. Alice would be dancing in her grave!

&

Alice had a left outlook and, in her words, was "in and out" of the Communist Party during the 1930s. Her friends included not only radical poets, such as Kenneth Fearing, but also CP union organizers, such as Pat Whalen and Michael Gold. She admired their courage and painted strong portraits of them. In the years before she died Alice loved to talk with my Marxist husband Kevin.

Profoundly touched by her experiences of the Depression, she transformed those experiences into images: a hearing of the Russell Sage Foundation when an impoverished woman confessed to living with her children in an overturned automobile; a string of workers in her neighborhood; a nighttime parade protesting the spread of fascism.

She sympathized with oppressed communities and working-class people who, she would say, "have gotten a rotten deal." She knew families who struggled financially and emotionally because of poverty. She often focused on African Americans and Latin Americans, giving them dignity and personality.

But she could be fierce when negotiating with patrons over the prices of her paintings and the fees for her public lectures. She wanted what she felt was hers. To my knowledge, of all the people who wrote about her and organized exhibitions of her work (including myself), she never gifted them with any of her pieces. All her works she wanted to sell and keep the money herself— a need inflected by her anxiety about poverty.

Alice delighted in being privy to the art gossip she heard in her portrait sessions with art-world types. In talking about the hectic rat race of New York, Neel's favorite motto was: "I'd rather be shot as a wolf than a lamb." The traits she seems to have been born with, such as stubbornness and grit, became her resources—what she needed to survive and flourish. She prided herself in refusing to compromise in what she saw as the fickle duplicity of art world fashions and commercialism.

Writing the book on Alice Neel became an intense experience for Alice and me, and I still want to write more. I want Neel to be remembered as an artist *in history* who had absorbed the lessons of cubism, fauvism, expressionism, and mid-century modernism, was alert to the sociological and political nuances of urban, professional life, and knew exactly what she was doing.

Thank you, Alice Neel.

25

May Stevens, 1974-Present

Critic Lawrence Alloway introduced me to the art of May Stevens by making a proposal. He and I had become friends in the early 1970s. He wrote in his *Nation* columns about my exhibitions at the Whitney, and I was flattered he gave me regular shout-outs. Once Kevin joined my life, we would get together for dinner parties with Alloway and his wife, artist Sylvia Sleigh. I loved his wit and her quirky British mannerisms.

In the summer of 1976 Alloway told me that the Everson Museum in Syracuse had scheduled a fall exhibition, *Three American Realists: Alice Neel, Sylvia Sleigh, May Stevens.* He suggested I write an article before the show opened. Knowing I was familiar with Sylvia's and Alice's work, Alloway convinced me that *Art in America* would accept my article. I did not yet know May, but I promptly made an appointment for a studio visit. May and I hit it off that first meeting, and I wrote my article on the three artists. Editor Betsy Baker said she liked the piece, but I had missed the deadline.

Meeting May, I also met her husband, Rudolf Baranik. They were a very close couple who embraced the same lifestyle: a spartan rejection of materialism, a devotion to their art, active in progressive causes, and indifferent as to whether their paintings sold or not. Both independent socialists, with May also a feminist, they wanted to live and to love on an equal plane.

Rudolf's family, secular Jews, had been murdered by Lithuanian fascists in 1939. Rudolf, who had traveled to Chicago in 1938 to attend art school, joined the US Army and fought in Europe. His brother escaped Lithuania to fight in the Soviet Army just before the mass murder of Lithuanian Jews. Family lore recalls he "escaped on the last train" before the German Nazis arrived. May, in contrast, had grown up in a working-class neighborhood of Quincy, where her father worked as a pipefitter at Bethlehem shipyards.

May and Rudolf met in 1947 at the Art Students League, where Rudolf had returned from the war to become an instructor. May was enrolled as a painting student. They fell in love, married, and in 1947 went to Paris—living on Rudolf's Army GI Bill stipend. They became parents to Steven, born in Paris. Even though May took on the responsibility of being the primary caregiver, she still focused on her art. The couple submitted works to exhibitions in Paris, such as the Galerie Huit, which showed the works of American expatriates. Both were exposed to leftist artists and to the ideas of Existentialism then flourishing in post-war Paris and represented by Jean-Paul Sartre and Albert Camus.

May spoke of her experiences as extraordinary. She developed a horror of living an ordinary life. She said to me in an interview that she rejected "the life of my parents, a life that didn't have action and excitement and struggle and trying to change things and trying to reach for things." Indeed, May and Rudolf did not live a conventional life. They preferred to be in their studios creating art or attending meetings focused on bringing together communities to change the world for ordinary people.

A long-lasting friendship developed between our family and May and Rudolf. Like Alice Neel, May and Rudolf also shared with us the politics of anti-racism, anticapitalism, anti-authoritarianism, and social change. We swapped stories about our political thoughts and engagement in activism. At this time Rudolf was also editing a Lithuanian-language socialist newspaper in New York.

A short time after I met May, she asked me to write a short catalogue essay on *Big Daddy,* a signature image of hers and the theme of a new exhibition. She based *Big Daddy* on photographs of her father. He was racist and antisemitic, but he adored his art-school daughter to the point that he would slip home un-stretched canvases from the shipyard on which she could paint. She created the grinning, bullet-headed figure of *Big Daddy* as a symbol of patriarchy and military male authority. In 2004, she recalled the anti-war mindset of herself and friends during the late 1960s: "Why not use art's power to help stop a war?"

My involvement with contemporary anti-war artists such as May reinforced my convictions about the necessity to create a new political art by blending political feminism and anti-racism with radical activism.

Kevin and I began to meet and socialize with others in her circle—artists such as Leon Golub and Nancy Spero. I renewed my friendship with the critic Lucy Lippard, whom I had worked with in the early 1960s at MoMA. Through May, I also met feminists such as Linda Cunningham, Moira Roth, Harmony Hammond, Joyce Kozloff, and Joan Semmel.

When I became pregnant with Andy in 1977, May took photos of me, along with photographs of other artists and critics for a painting that would be part of a series of women posing in her studio. The Vietnam War had ended, and she had moved on from Big Daddy. She had already finished *The Artist's Studio (After Courbet), (1974),* and *Soho Women Artists* (1977-78). Her new painting, *Mysteries and Politics* (1978), would include women art historians as well as artists.

The cast of *Mysteries and Politics* included Betsy Damon, Pat Steir, Poppy Johnson holding her twin babies, Carol Duncan and a pregnant Patricia Hills (pregnant with Andy), May Stevens (averting her face), Suzanne Harris,

Amy Sillman, Elizabeth Weatherford and Joan Snyder, seated. On the wall behind the figures is a painting of Mary Beth Edelson's torso and large black and white images based on photographs of May's mother holding May as a baby and Rosa Luxemburg in a large white hat. The series showed at the Lerner Heller Gallery in 1978.

May's heroine had become Rosa Luxemburg, the Polish-German theoretician and revolutionary who, with Karl Liebknecht, founded the German Communist Party and was murdered by a proto-Nazi group in January 1919. May transitioned from Big Daddy images to the pairing of her mother and Luxemburg. She called the Alice/Rosa series *Ordinary/Extraordinary*, as she was intrigued by the different lives of the two women.

Luxembourg was extraordinary. In contrast, May's mother Alice Stevens was a working-class, uneducated Irish Canadian living in Massachusetts and working as a waitress when she met May's father. She devoted her life mainly to caring for May and her brother Stacey, who had childhood diabetes. Over the course of Alice's marriage, Stacey died, May left to study art in New York, and Alice withdrew into silence and depression. Eventually, her husband placed her in a nursing home and took up with another woman. Alice lived to an old age in the fog of dementia. She was ordinary. But May always explained that the reverse could also be true. The women had taken different paths—not always of their own choice. Both women deserved our respect. May referred to both as her "two mothers."

Outside of making art, May's political activism during the 1980s was focused on her involvement with the Guerrilla Girls and *Heresies*, a publication focused on women's art and women's causes.

Rudolf and May's lives were interrupted when their son Steven committed suicide in 1981 by jumping off the George Washington Bridge. He landed on the shore of the Hudson

River. He left a suicide note, the contents of which she never discussed, but Steven's death threw her into a depression. May looked to a therapist to help her. Her mourning channeled itself into painting more pictures of the martyred Rosa. On a visit to her in 1982, I could see her fragility approaching an unbearable plateau. I felt that I needed to reach out to her, perhaps I could buoy her spirits.

Since I was then Director of the BU Art Gallery, I realized I had the power to help May think of her own future in positive terms. I suggested a large show of her recent paintings for the BUAG. She agreed and embraced the project with enthusiasm. *May Stevens: Ordinary * Extraordinary 1977-1984* opened at the BUAG on February 29, 1984. The show then traveled to the Art Gallery at the University of Maryland and on to the Frederick S. Wight Gallery at UCLA. May designed the 48-page catalogue.

I could not have wished for better catalogue essays than those by critics Donald Kuspit and Lucy Lippard, art historian Moira Roth, and British critic Lisa Tickner. I wrote the Foreword, the last paragraph of which reads: "The paintings are intense confessionals. But they also penetrate down into the epistemological underpinnings of art. They state the situation of Alice Stevens who lives *as* dead and Rosa Luxemburg who lives *in* death, but they also ask: how do we know who we are, how do we know the past, how do we know where we are going." I echoed May: Are we ordinary? Or are we extraordinary?

After showing May's work, I asked myself, *Why not mount a Baranik exhibition?* We heard that Jonathan Green of the University Gallery of Fine Art at Ohio State University was planning a show called, *Rudolf Baranik Elegies: Sleep – Napalm – Night Sky.* We signed on and the show opened at our venue in February 1987.

Jim Drobnick, an independent critic, suggested that the BUAG add a satellite exhibition to the show focused on Rudolf's series, "Dictionary from the 24th Century." We accepted Drobnick's suggestion with enthusiasm. The "Dictionary" photostats would fit nicely into the 14 x 8 foot empty storage space, adjacent to the large 2,500 sq ft gallery that would show the paintings. I curated the installation of the definitions Rudolf had given me, which were typed out on sheets and made into negative photostats. Rudolf designed the 36-page catalogue for which Drobnick wrote the essay, "Commemorating in Anticipation – Rudolf Baranik: an Interview." Included were five examples of Rudolf's dictionary definitions.

As curator, I wrote the Preface. The last paragraph reads: "Baranik, also, in many of these excerpts, implies a dark age of repression and oppression before the enlightened era of human harmony. We may or may not share his gloomy view of the present and we may or may not agree with his scenario—but we cannot dismiss his moral concerns. All moralists are optimists no matter how disguised in the cloak of ironic pessimism or selfparody. Baranik embodies the ideal that Antonio Gramsci recommended for all revolutionaries: 'Pessimism of the intellect, optimism of the will.'"

Later in 1990, Drobnick produced an expanded 54-page booklet that added 20 more of Rudolf's definitions—often whimsical, ironic, but often sharply pointed: "Alice," "Apartheid," "Central Intelligence Agency," "Disinformation," and "War" were some of them. For "Art," he ended the entry: "By the end of the 23rd Century all art objects ceased to be comprehensible and were either discarded, filed on laser prints, or deposited for study by specialists in museums of natural history."

&

Increasingly, May wrote poetry. An avid reader of feminist and political poets, she knew many of them. She often spoke fondly of the poet and activist Grace Paley. Paley was one of the leaders of the War Resisters League during the 1960s, when May and Rudolf were also active. Jane Cooper, a poet who taught at Sarah Lawrence College, was one of her best friends. Jane saw May often when they both had Bunting Institute fellowships at Radcliffe College in Cambridge. And Jane always attended May's New York gallery openings. May also knew the Cambridge poet Martha Collins, who reproduced one of May's paintings on the cover of a book of her poetry.

In a packet of writings May sent me in May 2009, she included many of her own poems as well as older poems she had written down by poets Stephen Spender, Frederico Garcia Lorca (in Spanish), and many by Wallace Stevens. The words of theorist Julia Kristeva and Virginia Woolf were poetry to May, and in a later series of paintings she imbedded their words in paintings on the theme of women and water.

Her favorite poetry couplet came from one of Pablo Neruda's Spanish Civil War poems, "Explico Algunas Cosas" ("I Explain a Few Things"). He wrote: "... y por las calles la sangre de los niños/ corria simplamente, como sangre de niños" ("and through the streets the blood of children/ran simply, like blood of children."). "The blood of the children" came to her mind when creating her "Tic-Tac-Toe" series of drawings about abused children. Stevens commented:

"There is no place where you can take that phrase ... and exaggerate it and make it worse, or make a metaphor or an artistic expression which will make it stronger or more meaningful. It's unspeakable."

May and Rudolf were very fond of my children and delighted in visiting our family at our Jersey Shore summer house. When we visited them in SoHo, Rudolf would let Brad operate the decrepit elevator of their Wooster building to the 6th and 7th levels where they had their respective lofts. They later saw Christina and Brad leave home, and then return for holidays. In 1990, when May taught at the State University of California/Long Beach as Visiting Artist, Christina (then enrolled as an art student at Long Beach) took May's semester-long course in mixed media and loved it. Christina's best friend Carrie Hamilton, a student of Rudolf's at Pratt, provided the voice-over (on a tape cassette) that served as the audio component to May's 1992 eleven-foot-long painting, *Women's History: Live Girls*.

Both Rudolf and May were especially close to Andy. They met him at his baby shower, which he attended in swaddling clothes—having been born a month early. They delighted in his curiosity and willfulness as he grew up. They were especially amused by how Andy lavished attention on his pet guinea pig, Brownie, to whom Andy would feed endive. Embarrassed by the extravagant expense of endive, I would explain that the local grocer knew of Brownie's culinary favorite and gave Andy free endive. One holiday, when Rudolf and May were visiting, May took out her paints and created two pictures on velvet: one of Brownie and the other of the endive.

In June 1987, when May and Rudolf had summer residencies at Peterborough in New Hampshire, Andy (then nine years old), and I drove up to visit them and spend the night. Andy slept on the floor in front of the fireplace. To him their cottage was an enchanted place. Many years later Andy improvised an audio cassette with music he knew May would like. May gave Andy some of her art, as she did the rest of us.

I saw her weekly—even daily—when she held her Bunting fellowship during 1988-89 and lived in Cambridge. Before she took up residence, I went to the director and insisted that May needed a very large studio. The Bunting people obliged. There she painted her very large five-panel painting, *Alice in the Garden*. Andy had received a camcorder for Christmas, and he taped many video sessions with her that spring, including one of May and me talking and walking through a forest-like park.

May was also fond of my mother Glennie who lived with us the last few years of her life. May delighted in hearing Glennie's stories of her love life with "Howard Hughes" and wrote a poem for her when Glennie died in 1991. May asked me to tuck the poem— "The Wildness of Women / For Glennie Baker, Aged 82"—into Glennie's casket, which I did.

Their son's depression and death still haunted Rudolf and May in their late years. Together they printed a small book on their son's series of photographs he had called *Burning Horses*. The photographs consisted of closeups of small plastic horses that he had set on fire, leading to the melting of the plastic into contorted shapes. I shuddered when I saw them—to me the symbolism of his personal pain seemed so overt. During 1990-1991, May made her own large drawings freely incorporating shards of Steven's photographs. The symbolism of those gestures made me overwhelmingly sad—especially when one knows the backstory.

In 1994 May and Rudolf moved from Wooster Street to Church Street near the World Trade Center towers. On one very long day, I helped them move, which consisted of trying to consolidate two SoHo lofts into a space half the size of just one of their lofts. I urged them to arrange for the movers to move the excess into a Manhattan storage space.

They did not stay long at Church Street. They loved New Mexico and their friends Lucy Lippard, and Harmony Hammond, who lived in Galisteo, outside Santa Fe. In late 1996 they bought a substantial fake-adobe house in the El Dorado section of Santa Fe about 15 minutes from Galisteo. Kevin, Christina, Brad, Andy, and I visited at Thanksgiving in 1997.

Rudolf was sitting in his chair one morning in late winter. May called to him, and he didn't answer. She went to him and feared he had died. It was March 6, 1998. May telephoned Lucy, who came right over. Together they called a funeral home.

Rudolph had had heart problems. His death, therefore, was not unexpected, but still an emotional strain for May. She held a memorial service in Santa Fe and another one in New York. Many tributes were spoken by critics, artists, and friends, including myself who raised my right fist at both services in solidarity with Rudolf's politics. May's soulmate had slipped away.

Two years later May wrote "Lovesong," which she dated November 24, 2000.

WHEN YOU WERE ALIVE
YOU WERE EARTH TO ME
YOU WERE THE GROUND I WALKED ON.
NOW YOU ARE DEAD. YOU ARE AIR
YOUR WORDS LEAP
GLITTERING IN THE LIGHT
TELLING ME WHAT I MEAN SAYING WHAT I
WANT TO SAY.

AT NIGHT THE COLD STARS BURN WITH A
LASER LIGHT
UNDER THE COVERS IN THE WARM DARK
I AM LAPPED BY THE TONGUE OF YOUR
TENDERNESS.

While mourning Rudolf she also mourned her son Steven. She dwelled on the events of her son's life—of his struggles, his mental health, his swimming in the Hudson River near their apartment building, his dog, and burning his draft card during an anti-Vietnam rally in the 1960s. In 2002 she wrote a poem, "Late October—for Steven Baranik" that alludes to his memorial service in which one of his paintings, placed on the floor in her studio, was covered with gingko leaves gathered by her and her friend Linda Cunningham.

But her career was doing well. In 1999, she had a major exhibition, *May Stevens: Images of Women Near and Far,"* at the Museum of Fine Arts in Boston. The exhibition included many of the large Alice paintings as well as many she had done the previous decade of women in boats. It was, to May, a homecoming to Boston. The MFA acquired two large paintings by May.

By this time May was regularly visiting my family in Cambridge almost every Christmas until she entered the Santa Fe assisted living facility in 2013. In 2002 and 2003, I began to tape-record my conversations with May, believing that her personal reflections needed to be preserved.

Meanwhile, May's dealer Mary Ryan was negotiating with museums to showcase an exhibition of May's work. The Minneapolis Museum of Art stepped forward and scheduled a show, *The Water Remembers: Recent Paintings by May Stevens 1990-2004* for 2005. A writer was needed for the exhibition. Another art historian, who for many years had promised May she would write a book, backed out of this new project.

I stepped in as the author. I eagerly took on the project to write a book of May's life and art based on our interviews. The months were passing. Mary Ryan helped to secure Pomegranate Press, and we accelerated the book schedule. The layout was spectacular, and the lavish color was true to the images. We barely had time to meet the deadline. The Pomegranate editor jokingly called it "the fastest book in the West." But at least one copy arrived in time for the opening.

May Stevens followed the format of my Abrams book, *Alice Neel.* The front part of the book—my essay "May Stevens: In Conversation"—consists of a series of May's long, self-reflective, mostly autobiographical passages from my interviews with her as well as interjections by me to give shape to the narrative flow. The one-page forward, "Writing on Water," was penned by literary critic and Wesleyan University professor Phyllis Rose. My own essay follows the interviews—"May Stevens: The Dialectics of Representation, the Praxis of Painting"—and includes photographs of May, her family, and her friends. Eighty-six color plates along with bibliography and chronology make up the last part of the book.

May talked about, but we did not include in the book, the episode of her late life when she rekindled a romance with her former MassArt boyfriend. She was 77 when she wrote to him in early 2001, just asking how he had been all those years. He replied he was retired and living in Los Angeles, and he suggested they get together. She confided in me at the time just before she went to visit him in his L.A. home. She was absolutely giddy—like a teenaged girl—when she flew to L.A. from the Headlands in Sausalito, where she then held an artist's residency. The romance lasted for several months— maybe even a year with several exchanges of visits. Each time she would return, she would confide in me about his right-wing attitudes and the non-stop television broadcasts on Fox News. As charming as he was, she finally broke off the relationship because she found his politics too offensive.

The romance, although brief, buoyed her, and made her feel like her younger self. She admired the fact that this man had pride in his body at his age, that he walked around naked, and that he made clever little drawings of their love-making. I believe that this final experience of male intimacy was the catalyst for her late work. She went on to produce stunning paintings about women, water, and the flow of life.

Attracted to Buddhism, she would go on retreats, in which meditation and silence were major factors. But she complained that she was not allowed to do her usual talking. During her later years she wrote imaginary letters to her deceased family—her father, mother, Rudolf, Steven, and most poignantly, her brother Stacey who had died of childhood diabetes. These draft letters were in fact memoirs of her feelings. Evidence in her archives indicates that it was probably her psychotherapist who suggested she do this, as a draft of a letter from "May" to "Alice" is not in her handwriting. I suspect the therapist wrote it as a model for May.

For several years past her 80th birthday she continued to paint. She planned to make paintings of her own nude body swimming in water and asked a photographer friend to take photos of her. She began at least one large painting but struggled to complete it.

During this time, May's dementia slowly crept into her brain. She picked fights with her old friends; she repeated stories she had just told five minutes earlier; she kept having car accidents; she could not get out of her bathtub and spent the night there until Harmony Hammond, as a member of the volunteer fire department, lifted her out. Moreover, it became increasingly difficult for her to keep up her routine of visiting us in Cambridge for the holidays. One Christmas, Andy flew from California to New Mexico, picked her up, and flew with her to Boston; they returned the same route. Andy reported that when she entered her house, she didn't know where she was and became angry at him for bringing her to such a strange place.

Her mental health continued to slip. In the spring of 2013 it became clear to Lucy Lippard, who held Power of Attorney, and to me, the executor of her will, that May had declined to the point where she needed full-time help, as well as an environment filled with people interacting with her. Lucy found a Memory Ward in Santa Fe where she was welcomed. Lucy got people to visit her, made sure the accommodations were satisfactory, took her to doctors, and handled her finances. Strong physically, May lived until December 9, 2019, when she died peacefully at the Memory Ward at the age of 95 ½ —exactly.

Lucy took care of the immediate arrangements after May's death, then I stepped in as executor. Lucy, along with their New Mexico friends, scattered some of May's ashes in the Galisteo River. May treasured the idea that ashes were the physical reminders of a once living person. In her late paintings she had blended Rudolf's ashes within the paint of her art. She had even given me a small bag of Rudolf's ashes.

Because of the COVID-19 pandemic, the Memorial Service for May was delayed until June 23, 2021. Kevin's daughter Emily organized the program with the help of Mary Ryan of the Ryan/Lee Gallery where the event took place. Speakers included Emily as master of ceremonies, Andy, and myself, along with artists Joyce Kozloff and Adele Ursoni, MoMA curator Esther Adler, and art historian Aljandro Anreus, a scholar of Rudolf's work. Also included were video tributes by Lucy Lippard, the artist couple Dread Scott and Jenny Polak, and artist Harmony Hammond. More video footage, shot by Andy when he was 11-years-old, showed May and me as we walked through a wooded area in 1989 as she recited one of her poems.

Holland Cotter wrote an obituary for the *New York Times* calling her an artist "who turned art into activism." Lucy Lippard wrote an obituary for *Artforum* (March 2020) that captured the spirit of May as we all knew her: "May was a great reader, and a poet and writer with an original voice … She hated pretension. She was inquisitive, outspoken, and sometimes tactless—in which case, Rudolf would say, 'That's not the real May.' She was publicly tough but privately vulnerable, given the tragedies she had survived."

Most of the remainder of May's ashes, which Lucy sent to me, along with a small bag of Rudolf's ashes I had, were taken to Berlin by my friend artist X Bonnie Woods in fall

2022. Bonnie made arrangements to have both of their ashes scattered in Berlin's Landwehr Canal on "Rosa Luxemburg Day"—the day that marked the murder of Luxemburg and was memorialized by a crowd of feminists. Bonnie took photographs of that solemn event.

May will be known as a powerful painter focused on the issues that confronted women in the last half of the 20th century and the first decade of the 21st century. Her subjects covered the many topics that drew activists to the streets in protest, and that touched her. These subjects ranged from patriarchy, racial violence, child abuse, and book banning, to the courage and resiliencies of women, and, finally, to the peace of memories in words and water.

An extraordinary woman.

&

Widowed and without living children, May thought about her legacy of work and activism. In 2005 she wrote a will and trust with the goal of setting up the May Stevens and Rudolf Baranik Foundation. Optimistic about its operation, she hoped that students, artists, and art historians would study the artworks, poetry and writings done by her and Rudolf—and that they would embrace May's and Rudolf's art as guides for an art of social justice. I was fully on board for this and became a trustee of the Foundation, as did Andy who was always so close to May.

I end with the mission statement of the Foundation, which was approved as a 501(c)3 by the IRS in November 2021:

> The mission of the May Stevens and Rudolf Baranik Foundation is to preserve the legacy and work of May Stevens and Rudolf Baranik; encourage the education of artists on the ways that social issues

and social engagement intersect with the art of the past, present, and future; assure public access of Stevens and Baranik's work through archival research, exhibitions, educational programs, and internet access.

We will do our best, dear May, to carry out your wishes.

26

Jacob Lawrence, 1983-Present

Jacob Lawrence (1917-2000) will always remain a giant in the field. To me he was charismatic, and I was determined to probe deeply into his past, to meet frequently with him, to explore his later outlook on life and art, and to synthesize all of it into a book.

I conceived *Jacob Lawrence: Painting Harlem Modern* (2009) not as an annotated interview (that had characterized my books on Alice Neel and May Stevens), but as a plunge into that Harlem world. That meant trying to understand the life and art of someone who was Black, male, and came of age in the 1930s.

Lawrence began as a rising star in the Black arts community. Art world people, such as Howard University professor and art writer Alain Locke, wrote about him as early as the late 1930s. Only in his early 20s, Lawrence had painted his series on the historic figures Toussaint L'Ouverture, Frederick Douglass, and Harriet Tubman. An exhibition of the complete sixty paintings of his *Migration* series traveled across the country from 1942 to 1944. During World War II, MoMA held an exhibition of his Coast Guard paintings.

I became aware of Lawrence in 1974 when I saw his large Whitney Museum exhibition organized by art historian Milton Brown, with the aid of Louise A. Park. Since I was also working at the Whitney, I visited the show many times.

I was blown away and took slides, intrigued by the designs of his paintings, his limited palette, and the subtleties of his storytelling. I marveled at how shards of color could tell a deeply moving story.

Called upon to give lectures on Lawrence to Black audiences outside the classroom, I learned more about him. I also wrote essays on the artist published in catalogues for the traveling exhibition *Social Concern and Urban Realism: American Painting of the 1930s* (1983), and for the Seattle Art Museum's *Jacob Lawrence: American Painter* (1986).

Were I to write with any authority, I could not just rely on my studio arts understanding of composition and handling paint. Nor could I rely on my art history training of formal analysis and of knowing the trends of cubism and modernism. I would need to probe deeply into the sociological geography of Black communities, class analyses, social psychology, regional argots, local expressions, styles of humor, the Black church, established ethical choices, social sanctions, sexual orientation, and attitudes toward gender. Also relevant are family cultural legacies, including the legacy of self-definition discussed by Henry Louis Gates, Jr. in his Preface to *The Black Box: Writing the Race* (2024). Since writers and artists can speak for their communities, I plunged into reading novels, historical studies, and memoirs, listening to the music, seeing films directed by Black professionals, and living in Harlem.

Although I had carried out extensive interviews with Lawrence and his wife Gwendolyn Knight in the 1980s, I also needed to find mentors and Black colleagues to help me in my journey. In other words, as a white scholar I needed guidance to learn more, to take criticism, and to be mindful of cultural nuances recognized by Black scholars.

With the encouragement of Harvard professor Nathan I. Huggins, then director of the W.E.B. Du Bois Institute for African and Afro American Studies [now called the Hutchens

Center for African and African American Research], I applied for and received a residence Fellowship at the Du Bois Institute for the academic year 1991-92. My aim was to work on two projects: the representations of Blacks in American art of the 19th century and Jacob Lawrence. Little did I know how the Du Bois would change my life.

Huggins retired and literary historian Henry Louis Gates Jr. arrived that fall. As the new Director, Gates came in with champagne bottles popping at his welcoming party. With smart innovative ideas to make Harvard a leader in African American Studies, Gates brought rapid changes to the Du Bois Institute—expanding the staff, recruiting scholars from around the globe, achieving the total support of the Harvard administration, and raising funds. He eventually established The Ethelbert Cooper Gallery of African & African American Arts at the Hutchins Center. Indisputably, Gates was the main influence and shaper of my future scholarship.

I was off and running. Gates invited me to return several times as a Du Bois residence scholar, and I appreciated the desk, computer, research assistants, Harvard's extraordinary library, and the camaraderie with other fellows that the Du Bois Institute supported. Best of all were the noon seminars on Wednesdays presided over by Gates, where fellows (including myself), presented new research. In the late afternoon lecture series, we saw and heard renowned scholars from all over the globe talking about various aspects of contemporary African and African American history, sociology, culture, and literature. It was a diverse group. And since my home in Cambridge was just a ten-minute walk from the Du Bois Institute (and I routinely scheduled my BU classes not to overlap with the noon seminars), I was almost always in the audience. Even in those years when not formally affiliated, I felt part of the family—even attending dinners following the late afternoon talks.

"Skip" Gates (as everyone called him) personally

welcomed me into his Black scholars community at Harvard. He was open to all ideas and insisted that he had no interest in the race of an author or a scholar "as long as they did good scholarship." That message meant so much to me. This community gave me an unparalleled education and provided me with a vantage point to see Black history.

From these experiences and mentoring I learned to be mindful of the various permutations of racism today (subtle and overtly violent). We all must boldly acknowledge the vicious contradictions in our history's "democracy." Although our country was founded on the principle spelled out in the US Constitution—that all men are created equal— the slaveowners who wrote the Constitution hypocritically maintained their right to own men and women as their property and to count them as three-fifths of a person when it came to congressional representation.

Since then, the US has had a long history of law-sanctioned physical violence directed toward the descendants of African people. And that's not even mentioning the emotional trauma inherent in being removed from their homelands, the breakup of families, chattel slavery, the rape of Black women, the mutilation and lynching of Black men, the failure of Reconstruction after the Civil War, the terror of the Ku Klux Klan, forced peonage, and the confiscation of Black property. Jim Crow statutes reinforced racial segregation in public transportation and institutions including buses, railroad cars, schools, auditorium halls, restaurants, and voting polls. There were restrictions placed on private life activities, such as social gatherings and marriage. And let's not forget segregated baseball leagues. Decade after decade Black people had to dodge or negotiate systemic and systematic racism.

I was affiliated with the Du Bois Institute, off and on from 1991 to 2016. Ideas and histories from the lectures, conversations and courses I audited on Black studies, as well as new research I unearthed from Harvard's library archives and special collections, spun around in my head. I was exhausted by the pleasure of learning and being challenged by other scholars' provocative ideas. With that behind me I felt ready to write serious scholarship on Lawrence.

&

In 1992 Elizabeth Hutton Turner, the curator at The Phillips Collection in Washington, D.C., began organizing an exhibition on Lawrence's *Migration* series of 60 paintings. Half of the works were in the Phillips, the other half at the Museum of Modern Art. Lawrence's *Migration* traced the Black Migration from the South to the North and West in the years during and after World War I, when industry needed Black workers for the war effort. That history and Lawrence's paintings needed to be conjoined.

Turner convened a group of scholars to brainstorm on Lawrence and his work. The full-day event was one of the first such convenings that museums, often funded by the National Endowment for the Humanities, have regularly staged to jumpstart ideas about an artist or art movement for exhibition development. Turner's stellar group included Gates, historians Lonnie G. Bunch III and Jeffrey C. Stewart, art historian Richard J. Powell, photographic historian Deborah Willis, and me. Turner assigned topics to each of us for the catalogue essays.

My essay for the catalogue tackled *The Migration* as an ensemble focused on a close analysis of the rhythms of the 60 panels as they relate to the narrative themes within the larger story: the conditions of the South, the human movement between South and North, and the conditions for Black people in the North. Lawrence did not sugarcoat the story of migration. The series delivered an uplifting message that the oppressed need to take history in hand and change it.

After the opening exhibition at the Phillips, the exhibition traveled to five other venues, the last of which was the Museum of Modern Art. At the dinner following the MoMA opening, Henry Luce III, whose Foundation had largely underwritten the New York exhibition, spoke at length. Lawrence also rose to speak of his gratitude to his community. He thanked a long list of individuals and institutions: "And I thank the Schomburg, the streetcorner speakers, the communists…" At the mention of "communists" Luce exploded into a coughing fit while Lawrence continued to thank other groups. It was a moment that brought silent laughs to several of us.

I have found no evidence that Lawrence and Gwendolyn were members of the Communist Party, but he admired their activism to achieve social justice, and he benefitted from the communist art teachers who instructed him. The CPUSA's newspaper *The Daily Worker* praised his exhibitions. We can assume he was in the CP's orbit, like many artists in the 1930s. The FBI, however, still kept tabs on him—including reports on the shows. Later the State Department made it difficult for Lawrence to take up residence in Lagos because of his friendships with leftists.

Inspired by the Du Bois scholars and fellows, I plunged into more research on Lawrence's world of Harlem artists, writers, intellectuals, and organizations. By the mid-1990s, I decided that writing a book-length study of Lawrence and Harlem would be my priority. I applied for funding from the National Endowment for the Humanities. I was turned down twice by reviewers who did not consider Lawrence worthy of a book. I finally succeeded and took my NEH leave in the spring semester of 1995, but it was not enough time to make much progress. After that I had to set the project aside to attend to other Boston University projects, although I continued to read about Lawrence and his milieu, to visit the Lawrences on our trips to Seattle during the late 1990s and to attend the Du Bois Institute lectures and functions.

Lawrence died of lung cancer in 2000. He and Gwendolyn had moved to an assisted living facility in downtown Seattle a few years before. When his condition worsened, he was moved into a hospice unit in the same building. Gwendolyn took Kevin and me down to his bedside. He was sleeping, but Gwendolyn nevertheless said to him, "Pat is here." He lifted his head, blinked me a greeting, and then his head fell back on his pillow. He died a few days later, on June 9, 2000. His Memorial was a huge affair that took place at Riverside Church in Manhattan. Major civic leaders and notables spoke. I managed to find a place in the pews at the back of the church.

Reading in the area of Black studies, I constantly circled back to Lawrence. I drew up a revised proposal for a book and applied for residential grants to help fund a yearlong sabbatical year for my research. Kevin had retired, no small kids were around, and so we could live in new places.

I secured three grants: three months of research at the Schomburg Library in Harlem, sponsored by the Gilder Lehrman Foundation, four months as a senior scholar researching at the Smithsonian American Art Museum (SAAM) in Washington, DC, and three months at the Georgia O'Keeffe Museum Research Center at the O'Keeffe Museum in Santa Fe, where I began my writing.

Kevin and I rented our house to a visiting MIT professor and his family, packed up, and moved to Harlem, Washington, D.C., and Santa Fe. All memorable experiences.

I spent three months at the Schomburg Library in Harlem exploring their archives. For three weeks I carefully read the *Amsterdam News* page by page on microfilm from the years 1930 to 1942. These readings gave me the day-to-day context of Lawrence's life and the newsworthy events that shaped him and his neighbors. I absorbed the attitudes about race, hair products, entertainers, books, theater, boxing (e.g., Joe Louis the "Brown Bomber"), real estate, philanthropy, Black society and debutante balls, successful businessmen, exhibitions, artists of note, the projects of the WPA (Works Progress Administration), the Harlem Community Art Center (funded by the Federal Art Project of the WPA), and the failures of the Roosevelt administration to push through an anti-lynching bill. Almost every issue of the *Amsterdam News* had an article accompanied by pictures of that week's lynched people—always identifying those lynched and offering information on their family backgrounds. Such news was personal—not a statistic. The *Amsterdam News* also ran stories of people who had escaped lynching—often walking on foot at night from the South to Harlem.

When World War II began, the *Amsterdam News*, like other Black newspapers throughout the US, focused on supporting the war effort. They campaigned for the "Double-V"—victory over US racism and segregation at home, victory over the Nazis and fascists in Europe and Japan.

At the Schomburg, I met curators who shared the art treasures there. Renting a brownstone in Harlem from a Schomburg librarian, I had a passing acquaintance with people who sat on their stoops in the early fall evenings. Kevin and I also attended Lawrence's family church—the Abyssinian Baptist Church on 138th Street, made famous by Adam Clayton Powell Sr. and his son, the charismatic US Congressman Adam Clayton Powell, Jr.

I firmly believe that one's research on an artist or art movement should be sensory as well as academic—not just "talking the talk" but "walking the walk." In the theater we think of method acting. I am suggesting the equivalent for the art historian. That meant following in Lawrence's likely footsteps, walking the sidewalks, negotiating the curbs, feeling the inclines of the streets. All the senses come into play—seeing the sky, the urban buildings, and the outside of the houses where Lawrence lived and may have visited; hearing children and street noises; breathing the air and smelling the cooking food wafting out from open windows. It meant meeting and touching people he had known, or their descendants. I did that when we lived in Harlem.

Driving to Washington, D.C. in November, we found a two-bedroom condo in Chinatown near the Victor Building, the home of the SAAM scholars' program, the Archives of American Art and its Library. As a senior scholar, I was expected to be responsive to the younger scholars' queries. In my little cubical about six feet away from several of them I found myself in many conversations that helped my own research. There were weekly lunchtime seminars, organized trips to collections, and then at the end, the scholars' talks.

While in Washington I made a point of seeing many museums, taking field trips to George Washington's Mt. Vernon and Harper's Ferry, where John Brown and a small group of abolitionists attempted to raid a building where armaments were stored. I usually had lunch with the fellows, SAAM curators and other visiting scholars. I immersed myself in SAAM's Library, the Archives of American Art's archival boxes of research, and made trips to the Library of Congress—a great resource.

I was determined to continue my quest for these sensory experiences when we traveled through the South on our 16-day motor trip from Washington, D.C. to Santa Fe.

On March 9 we left Washington and stopped at museums that had works by Lawrence and other Black artists, at towns where he would have visited, at archives holding writings of Black creative people, and at sites important to Black American history.

We first hunted for Lanexa, Virginia, about 50 miles from Richmond, where Lawrence and Knight spent several months in 1942 living with his relatives. According to

Wikipedia, Lanexa is an unincorporated community by the Chickahominy River. No sign on the highway announced Lanexa. After driving back and forth on the highway, we were led off onto several country roads, but never found much other than a few small houses but no stores. When Lanexa had previously come up in conversations with Jake and Gwendolyn, she aloofly commented that Jake's relatives "were country people," not the type for a sophisticate like herself. After spending the night with friends in Virginia, the next day we visited the Chrysler Museum in Norfolk, which had art on view by Black artists such as Benny Andrews, and Civil War photographs of Lincoln's assassins. No pictures by Lawrence, but ones important to Black history.

Driving south along the Atlantic, we stayed with my former students Charlotte Emans and Will Moore, in Wilmington, North Carolina. They told us the history of the 1898 riot there when whites terrorized, drove out of town, and killed the citizens of a large Black community. Charlotte also drove me to see the gatehouse where the North Carolina Black artist Sister Gertrude Morgan had stood watch. In her spare time Morgan painted "outsider" paintings inspired by her religion.

On March 12 we drove to Kiawah Island—one of the Sea Islands off the South Carolina coast, near Charleston. We spent three nights in a gated community (in the empty condo owned by the parents of another former student) and explored the area. We drove to Beaufort, where still another ex-student had invited me to give a Jacob Lawrence lecture to his class at USC/Beaufort. Jake's father's family had hailed from Beaufort. We also saw galleries with local Black artists.

Kevin and I drove to nearby St. Helens Islands to see traces of the Gullah people—a group of African Americans whose ancestors had worked as enslaved people on the rice plantations, but who had kept the culture of their African ancestors alive. The Penn Center, a small museum that celebrates Gullah culture, was informative. But I realized that our trip to the Sea Islands was becoming not a Lawrence experience, but a Carrie Mae Weems experience. Weems, a contemporary photographer focused on contemporary Black culture, was "looking for the Gullah" in her photographic *Sea Islands* series of the early 1990s. She hoped to find Gullah remnants as I, too, hoped to find. Instead, I mostly found gated communities, golf courses and a few hamlets with convenience stores.

Back in Charleston, we saw the museum and I bought a sweetgrass basket from a weaver who had set up her wares on the steps of a church. When we left the Sea Islands area, we were at the 1,045-mile mark of our journey.

We arrived in Savannah on March 15 to meet with Dr. Walter O. Evans, president of the Jacob and Gwendolyn Lawrence Foundation, and a noted collector of Black art. We visited him in his townhouse in downtown Savannah, which has one of the most beautiful series of parks in the South, and had dinner with him and his wife. As far as the art scene is concerned, the economy is dominated by the Savannah College of Art and Design.

From Savannah we went to Atlanta, where I combed through the archival collections at Emory University and found most useful the Benny Andrews and Romare Bearden archives. We visited the High Museum and spent two nights with Amy Lighthill, another former student.

We left Atlanta at the 1,448-mile mark and headed toward Tuskegee University, a place visited by Lawrence when he quickly toured the South in 1947 on assignment for *Fortune* magazine. The small museum there focuses on George Washington Carver and his impact on the university, the community, and peanut farming. I asked, but no art museum was located at Tuskegee.

We continued on to Selma, Alabama. In college during

the mid-1950s, I had spent the summer months at Craig Air Force Base a few miles from Selma, and I wanted to make a sentimental journey there. The Base was gone, abandoned by the Air Force in the 1970s when cuts in the military budget prompted such closings. Not surprisingly, since the economy of Selma rested on servicing airmen and their families, the town of Selma was now a shadow of its former self, with stores boarded up and little traffic on the main street. Nevertheless, a lively art opening of local artists was taking place in a gallery on the street next to the bridge, and I chatted with the artists about their experiences living and working in Alabama.

Of course, I also wanted to revisit the infamous Edmund Pettus Bridge, the site of Bloody Sunday—the most famous anti-segregation march in US history and the subject of one of Lawrence's most notable prints, *Confrontation at the Bridge* (1976). The bridge's span looked different from my memories of a steep, rounded bridge. But that memory has been crowded out by recollections of the often-reproduced photographs of John Lewis, the Reverend Hosea Williams, Martin Luther King Jr., and hundreds of other protestors (Black and white) advancing and retreating as they attempted to march through a phalanx of armed Alabama state troopers.

Since Jacob Lawrence had done a painting called *Gee's Ben* inspired by his 1947 trip, Gee's Bend became a must-stop destination. I knew of the Farm Security Administration (FSA) photographers who had visited Gee's Bend and had photographed the poverty of people living in dilapidated homes, later replaced by government-built houses. I also wanted to see the famous Gee's Bend quilts, and the places where the quilters lived.

Kevin and I took many twists and turns off the main highways and finally found Gee's Bend, a hamlet not much more than a scattering of houses along a rural road. Although it was getting late in the day, I was determined to find the building that houses the famous quilts of the Gee's Bend Collective. We finally located it in Boykin, Alabama.

Let me explain: the Alabama River does a bend, and the peninsula thus formed has two hamlets—Gee's Bend and Boykin.

The long, one-story building that warehoused the quilts was locked up, so I went to the nearest house, one with a Coca-Cola vending machine on the porch. A woman there told us we could get help if we went over to Mary Bendolph's house on the next road. We did, and Bendolph invited us in. She volunteered to call Mary Ann Pettway, who had the key to the building and who could show us the quilts of the collective.

We had to wait, however, because Pettway was cooking dinner and could not immediately meet us. In the meantime, Mary Bendolph showed us her quilts (gorgeous!) and her one-story house, which had originally been built in the 1930s by the Farm Security Administration (FSA). She had made several additions to the house but pointed out the basic 1930s plan of three bedrooms, bathroom, kitchen, living room and porch. To learn all this about 1930s government architecture was a bonus. Bendolph's daughter lived next door, and her house still had the original FSA floor plan.

Eventually, Bendolph took us back over to the Collective's building, and we met Mary Ann Pettway there with her keys. We looked at the quilts, which were $2000- $2500 apiece [$3200-$4000 in 2025]—no doubt reasonably priced—but out of our price range. Kevin nudged me and whispered, "We gotta get out of here!" But I felt an obligation to buy at least a small quilt because of the time they had spent with us. I finally bought a modest red and white quilt for $500 [$800 in 2025] made by Quinne Pettway and signed by her. Later I told Bendolph that I really liked her quilts and wondered what her prices were. She looked me in the face and said,

"You don't want to know the prices." In other words, she had shrewdly assessed me and had concluded that I could not afford her quilts. She was right. I learned that the real Gee's Bend women are nothing like the sentimentalized portrayals of them on the PBS documentary.

Late at night we arrived at a motel in Mobile, Alabama, exhausted and hungry— having driven about 600 miles that day.

We were up early the next day and traveled west on US 10 along the Gulf of Mexico. It had been six months since Hurricane Katrina had slammed the coast of Mississippi, but the damage was still evident. Most of the wreckage from the storm-beaten homes had been removed—leaving just the concrete foundations. Big backhoes were still at work clearing away other severely damaged houses. Barriers along US 10 were erected to re-route us onto roads not washed out by Katrina. I recall, perhaps falsely, seeing an automobile stuck up in the trees.

Arriving in New Orleans in April 2006, we found a city still trying to pick up the pieces after Hurricane Katrina. Hotels were barely open and rooms difficult to reserve. We settled on an old inn on the Loyola campus, in which we shared a bathroom with other guests—mostly students from a private East Coast high school there to help the city rebuild. The bathroom sharing became a problem when we both got sick with a mysterious stomach sickness.

We felt the culprit had been the wine offered to us by a curator friend of a BU colleague who had invited us for drinks our first night. He told us he had survived Katrina by bedding down in the New Orleans Art Museum and living off the snacks in the museum's vending machines. He was now living back in his Latin quarter home and complained about the flood-soaked wine he had stored in his basement. I recall him saying, "And the curious thing is that there were these worms crawling through the corks of the bottles." Within 30 minutes of drinking the wine, Kevin was sick.

Nevertheless, we went to a restaurant as planned. Kevin did not eat. I got sick an hour later. We both got *very* sick.

I had an appointment with the director of the Ogden Museum of Art, where Lawrence's Toussaint L'Ouverture series was on view. I had to see them, having planned to devote half a chapter in my book to this series. I felt awkward being sick, running to the restroom every fifteen minutes during my meeting with the director. The next day Kevin and I went to the hospital and received intravenous fluids as we were severely dehydrated.

I still needed to look at the neighborhoods that would have been familiar to Lawrence and Knight during their brief sojourn in New Orleans in the winter of 1941-42. The couple had chosen New Orleans because they wanted to experience Mardi Gras, but that was cancelled with the advent of WWII.

So, before we left New Orleans we toured the city to get a sense of what they might have seen, such as the Latin Quarter streets where jazz was played. But we were also interested in seeing the destroyed houses in the 9th Ward that had been abandoned during and immediately after the 2005 hurricane. The large X's on the doors of New Orleans' devastated wards indicated that responders had already searched the houses and that no new bodies would be found. But New Orleans was still finding bodies. Another was reported in the *New Orleans Picayune* on the day before we left. Our experience of New Orleans was certainly not the experiences of Jim Crow that Lawrence had as he confronted Southern racism for the first time. But I did get a sense of the timeless geography of historic New Orleans.

Armed with Gatorade (to prevent dehydration), we pushed on, through Orange, Texas, to Port Arthur, the birthplace of the artist Robert Rauschenberg. The town seemed pure Texas—rough oil refineries everywhere and motels set up for the sex worker trade. Certainly not genteel.

From there we went to Austin to visit another ex-student and her husband. Austin seemed like an island of great sense and rationality within the wide expanse of Texan bluster. After 18 days on the road, we finally arrived in Santa Fe, where a small two-bedroom rental apartment awaited us.

My three months at the Georgia O'Keeffe Museum Research Center proved productive. I met many great colleagues, including scholar Lois Rudnick. At last I was writing about Lawrence. I continued to do so over the next two years as I gave lectures on my chapters and received feedback.

When my manuscript on Jacob Lawrence went through final edits in early 2009, the editor suggested I ask Henry Louis Gates Jr. to write a forward. I went to Skip's Harvard office and proposed the idea. He told me he was too busy with his television series, but happy to write an endorsement on the back of the dust jacket. I told him that the publisher felt that since I was a white woman, I needed introductory remarks by a Black scholar. He told me I did not need such endorsements for my scholarly books. Then he leaned forward across the desk and said: "If they ask that of you again, just say to them 'Kiss my Black ass!'"

This sentence has had a lasting effect on me. Of course, I am not Black and don't claim to be. But that message meant that we can all do this scholarship—although white scholars must be prepared to go the extra mile when confronted with historical circumstances of which they know little.

The operative word for Lawrence's past and his legacy for the 20th century is *struggle*. I ended my book on Lawrence with a focus on this word:

The word struggle, so often used by the Left to suggest what is necessary to gain justice and freedom for all groups, had a deep meaning for Lawrence and frequently came up in his conversations.

Consistently, it was the one word that symbolized his views on art and life. He told a Seattle *Times* reporter in 1998 that early in his career he had to struggle because he wasn't very skilled. "So, with formal problems and other things, I had to work harder. So there was a tension in the works. Now I have more skill but I would hope that there still is some struggle. When you don't feel struggle, there is no passion. It's true in civil rights, and in art."

In a 1982 lecture he had remarked: "Man's struggle is a very beautiful thing … The struggle that we go through as human beings enables us to develop, to take on further dimension." For Lawrence, the experience of struggle defined his identity. In 1930s Harlem, struggle defined his modernism. It stayed with him all his life.

27

Diversity, Equity, Inclusion, 2015-25

Art historians have led the way in confronting past art that today might be considered racist imagery—images demeaning to non-white people or images promoting white racial superiority. I think of those 19th century statues that represent white men leading Black men or, in the words of Kirk Savage's book title: *Standing Soldiers, Kneeling Slaves.* Art historians have been actively participating in the controversial public debates and culture wars over public murals and sculpture in schools, universities, libraries, and parks, that show imagery offensive to some groups of people. How do we handle not only the historically racist images, but also the language then used to describe them? Can we turn such images and language into teachable moments?

Artworks that call up disturbing historical institutions and events can understandably traumatize many groups. It is the brave and even risky museum curator and their colleagues who needs to confront the problem and invite audiences to ponder the issues and suggest solutions.

A good example of the controversies that arise are the paintings of Philip Guston satirizing KKK-type figures with their hooded robes. Over the decades these paintings have been disturbing to many people. In 2020 the Hauser and Wirth Gallery displayed these works (which I saw) in two large rooms of their New York gallery in anticipation of a large retrospective exhibition project that would open at the

National Gallery in Washington and travel to other venues. However, with a new sensitivity toward systemic racism generated by protests over police brutality toward Black men and women and the Black Lives Matter movement, the National Gallery decided in 2020 to postpone their Guston show. One assumes they wanted to be mindful of the emotional hurt such images might elicit. But, whatever the well-intended reasons for the postponement, the actions were still censorship.

The museums involved did not anticipate the pushback from the artists' community. Barry Schwabsky, writing "Don't Hide the Art of Philip Guston" (*The Nation*, October 30, 2020), brought attention to the fact that 2,600 people (including both Black and white artists) signed a petition protesting the cancellations.

Black artist Steve Locke, familiar with the images from the Hauser and Wirth Gallery, wrote "Guston, Whiteness, and the Unfinished Business of the Vile World," a personal account for *Artforum* (December 2020). He recalls first encountering the images as an MFA student in art school. He was profoundly disturbed but learned from the experience. He came to understand that "the artist is a conduit through which the entire culture is filtered. Artists are not simply expressing themselves; they are expressing an embodied experience of our shared culture."

Locke argues that one should not turn away from the reality of such difficult subject matter, even when one is white. "To claim that one's whiteness prevents one from presenting works of art that are *about* whiteness troubles me as much as the need to present Black voices as interlocutors for a discussion about race," he wrote. The issue is accountability—which Locke saw as Guston's motivation for painting the KKK pictures.

Finally, the Guston show was reactivated and went ahead with the inclusion of the offending pictorial figures. I viewed the MFA's installation in Boston in summer 2022 and noted that the MFA staff still felt obliged to comment on the wall labels about certain works. Ginger Klee, a consultant to the "Philip Guston Now" curatorial team, penned a statement printed in a handout available at the entrance of the gallery:

> It is human to shy away from or ignore what makes us uncomfortable, but this practice unintentionally causes harm. You have an opportunity to lean into the discomfort of confronting racism on an experiential level as you view art that wrestles with America's past and present racial tensions. You have every right to feel your feelings throughout this exhibition. I encourage those who have experienced oppression, and allies, to name your feelings, sit with them, and learn from them. But it's also important to identify your boundaries and take care of yourself. Critical to the fight for equality, equity, and justice is self-care, rest, education, and community.

This admonition has an admirable down-to-earth appeal and is strongly applicable to the works cited above. Note that Klee's appeal includes "allies."

We are all in this together. All voices need to be heard. But it is imperative that we recognize that decisions are generally based not only on our personal ethics, but also by the exigencies of the times.

&

Having discussed problematical imagery, we turn now to "Diversity, Equity, Inclusion" (DEI). These are big words, positive words, and necessary to carry as banners into the 21st century. And those words bring into dialogue not only issues of what exhibitions to stage in museums, what education programs are relevant, what audiences to target, but also areas of staff responsibility and decision making.

First, some background.

As a result of the Civil Rights Act of 1964, non-profit museums, universities, libraries, national parks, as well as private corporations, revisited their hiring practices in order to embrace and advance the goals of affirmative action. The idea was that "all qualifications being equal," institutions and corporations should hire and/or admit to universities, those gender, racial, and ethnic groups previously underrepresented. Eventually the word "diversity" became the umbrella tern to counter systemic racism and sexism in universities and the workplace.

The reason for continuing diversity of staff today is to have a knowledgeable staff in "mission-based decision-making positions," as Frist Museum Curator Kathryn E. Delmez succinctly phrased it to me. Each of the staff then can bring different voices from their backgrounds and current vantage points, knowing that collectively all suggestions will be respected. This means that people coming from various cultures of family, race, class, gender, ethnicity, geographies, education, and self-definition can offer new information and opinions at the table. All staff need to be trained in the specific culture of the museums in which they work so they can jump into the give-and- take of ideas, and they need mentors. Some major museums have made curatorial hires—following what they consider practicing diversity— and then betrayed the new curators by not showing them the ropes. Indeed, museums should encourage a learning environment supportive of those new hires.

A diverse group of interns also needs to be mentored and paid well. At PS 1, an adjunct MoMA space in an industrial neighborhood of Queens, local working-class high school neighbors are given jobs as docents to show visitors around PS 1 and its grounds. Their knowledge and enthusiasm always gave me a rich museum visitor experience. These young people, as they are fulfilling their duties, are also connecting to the art world and might possibly go on to be curators and staff members at a museum or gallery where they can share their experiences and ideas.

Diversity means not only that staff should be diverse, but also the artists and the content that is being developed and displayed. The high art of painting and sculpture can be shown alongside the diverse visual culture of advertisements, posters, costumes, everyday pottery and furnishings, book illustrations, bank notes, sheet music covers, comics, family photos and videos of performances. The *inclusion* of art from a *diverse* range of geographical locations and ethnic communities or from different centuries is always stimulating.

The re-hanging of paintings, sculpture and furniture in the new installation of the American Wing, carried out by the Metropolitan Museum of Art during 2024 with Sylvia Yount leading a team of curators, is a model of what diversity and inclusion means in the museum context. The introductory wall label states:

> Visitors to the American Wing will experience three floors of art, design, and culture from the mid-seventeenth to the mid-twentieth century—along with select contemporary expressions—by a diverse array of makers from across North America. Since our founding in 1924, this curatorial department has evolved its collecting practice to include artworks in many mediums by African American, Asian American, Euro-American, Latin American, and Native American figures, affirming ever more inclusive definitions of American art and identity. Visitors can explore fresh dialogues between artworks informed by multiple perspectives

throughout more than 75 galleries. The current display highlights an increasingly fluid and nuanced understanding of what it meant to be American at different points in the Museum's history—and what it means today.

The installation did just that.

Many of the Met's American Wing's galleries mixed up the cultures and focused on a theme, such as Gallery 731, named "Global Trade and Cultural Exchange." One exhibit, set aside in a small alcove, displayed Missouri artist George Caleb Bingham's *Fur Traders Descending the Missouri* (1845) and Black sculptor Edmonia Lewis's busts of fictionalized Native Americans, *Minnehaha* and *Hiawatha* (1868). Also central to the display was a *Haudenosaunee Paddle* (1850-1875) made by an anonymous Native American. Their juxtaposition made the viewer think about the ways art can suggest the compatibilities and differences between peoples of different backgrounds.

At the Met and at other museums, lengthy text labels can consolidate this cornucopia of diverse visual objects with history. For more contemporary shows, the visitor can expect an artist's personal ephemera in cases that display personal letters, magazines, and documents with the purpose of expanding the context of artists and their era. While teaching us about our past and contemporary worlds, museums can create interactive experiences about the visual pleasures of art and design, and thereby give catharsis and mend wounds.

Today we have many more exhibitions that focus on artists previously overlooked because of their race, ethnicity, gender identification and/or queerness. Examples are the group exhibitions of 1950s abstract expressionist art that now routinely include Black artists such as Ed Clark, Norman Lewis, and Beauford Delaney and women artists such as Lee Krasner, Joan Mitchell, Helen Frankenthaler, and Grace Hartigan.

Contemporary photography shows have embraced Black photographers—especially documentary photographers such as Gordon Parks and Roy DeCarava, who recorded patterns of life among Black people of an earlier generation. Younger photographers are getting space in newspapers, galleries, and on the internet.

One of the most satisfactory recent exhibitions that exemplified diversity and inclusion was *With Pleasure: Pattern and Decoration in American Art, 1972-1985* at the Los Angeles Museum of Contemporary Art in 2019. Instead of focusing on the original 1970s New York artists whom we know as leaders in the turn toward pattern and decoration, the MoCA curator Anna Katz and her team spread the net to include Black artists Emma Amos, Sam Gilliam, Howardena Pindell, Faith Ringgold, and William T. Williams. While this show celebrated talent, it implicitly critiqued an art world that had long ignored the talents of the full range of artists.

Increasingly, museums are publicly acknowledging *all* the people—the staff, guest curators, and even vendors who participate in making an exhibition—by including their names on introductory wall labels as well as in exhibition catalogues. An example: Installed at the beginning of the Oscar yi Hou show at The Brooklyn Museum in 2022 was a large text wall label reading: "Every exhibition at the Brooklyn Museum is a collaboration. Many thanks to all those listed below as well as many others who directly shaped the development and production of Oscar yi Hou *East of the Sun, West of the Moon.*" The text went on to thank the departments and listed the individual names of more than fifty staff people. I was struck at how similar the wall label was to the rolling credits of movies. Visitors need to be aware that it takes a village to make an exhibition.

Another trend in museum practice of inclusion entails

reaching out and inviting non-curators to curate exhibitions based on their experiences—unfamiliar to in-house curators.

One of the first exhibitions about the history of bondage and enslaved people to be curated by an artist occurred in 1992 when the Maryland Historical Society invited Fred Wilson to curate a show from their collection. In *Mining the Museum* he featured the Society's own collection of high art along with artifacts of slavery also owned by the museum, such as iron collars and handbills about runaway slaves. Wilson's ironic wall labels heightened the contradictions between the privileged lives of slave owners and the struggles and rebellions of the enslaved people. Wilson knew that as an artist-curator he had the opportunity to push the envelope and to speak out in ways that staff could not. The exhibition was an overwhelming success.

Museums have invited other non-art historians, such as historians, poets, and even non-curatorial staff, such as guards and art handlers, to develop exhibitions. And for shows developed by in-house curators, wall labels have often been written by school children and neighborhood people. Comments have been encouraged through Post-its which visitors affix to the walls, turning the museum into a public forum.

However, we need to tread lightly when we see inclusion turning into its opposite—*exclusion*—and be aware that one person's perceived inclusion is another person's perceived exclusion. Our recent history is filled with court cases focused on college admission policies where colleges were perceived as giving preferential treatment to a disadvantaged racial group at the expense of others. The colleges employed this inclusion to encourage diversity. The issue peaked in June 2023 when the Supreme Court ruled against affirmative action because it violated the Equal Protection clause of the Fourteenth Amendment. While promoting *equality*, the Court ignored the issue of *equity* which the colleges had argued was needed to bring about a more just society.

Some of the backlash against the Court's ruling led to arguments advanced by liberals that the experiences and cultures of oppressed groups could only be owned by that dispossessed class. They argued that another group can never borrow the speech, the art techniques and the subject matter traditionally owned by the discriminated group.

I think history shows a contrary situation. I believe that all culture is a synthesis of many cultures. Since early Homo Sapiens we have been looking over our shoulder to see what other people and groups are doing in their daily lives, and then borrowing what seems useful, sensible, exciting, and aesthetically compelling. How do we reconcile the dialectic? Encourage diversity, but improve the pre-college educational system, and focus on social justice issues such as adequate housing, food, clothing, medical care, quality education, and access to leisure-time activities in order to promote an even playing field.

Let us explore more fully the concept *equity*—something very different from *equality*. Equality would mean that every person would get the same platform to stand on even with their varying needs and skill sets. Equity goes further by arguing that people should be accommodated by adjusting to their needs.

A sidebar: One aspect of equity that museums avoid discussing are the skewed salary differences between museum directors, whose annual income amounts to millions of dollars, with perks such as luxurious city apartments and generous expense accounts, while guards are lucky to get the federal minimum wage. These workers are joining unions in order to benefit from higher wages and better working conditions. Following the corporate business model, few museums look favorably on this unionization. Nevertheless, many staff have won the right to engage in collective bargaining. I'm all for it.

Unionization of staff (minus the curators, who are considered management) has recently become the norm in large museums. "Museum Employees Embrace Union Pitch," *New York Times*, Feb 22, 2022, mentions unionization efforts at the Walker Art Center, the New Museum, Boston's Museum of Fine Arts, the Museum of Contemporary Art in Los Angeles, the Philadelphia Museum of Art, the Art Institute of Chicago, and the American Museum of Natural History. These are in addition to unions established decades earlier at New York's Museum of Modern Art and the Whitney Museum of American Art. By 2025, we see many other unions established in museums.

More recently, conservative politicians have attacked DEI programs. The arguments for DEI were ignored and the problematic aspects exaggerated. Much of the invective targeted public institutions and the ways that a critical history was gaining traction. Museums were aware of this backlash. *Museum,* the journal of the Alliance of American Museums, devoted its January/February 2025 issue to discussing the backlash and ways to maintain the spirit and positive outcomes of DEI programs.

Museum staff like to add the word "access" to DEI to create DEIA—a broader concept. *Access* helps to clarify the search for solutions to bring art to the general public through admissions policies, accessible pathways for people with disabilities, outreach to the community, bilingual wall labels, and making available the treasures the museums hold by eliminating admission fees. The March/April 2025 issue of *Museum* devotes several articles to what museums have done and what needs to be done. This dialogue on accessibility extends to public parks, zoological gardens, music concerts, and theatrical events.

"Art for the people" does not mean charging $60 for two people visiting the Guggenheim Museum in New York. Access means more generous opening hours and free admission—especially for children, students, and elders. Already some museums have negotiated with corporations to give free passes. As examples: the Metropolitan Museum gives free admission to New York residents and the Museum of Modern Art has free Friday nights. Nevertheless, it is time for city, state, and federal government to support art and culture as they do in Europe without imposing censorship on the historical content of exhibitions, their catalogues and wall labels. Let's keep free speech alive.

&

I believe that museums can better serve the public when they behave like beacons in the night. When museums reach out to all ages, genders, classes, and ethnic groups and involve those groups in decision-making, those visitors learn that art can be both pleasurable and educational. Compositional designs, color, and illusions of space in representational and abstract art can be visually thrilling as well as be tools to remind those visitors of the cultural and political history that forged them.

28

My Last Hurrah, 2015-25

My biggest professional project/distraction in the last twelve years was completing the Eastman Johnson Catalogue Raisonné (EJCR). I had begun my Johnson project in the early 1970s when working on my dissertation, even though I had no such plans for a catalogue at that time. But at the time of the 1999 Brooklyn Museum retrospective of Johnson's work, those 5 x 8 inch cards had grown from a few hundred to over 1,100.

Then Abigael MacGibeny stepped in. In 2012, Abigael, a BU master's degree student, urged me to build a Eastman Johnson database and took on that task. She built and populated the database with the vast amount of information I had collected over the decades, plus information she was gathering. She dove into serious provenance research, hunted for unlocated Johnson paintings, and discovered new works—eventually bringing the total to 1400 works of art.

It became clear to us both that we were working not just on a database but on a catalogue raisonné. Like other catalogue raisonnés, it would be a compilation of all Johnson's paintings, drawings, and prints. We would include titles, alternative titles, dates, medium, measurements, provenance (the history of ownership) exhibition history, plus photos and commentary. From 2014 to 2016, I applied for and received a small foundation grant to continue the project and pay Abigail.

We looked for a long-term steward to maintain the EJCR in "perpetuity." We approached many museums, including the Brooklyn Museum and the New-York Historical Society. I suspect they declined because they perceived maintenance costs and the staffing required to update a CR website would get out of hand. Meanwhile, we needed more funds.

With the encouragement of gallerist Warren Adelson we secured a large grant in 2018 that would keep us going for a year or more while we kept looking for a long-term steward. Museum director Paul d'Ambrosio (my former student) of the Fenimore Museum in Cooperstown sponsored that grant. The process of gathering information, getting the details right, and scrutinizing each entry took months of our time. We met two afternoons a week to study images and finalize the published information.

For me, the intensive work was a welcome distraction from this wretched time when we had to confront Covid-19, as well as Kevin's increasingly debilitating Alzheimer's disease.

Finally, Jeremiah McCarthy, Curator at the National Academy of Design (NAD) came to our rescue. He persuaded the director of the Academy, Greg Wessner, to sign on as the long-term steward of our catalogue raisonné website, with the proviso that I raise a substantial endowment to fund the website's annual maintenance. During 2020-2021 I wrote dozens of letters and applied for more grants.

Abigael and I brought on three art historian advisers, all with PhDs, all retired from the museums and universities where they had worked, all familiar with Johnson's style, and all still active in the field. They included, Brian Allen, Linda Ferber, and Marc Simpson. They advised us regarding grant proposals, potential donors, and strategies for securing the long-term stewardship.

Jeremiah raised the issue of racist language. We all agreed that the words of the 19th century are often inappropriate when used today. We now faced a dilemma when writing EJCR entries—to ignore the problem or to banish the words. To help us, we added "consultants for interpretation": Rika Burnham, Adrienne Childs, Scott Manning Stevens, Jeffrey Stewart, and Alan Wallach. They advised us how to handle offensive language in 19th-century commentaries on Johnson's work. Collectively we wrote a statement included in the EJCR about the ever permutating racist and sexist language that has dominated discourse throughout the centuries.

We met our fundraising goals. We launched the Paintings section of the EJCR website on July 29, 2021—the anniversary of Johnson's birth. As Kevin was dying during these days, I was grateful that Abigael could organize the details of the launch and its accompanying festivities. We introduced the Drawings and Prints section to the public on April 5, 2022—Johnson's death date. The NAD staff pitched in. Students, gallerists, museum curators, owners, and academics are now going to the website for information about Johnson and his environment. We succeeded.

29

Losing Kevin, 2015-25

When Andy, Kevin and I left Beth Israel Deaconess Medical Center in Boston on a chilly mid-December day in 2015, we were not prepared for the news we had just heard—that Kevin was in the middle stages of the debilitating disease, Alzheimer's.

A few weeks before, Kevin had taken a battery of cognitive tests. He knew he was having trouble retrieving words, and sometimes seemed confused about who were the people around him. For some time I noticed his mental decline but had pushed aside scary thoughts. Even then I had to acknowledge there were tasks he increasingly could not do.

Kevin, who had learned how to code and built his own computer in the early 1980s, could no longer service my computer. He lost the ability to make critical comments on my articles. In 2013, when we lived in Berlin, he admitted he could not follow instructions from our German tutor, even though he once had fluent command of the language. His 80th birthday party created anxieties that only exacerbated his word and memory problems. A few months later he stopped cooking his wonderful Chinese dinners because he found it difficult to follow a recipe. His driving was erratic. He had two car accidents—minor ones, thank goodness.

Our Beth Israel visit sealed the diagnosis. The 11-page report detailed the interviews Kevin and I had with the neuropsychologist, the tests, and their results. The diagnosis: "major neurocognitive disorder due to possible Alzheimer's disease." It came as a shock to us all.

The report also cautioned: "Having a family member with a neurodegenerative disease can place significant burden and stress on family members and caregivers. We recommend that individual family members seek support." Unfortunately, I did not heed that recommendation until more than five years had passed. I deluded myself that the problem was only temporary.

In November 2015, Kevin's brother-in-law Frank Irwin had a fall at home. He died six or so days later. Kevin's sister Marianne invited us to live with her in her Brooklyn apartment. Marianne offered us a small guest room—a space about 9 x 14 feet with one window facing a side street. In contrast, our Cambridge house had two floors, a finished basement, a storage attic, a garden, furniture, hundreds of books, artworks, and at least 50 boxes of research files. Although we declined her offer, I loved Marianne and assured her we would visit three to five days each month.

The following April, Marianne held a memorial service for Frank and a reception at her apartment. Her neighbor Paul came. We had become friends because of alternate side of the street parking, which meant moving our cars twice a week to accommodate street cleaning and waiting for the meter maid to finish her rounds ticketing unmoved cars. Paul off-handedly asked whether Kevin and I would like to move into the doctor's office he occupied next to Marianne's apartment. He planned to sell it. Kevin, our children, and I promptly stepped into his place and fell in love with the space and with the idea of living in Brooklyn next to Marianne. We replied with an emphatic "Yes!"

We already had decided to leave Cambridge. Emily lived in Manhattan, and the West Coast children enjoyed coming to New York City. We moved the summer of 2016. All five of our children flew to Cambridge to help. We gave away or sold much of our furniture. We gave many books to colleagues, to the BU library, to the American and New England Studies Programs, and to Roxbury Community College. We sold 68 boxes of books to a bookseller.

I knew I would miss Cambridge and Boston—so many friends, colleagues, and ex-students there. Kevin enthusiastically embraced the idea of moving to New York. To amuse people, he would say, "There's New York, and everywhere else is Hoboken!"

In late August 2016 we hired an architect and contractor to transform the Brooklyn doctor's office into a livable apartment. Because of paperwork and delays, it took the contractors until June 2017 to finish the project. But we had a splendid apartment.

After moving to Brooklyn, Kevin's symptoms gradually worsened. I realized that each day, thousands of brain cells and their neurons broke down so that functional cognition was slowly disappearing. I brushed off the dark thoughts and made the best of it, trying to keep Kevin comfortable and safe. I hoped (by some miracle) that he would get better, encouraged as I was by newspaper articles about cures for Alzheimer's. Those were my years of magical thinking.

But even with aphasia, Kevin could still participate in conversations. However, dinner parties with non-family members presented difficult moments. His inability to call up words and the thoughts those words represented became increasingly frustrating to him. He was still Kevin, but had this bitter handicap.

During 2017 and 2018 he was still somewhat independent, so I enrolled him in memory classes at Brooklyn Methodist Hospital. The hospital was a 20-minute walk from our home, where he walked by himself twice a week wearing a GPS on a key chain in the event I needed to track him. Eventually I had second thoughts, worried about his getting lost, and decided to accompany him on each trip.

At first Kevin functioned somewhat satisfactorily in the class. Inspired by a picture the therapist must have distributed to the class, he wrote a credible description, dated May 8, 2017. Later, responding to a picture-book image shown by the therapist in September 2017, he wrote a clever story slightly surrealist in its subject, lucid, and even poetic.

When we journeyed on our Viking River Cruise down the Rhine with our children in the summer of 2017, he seemed fine: independent, able to coax the words from his memory, and enjoying the company of family members. Even when we went on a 10-day trip to Sicily in November 2018, he was alert to the sights around him, to the Greek and Roman sculpture in the museums, and to the lectures by the guides. But he turned taciturn during the tour group's socializing. After Sicily and back in Rome, he complained of being tired and wanted to "go home." Nevertheless, traveling energized Kevin—especially traveling with family and friends.

Even though I had my projects, I also needed a private outlet for words to describe our sad family situation. I began to keep a journal in January 2019. My words of concern about Kevin and his condition were also reminders to me that I needed to keep my own personhood intact. Besides working on the Eastman Johnson Catalogue Raisonné, I also did research on the artist Joyce Kozloff for a book I planned to write. I finished writing and publishing two long scholarly essays in the field of African American art and two short exhibition catalogue essays.

Reviewing my journal for those years, one of my first notes of January 2019 commented that Kevin could still load the dishwasher but became confused as to where dishes should be put away. He could still make his own coffee but needed help. Opening the front door after a walk, he frequently pulled out his wallet, and I had to remind him that he needed a key for the lock.

On June 1, 2019, I wrote in my Journal:

Yesterday morning we went to a speech pathologist … who is trying to help us help Kevin. Kevin's short-term memory is about 5 seconds, but he can recall some things from his deep memory. He could not remember the names of any of the children or where they lived. But at home, he can still bathe and clothe himself … and walk to Foodtown to buy himself some hummus, which he likes. The doctor suggested we make a booklet for Kevin with pictures of the children, their names and where they live. A simple book. I made the book, and he enjoyed turning the pages.

Kevin's sister Marianne, who lived next door, was moving in the same direction of dementia. I wrote: "She cannot remember the names of Kevin and my children and is upset about it. But she manages to prepare food for herself, go shopping, go to the bank, and do other errands." I realized I was then also becoming a part-time caregiver to her as well. I was saddened to see them both declining: he accepting his fate and Marianne fighting against it.

On September 4, 2019, I wrote in my Journal, in language that recalls the Beth Israel 2015 report:

As to Kevin's condition: He is more and more tongue-tied, and unable to express his thoughts. And then he forgets his thoughts … But his new chore is making the bed, which he takes a long time to do … When he showers, I must help him get dressed. Dressing by himself takes a long time, and he has a hard time figuring out how to get his arms through the sleeves. But he still has his sense of humor [and seems] engaged (but silent) in most conversations.

It is hard for me to fathom what goes through his brain. He liked sitting on the porch in Ocean Grove, [New Jersey] seeing people passing by. I try to get him to walk at least 30 minutes a day; but during the constant heat waves he mostly sat on the porch. He likes having people around him as company. Here in Brooklyn, it is very lonely for him.

On November 11, 2019, I wrote:

Kevin is not doing so well. [On a walk] he almost stumbled a couple of times but was able to walk and carry groceries. But that is not the case last night, when he looked like he was going to fall and had difficulty getting up from the couch. He complained of his ear hurting. Checked his blood pressure (137/77, pulse 66). But he had difficulty undressing and lying down in the bed. We will see how he is today.

About this time, he could not tie his tie as he dressed for the opera. I went to YouTube, watched a video, and learned to tie a tie. For Jan 1, 2020, I wrote: "About a week ago, he came to me holding a razor and said that he didn't know 'how to do this.' So the next day I took him to a Dominican Barbershop on Washington Avenue. They gave him a shave for $9, plus a tip. That will probably be the new routine – every 5-6 days or so." That same entry reported on recent difficulties: "Yesterday we went to Foodtown market on Vanderbilt, and he carried back groceries to our apartment— about four blocks. He was stumbling at the end. He was utterly exhausted and had to lie down for about an hour."
In that entry I also summarized my own situation of lower back pain, and concluded: "Of course, some of the backache would be due to stress. Taking care of Kevin and

doing things he can no longer do. Working is my salvation. Being engaged in intellectual issues. My brain is in good shape, and I hope it lasts for a few more years."

By then I knew Kevin no longer enjoyed attending the opera. He did not seem to comprehend the story and, after a time, even the music seemed taxing to him. Nevertheless, he was a handsome, distinguished-looking man, he smiled a lot at me, and friends were baffled by his inability to respond.

At the end of February 2020, Kevin and I flew to Los Angeles to see my UCLA granddaughter perform in a play. We returned on March 2. On the return flight, I saw a passenger use sanitized wipes to clean her seat. I thought *how strange*. There had been news about a new virus, but government officials had not yet geared up to send out warnings from the CDC. President Trump and his aides seemed not too concerned.

By March 15, New Yorkers were in panic mode. During the March 22 weekend, Emily and her husband Robert Fader drove us (along with Marianne and Emily's dog Alfie) to Ocean Grove, New Jersey, where we had our summer house. While there we made the collective decision to decamp to New Jersey while the pandemic raged. The next week we drove back from Ocean Grove to Brooklyn, where we picked up suitcases, computers, boxes of my research materials, and household necessities. We were prepared to face this new pandemic.

Emily and Robert were wonderful trying to protect us as the vulnerable elderly people we were. They did the shopping, and Emily scrubbed down the Cheerio boxes, apples, etc. with liquid sanitizer. We stayed on our porch and did not allow anyone outside our pod to come into the house. We wore masks when she and I had business at the local bank.

But my health was not good. On Saturday, April 4, I blacked out for about 5 seconds. I already had a heart monitor implanted in early March at Brooklyn Methodist Hospital that relayed information to my cardiologist. I called him. He checked and said that my heart had "paused." Moreover, that I needed a pacemaker immediately to prevent future blackouts—or worse. Overriding hospital Covid-19 protocols, the surgeon scheduled the procedure for April 8. Andy overnighted me some N-95 masks.

Robert drove me into Brooklyn armed with a mask, wipes, hand sanitizer, etc. No one was in the hospital's reception lobby. No guards, nurses, receptionists. I went to the empty second floor and a small group of staffers was waiting for me. It entailed far more than a procedure, it was a real operation with two anesthesiologists, and about six nurses besides the surgeon. The pacemaker wires were threaded through vessels that went to the heart, and then the wires are screwed into the heart.

Robert was able to pick me up at 6 p.m. He took me to my Brooklyn home where I shed my clothes, took a brief sponge bath, and dressed in fresh clothes and shoes. He returned me to Ocean Grove, and Emily cared for me as I was then quite fragile. She semi-quarantined me in the second-floor room and banned me from the kitchen. I wore my mask in common areas. This went on for about five days with no temperature ... so we relaxed.

April, and then May passed, and then June arrived. On June 15, Andy and Brad arrived in a huge RV from Park City, Utah. They had not yet heard results of their Covid-19 tests taken days earlier, and we were all anxious about their staying in our house. What should we do? The clumsy handling of the situation created an unnecessary breach in the family unit, and Emily and Robert left the next morning for Manhattan.

Andy left after three weeks, but Brad stayed on for another couple of months. In July, Brad, Kevin, and I drove to Maine for a week's visit with my sister Gail, her family and other friends. The trip was taxing for Kevin, but he enjoyed himself. In early August Christina arrived in Ocean Grove, quarantined herself in a local hotel for five days and then stayed on for another three weeks in our summer home. It was wonderful having Christina visit, as it was seeing Brad and Andy. She gets along with everyone and tamps down family misunderstandings. Brad was lovely to have around, too. He is so funny, talented, an excellent writer and sharp on political topics and world events.

The pandemic continued to make us all crazy and, for some, a lot crazy, a lot depressed, a lot challenged. It seemed almost obscene to be asking rich people for money to fund the EJCR website project when there were so many troubles in the world, especially here in the US. We were hopeful for the Black Lives Matter movement, but the US was getting more politically polarized. It seemed socially risky to raise a contrary or related opinion. Nevertheless, we hunkered down to be supportive of the new anti-racist activists, to wear masks, and to love our family and friends, even if we could not hug them.

By early September 2020, Kevin and I moved back to Brooklyn. But fall was coming on and then began the wretched sameness of every day. No longer could we sit on the porch at the Shore and stroll on the boardwalk.

The routine in early 2021 was much like late 2020. I wake up and do exercises in bed for 15 minutes. I check out national news on my iPhone and try to do some work on my computer about household and financial matters before Kevin wakes up. When he does, I help him get dressed. Every two or three days I help him shower, and I shave him. I give him breakfast, his pills, and help him sit on the couch until 11 a.m. listening to classical music on the TV. I then turn on the news program *Democracy Now* (with Amy Goodman), which we both like to watch. For lunch I figure out how to be creative with leftovers. We take a 15-minute walk. Kevin naps and I have about two hours free time to write and answer emails—often Zooming with Abigael about the EJCR website. When Kevin wakes, he often sits in a chair in my office area just staring at me. Then Kevin and I take another walk about 5 pm—maybe slip into a local store to get food items that had not come in our food deliveries. Or we just walk around the block. I fix dinner. We eat dinner. We no longer drink wine because it seems like a bad idea.

After dinner, we sit and watch the news on the couch holding hands with fingers intwined. Then we watch a dark or dystopian movie or series (Netflix's "The Man in the High Castle" for example), or something on Channel 13, just as long as it is not cheerfully upbeat. Nature shows were a good watch because we knew the animals will eventually kill and eat each other, but the species will survive. We stopped watching the Boston Red Sox in 2020. Playing to empty ballparks, the Sox in 2020 suffered their worst season ever. They did better in 2021, but we had lost enthusiasm.

The routine continues: Kevin goes to bed. I tuck him in and tell him I love him. He wakes up during the night and I help him to the bathroom. I do the dishes and pick up, and I go to bed. Next day the same routine. And the same the next, and the next.

I am ashamed, however, of one incident. One night Kevin had to get up three times to go to the bathroom. Each time I showered him because he was a mess. At the third time I wailed at him, "Oh, Kevin, why are you like this?" He looked perplexed and shameful. I wish I could have taken back those words. I never said such things again.

Highlights for me were talking with old friends and family. I began weekly Sunday telephone conversations with my old college roommate Martha, who lives in Muir Beach, California. We would chat about old friends, husbands, our health, books we have read, and our kids who tend to bully us "for our own good." We recommend to each other the dark movies in tune with the dystopian malaise affecting us both. The movies match my own dreams. For example, of trying to move from an old house and discovering rooms with stacks of old furniture that I need to dispose of, and my efforts to get my family packed so we can catch a plane or get in a car and drive to some isolated place. It is never clear where we are going. A variation of my dream is when I discover that Kevin is driving the car and that upsets me. So, life feels like one bad movie.

I spoke with my sister Gail every day as we reviewed family issues, what we were doing, what we were thinking.

From Christina I had many, many calls in which she helped me plan my day, cautioned me about dehydration, advised me about medical and emotional issues, and talked about her faith. She flew in from California several times. Emily, a great solace, would walk over from her apartment on the Lower East Side, help me do chores, hug me, and generally cheer me up. I spoke with Brad and Andy frequently about trip agendas, their visits, and their own activities. Those calls and visits I have treasured and continue to feed me love.

I always realized that my situation was so much better than people fleeing their war-torn countries, carrying their possessions by hand, because of persecution, violence, poverty, and being members of the "wrong religion." They had to cope with the pandemic as well.

Nature became a balm for me. The sun on the leaves of the Japanese maple tree outside my window was beautiful, even though some of the leaves were partially obscured by the ugly scaffolding the building co-op had put up for exterior repairs. Seems like a metaphor. We will see a lot of ugliness before beauty can flourish again. Those were my thoughts, culled from my 2020 and 2021 journals—thoughts and dreams contrasting with realities—repeated day after day.

On November 12, 2020, I write in my Journal about

Trump, who refused to concede his defeat to Joe Biden. But I also wrote:

> Kevin is still declining. He still is good about toileting himself. No accidents as there were last August. He has problems feeding himself. He's not sure about what forks do, but usually gets food into his mouth with the help of his fingers. He spills a lot of food on the placemats. Some goes into his lap napkin; some food makes it to the floor. This just means I have to get plastic, wipeable placemats. Television still seems to engage him. We make a point to go on walks. Sometimes it is only a 10-minute walk around the block; other times it is walking to a close-by store or to Prospect Park. It is important that we both keep walking, walking, walking.

We held hands while we walked. More than one person came up to us and asked how long we had been married, that we seemed so fond of each other. I smiled and said that was true, and we had been married for more than forty-five years.

By February 2021, I had started enrolling Kevin in Medicare-funded home care organizations. First came Visiting Nurses, and then Caring Kind, with nurses, home care aides, and physical therapists coming to examine Kevin and help him do exercises. I hoped these brief visits would help Kevin recover his strength. He and I also went to physical therapy twice a week two blocks from our apartment. I received "Medicare Summary Notices" but ignored them—too much on my mind without having to fuss over potential co-payments.

The clock ticked away. The chimes of the ship's clock reminded me of the hours relentlessly passing. And the stress was taking its toll on my health. I noted in my journal that the A-Fib I had was debilitating. Edema was swelling my feet. Walking was so, so tiring.

May 18, 2021 was a day of contrasts. In the morning Kevin and I went to see our physical therapist. That evening he fell in the bathroom. Firemen came to lift him onto the couch. Early the next morning he slipped again. An ambulance took him to the ER at Brooklyn Methodist Hospital. Andy flew home from San Francisco and transformed our two-room apartment into a make-shift hospital. He set up a hospital bed in the living area, along with wheelchair and walker. After two nights in the hospital Kevin came home. Meanwhile, Andy and Emily began to interview home health aides. We found a trio from Trinidad led by Castree. They could provide 24/7 service, each with a twelve-hour shift. I realized the costs of care would burn through our retirement savings very quickly.

"But we have no intention of going the nursing home route" I wrote in my journal. Those were my words on May 22, 2021 and my mindset at the time. Kevin would stay at home for as long as he lived. Like many caregivers, especially during the pandemic, we reviled "nursing homes," considering them cold, heartless, Covid-19-ridden, understaffed institutions that allegedly drugged their patients, strapped them into wheelchairs, and prevented family from visiting. I continued with my May 22 entry: "A new chapter in our lives. Kevin has slipped to a much lower level of ability than last week. But I [am] beginning to find it difficult to lift his legs to dress him, help him up and down stairs, feed him, etc. [With the home aides] this lightens my caregiving."

I did not write again in my journal until June 11, when I filled in the three weeks that had passed, noting that Kevin was able to get in and out of a car with the help of the aides, still feed himself, and smile at his relatives. As to my condition: My lower legs were swelling up more and more.

My cardiologist confirmed I was back in the erratic A-Fib heart rhythm.

I began to question the wisdom of keeping Kevin at home. He was not safe. The aides could not really care for him. He was at times physically punching them. In the middle of the night, I could hear one aide, Rose, saying, "Kevin, don't hit me." The aides were doing their best. The space in the small apartment was inadequate for privacy. At the urging of friends, I began to research elder care facilities. Andy began probing his siblings about their views on assisted-living homes. Christina and Brad were open to finding solutions, while Mary and Emily argued to keep him at home no matter what.

Christina flew in on June 4, 2021 to help me. We talked about living facilities with memory wards, and we started visiting them. Emily did not go with us to visit the assisted living facilities.

Some of the places were truly awful, with dimly lit narrow corridors filled with old people slumped in their wheelchairs. We also visited some very expensive Manhattan facilities, but my favorites were the Sunrise facilities in South Brooklyn, with their friendly staff, good programming, sensible handling of Covid-19 issues, and their willingness to allow me to spend the night with Kevin if I wished. They also assured me that they could move Kevin to their hospice care unit when that time came. Although it would be expensive for us all to taxi there, their lower charges would compensate for the expense.

Christina and I visited Watermark, a new senior facility in Brooklyn Heights, with great views of the Hudson River and Manhattan. Their Memory Ward, recently renovated, had only two tenants in a ward that held beds and rooms for two dozen more. It had a swimming pool, gym facilities, and an art studio—none of which would have helped Kevin. More expensive than all the others, Christina and Andy agreed that its location would make it easier for Emily to visit from her apartment in Manhattan. A major drawback, as we came to learn, was its being short of staff.

Watermark required Kevin to have bloodwork, so we took him to his doctor. The next morning our doctor called to say that Kevin had to immediately go to the Emergency Room at Brooklyn Methodist, as he was dehydrated and had kidney failure. This ER visit—with severe visitor restrictions—lasted four days before he was released to Watermark. Brad had already come and set up our hospital bed in Watermark, and we had plans to bring in framed photographs and plants to make the room nice for him. We joined him for dinner the first and second nights, and I came at breakfast to help him eat.

Two days after he entered Watermark Kevin aspirated some food, and the ambulance came to take him back to Brooklyn Methodist. This time he stayed six nights in the hospital. On the seventh day, as he was being released from the hospital, Watermark informed me that they would not take him back. This meant that late in the day I had to scramble to find a facility for him. We chose Brooklyn Downtown Nursing and Rehab Center (BDNRC), recommended by the helpful people at Metropolitan Jewish Family Services, and only four blocks from my apartment. The "end-of-life" doctor wrote him a prescription for twenty days of rehab at DBNRC, after which Kevin could be transferred to their hospice care unit.

The facility was not rated tippy top. Although Medicare gave it a five-star rating, *USNews* called it average. I regretted we had not at the beginning chosen the Sunrise facilities in southern Brooklyn, which would have welcomed him back.

We arrived at DBNRC about 7 p.m. on July 21. With the Covid-19 pandemic still raging, we were required to suit up in gowns, masks, and face shields. Like the hospital, visiting hours were restrictive, following reasonable protocols set up during the pandemic surge in the summer of 2021. Most of us appreciated the Covid-19-weary, over-worked staff assigned to our floor. Kevin's roommate Jack, an elderly former rodeo cowboy, kept Kevin laughing. Friends and relatives visited, and they comforted me. Christina, Brad, and Andy supported me and worried about my health.

Partly because of family stresses, my A-Fib was really back in spades. Four days before Kevin died, I had a cardioversion to reboot my heart, but it did not work. The A-Fib exhausted my body and my mind. All the stress seemed to condemn me to a physically and emotionally wretched state. I remember those weeks of stress as the worst of my life. Later, as Kevin lay dying, Gail and her husband John were helpful advising and consoling me, when I didn't get the support I craved from some family members.

Kevin did his twenty days of rehab. It was delusional for me to think that rehabilitation would give him a new lease on life. He really appeared to be seriously dying the seventeenth day. He was not eating and drinking, and oxygen levels were low. Supplemental oxygen helped. On Kevin's 20th night at DBNRC he was moved into a hospice room.

The next morning—Thursday August 12—Andy, who had gone early to be with Kevin, telephoned us all to say the end was near. And so it was. When Kevin died at 2 p.m. Mary, Emily, Andy, and I were by his side. After his last breath, Andy blurted out, "I am so happy you have died and that you are now out of your misery." I felt the same. A great person—my loving husband—had finally escaped his awful disease. Several weeks before I had asked Kevin, "Do you just want to let go?" And he replied (his last full sentence), "Yes, I do."

He was gone. Four evenings after he died, Marianne, her family, Andy and Christina had dinner outside at a Thai restaurant in the neighborhood to celebrate Kevin's life.

A week after Kevin died, Brad, Christina and I drove to

my sister's Maine summer home on Belgrade Lakes for a few days. It was a great balm to be with close family, to gaze at the lake and marshes, and listen to the loons calling.

On September 22, 2021, I had an ablation operation to remove my heart's electrical nodes that were arbitrarily firing off and giving me the severe A-Fib. My sister and her husband came to attend to me and to help me sort out Kevin's clothes for Good Will. The ablation was successful, although the heart had been damaged and scarred by years of A-Fib.

I needed also to attend to my emotions. In late August I began a course of intense therapy sessions to help me cope with my grief over Kevin's death, with the family stresses, and my sleepless nights. Where did I go wrong? Why did I not argue more forcefully my position that Kevin needed to be safe, and that the safe place would not be our apartment but in a facility with trained staff.

I had many dreams about him. One vivid dream: I was standing in the middle of an atrium of a big shopping mall (like the Monmouth Mall in New Jersey). It was like a stage set. I see Kevin coming through a door at the back left and walking toward me. He wears multiple heavy coats. I say in my dream, "Where are you going?" He replies, "I was going to ask you"—a response he had for years preferred when he was gripped by confusion. I then grabbed his hand and said, "I'm going to take you home." He smiled and we exited out of the atrium through a door to the right—as if we were actors in a stage play.

A year and a day after Kevin died—on August 13, 2022—we held a Memorial Service for him in Brooklyn. About 80 people came on a beautiful day. Everyone in the family pitched in. Emily and Mary prepared a beautiful and touching slide show of Kevin's life. Christina organized the guest list and invitations. I found the venue, negotiated with the caterers, ordered flowers for the dining tables, and planned the program. Andy solved scheduling problems with the facility and secured musicians.

Brad did trouble shooting. My friend Deborah Gardner took photographs. Abigael MacGibeny helped, as did Pavla Berghen-Wolf, our assistant on the Eastman Johnson Catalogue Raisonné. The family all spoke or offered poems. Two of Kevin's old university friends—Dan Tompkins and Michael Goldman—read tributes. Two of his political comrades—Ruth Kiefson and Richard Anderson—spoke of his work in the movement. Classical guitarist Naeim Rahmani played Heitor Villalobos's Prelude Nos. 1 and 5. Violinist Adrianna Mateo and pianist Jonathan Cameron Kelly played selections from Prokofiev's Sonata No. 2 for Violin and Piano in D Major—one of Kevin's favorite pieces. We ended the ceremony with a robust singing of "The Internationale" with our political friends cheering. Then we had lunch. A splendid tribute and celebration of Kevin's life.

He was celebrated but gone—his body, his intellect, his wisdom, and his love. I miss his presence, his conversation, his understanding of the world, and our shared private affections.

In spring 2022, I wrote a poem, "The Empty Bed":

Easing into bed
And missing the cradled hollow
Of warmth and flesh,
Of murmurs and smells.
Instead,
Thrusting my feet into pockets
Of cool sheets in a flat expanse of space.
I feel no peace.
Only sorrow and loss.

Who was I now? My loving Kevin was gone. And I began this memoir.

Bibliography: Citations, Sources, and Recommended Readings

Sources: Memory, personal journals, correspondence, Patricia Hills papers gifted to the Archives of American Art, Boston University personnel records, newspaper articles, published and unpublished talks, and recollections by family, friends, and colleagues. Throughout the text the author has updated to 2025 the dollar amounts from the past by using the Consumer Price Index. See https://www.bls.gov/data/inflation_calculator.htm

Several quotations cited in the text come from Patricia Hills, *Modern Art and the USA: Issues and Controversies of the 20th Century* (Upper Saddle River, NJ: Prentice Hall, 2000); referred to as "Hills 2000."

Newspaper and journal sources cited by author in the text usually contain sufficient bibliographical information. Since these publications can be easily found on the internet, page numbers have not been provided. However, for specific quotations, page numbers can generally be found here in brackets.

Language about race is constantly changing, but author uses words that are in the general parlance of 2025.

Chapter 1 Dead End Jobs in San Francisco, 1958-60

Mills, C. Wright. *The Power Elite.* New York: Oxford University Press, 1956.

Chapter 2 Working at MoMA, Oh My! 1960-65

Miller, Dorothy. *Sixteen Americans.* Exh. Cat. New York: Museum of Modern Art, 1959.

Selz, Peter. *New Images of Man.* Exh. Cat. New York: Museum of Modern Art, 1959.

Temkin, Ann and Romy Silver-Kohn, eds. *Inventing the Modern: Untold Stories of the Women who Shaped the Museum of Modern Art*. New York: Museum of Modern Art, 2024. [The book focuses on founders and women heads of departments, but not the day-to-day work of the women mentioned in this chapter.]

Chapter 3 Coming of Age , 1965-68

Hills, Patricia. Papers, Archives of American Art. [Includes correspondence with Leo Steinberg.]

Steinberg, Leo. *Michelangelo's Sculpture: Essays by Leo Steinberg*. Sheila Schwartz ed. Chicago: University of Chicago Press, 2018.

Steinberg, Leo. *Other Criteria*. New York: Oxford University Press, 1972.

Chapter 4 Who Cares about American Art? 1968-72

Davis, Stuart. "Reviews: The New York American Scene in Art," *Art Front* 1, no. 3 (February 1935), p. 3. [Excerpted in Hills, 2000, Pp. 132-33.]

Eisler, Colin. "Where's Willibald? *Journal of Art Historiography* (2017). [On the history of the Institute of Fine Arts.]

Greenberg, Clement. "Abstract Art," *The Nation* 158 (April 15, 1944): 450-451. [Quoted in Hills 2000, pp. 150 ff.]

Guilbaut, Serge. *How New York Stole the Idea of Modern Art: Abstract Expressionism, Freedom, and the Cold War*. Chicago: University of Chicago Press, 1983.

Hills, Patricia. "'Truth, Freedom, Perfection': Alfred Barr's *What Is Modern Painting?* as Cold War Rhetoric," in Greg

Barnhisel and Catherine Turner, eds. *Pressing the Fight:* 2010. *Print, Propaganda and the Cold War*. Amherst: University of Massachusetts Press.

McCoubrey, John W. *American Tradition in Painting*. New York: George Brazillier, 1963. [pp. 8-9.]

Panofsky, Erwin. "The History of Art as a Humanistic Discipline" and "Iconography and Iconology: An Introduction to the Study of Renaissance Art," in *Meaning in the Visual Arts*. Garden City, NJ: Doubleday Anchor Books, 1955. [pp. 3-10 and 31-39.]

Chapter 5 Art Dealers, 1969

Bianchini, Paul, ed. *Roy Lichtenstein: Drawings and Prints*. Lausanne: Publications IRL, 1970.

Chapter 6 Change is Gonna Come, Late 1965-70

Anderson, Terry H. *The Sixties* [Revised Edition]. New York: Pearson Longman, 2007. For Sam Cooke's 1964 song see: https://www.youtube.com/watch?v=wEBlaMOmKV4

Chapter 7 Becoming a Feminist, 1968-72

Gornick, Vivien. "The Next Best Moment in History is Theirs." *The Village Voice,* (November 27, 1969).

Morgan, Robin, ed. *Sisterhood is Powerful: An Anthology of Writings from the Women's Liberation Movement*. New York: Random, 1970.

Nochlin, Linda. "Why Have There Been No Great Women Artists?" *Art News* 69:9 (January 1971), [p. 23]

Raven, Arlene, Cassandra L. Langer and Joanna Frueh, eds. *Feminist Art Criticism: An Anthology*. Ann Arbor, MI: UMI Press, 1988.

Chapter 8 Becoming a Radical, 1972

Baritz, Loren. *The American Left: Radical Political Thought in the Twentieth Century.* New York: Basic Books, 1971.

Kennebeck, Edwin. *Juror Number Four.* New York: Norton, 1973.

Israel, Matthew. *Kill for Peace: American Artists Against the Vietnam War.* Austin: University of Texas Press, 2013. Sale, Kirkpatrick. *SDS.* New York: Vintage Books, 1973.

Chapter 9 Four Whitney Exhibitions, 1972-74
Baur, John I. H. *Eastman Johnson.* Exh. Cat. Brooklyn, NY: Brooklyn Museum, 1941.

Hills, Patricia. *Eastman Johnson.* Exh. Cat. New York: Clarkson N. Potter, 1972. [Exhibition traveled to Detroit, Cincinnati, and Milwaukee.]

Hills, Patricia. *The American Frontier: Images and Myths.* Exh. Cat. (New York: Whitney Museum of American Art, 1973). [Exhibition traveled to six European cities with a reissued catalogue published by the United States Information Agency.]

Hills, Patricia. *The Painters' America: Rural and Urban Life, 1810-1910.* Exh. Cat. New York: Praeger, 1974. [Exhibition traveled to Houston and Oakland.]

Chapter 10 A Busy Time, 1974-78

Hills, Patricia. *Turn-of-the-Century America: Paintings, Graphics, Photographs 1890-1910.* Exh. Cat. New York: Whitney Museum of American Art, 1977.

Tuchman, Barbara W. *The Proud Tower: A Portrait of the World Before the War, 1980-1914.* New York: Macmillan, 1962.

Veblen, Thorsten. *The Theory of the Leisure Class: An Economic Study of Institutions [1899]*. New York: New American Library, 1953.

Chapter 11 Boston Ups & Downs, 1978-81
Patricia Hills Papers. Archives of American Art, Smithsonian Institution.

Chapter 12 BU Art Gallery, 1980-89
Hills, Patricia. *Social Concern and Urban Realism: American Painting of the 1930s*. Exh. Cat. Boston: Boston University Art Gallery, 1982.

Hills, Patricia. *Social Concern in the '80s: A New England Perspective*. Exh. Cat. Boston: Boston University Art Gallery, 1984.

Chapter 13 The Boston Women's Caucus for Art, 1983-89

Broude, Norma and Mary D. Garrard, eds. *The Power of Feminist Art: The American Movement of the 1970s, History and Impact*. New York: Abrams, 1994.

Hills, Patricia. "Personal Recollections of the Early Years of the Women's Caucus for Art in Boston," in Karen Frostig and Kathy A. Halamka, eds. *Blaze: Discourse on Art, Women and Feminism*. Newcastle, UK: Cambridge Scholars Publishing, 2007. [pp. 320]

Chapter 14 Blockbuster Exhibitions, 1986 and 2005

Hills, Patricia. *John Singer Sargent. Exh. Cat.* New York: Whitney Museum of American Art, 1986. [Exhibition traveled to Chicago.]

Hills, Patricia and Melissa Renn. *Syncopated Rhythms: 20th-Century African American Art from the George and*

Joyce Wein Collection. Exh. Cat. Boston: Boston University Art Gallery, 2005.

Chapter 15 The Daughter Track, 1989-91

Green, M. Christian. "'Graceful Pillars': Law, Religion, and the Ethics of the 'Daughter Track'" *Journal of Law and Religion*, 1:2 (June 16, 2016).

Miller, Dorothy A. "The 'Sandwich' Generation: Adult Children of the Aging," *Social Work*, 26:5 (September 1981), pp. 419-423.

Video "The Daughter Track": https://www.youtube.com/watch?v=BYKgzrbam8A

Chapter 16 Leda and the Swan, 1989

Hughes, Robert. "Sold! The Art Market: Goes Crazy." *Time* (November 27, 1989).

Chapter 17 A Combative Feminist, 1980s-90s

Fried, Michael. "Realism, Writing, and Disfiguration in Thomas Eakins's *Gross Clinic*," in *Representations* (No. 9, Winter 1985), pp. 33-104. [p. 57]

Hills, Patricia. "Thomas Eakins' Agnew Clinic and John S. Sargent's *Four Doctors*: Sublimity, Decorum, and Professionalism," *Prospects: A Journal of American Cultural Studies,* Vol.11-Essays (1987), pp. 217-30.

Hills, Patricia. "Half the Story." Review of Robert Hughes, *American Visions: The Epic History of Art in America* published in the *Los Angeles Times Book Review* (April 27, 1997), p.3.

Lubin, David M. *Act of Portrayal: Eakins, Sargent, James* (New Haven: Yale University Press, 1985). [pp. 72-74]

Macey, David. *The Penguin Dictionary of Critical Theory.* London: Penguin Books, 2000. [p. v]

Prown, Jules D. "Winslow Homer in His Art," *Smithsonian Studies in American Art* 1:1 (Spring 1987), pp. 30-45. [pp. 31, 37, 39].

Sim, Stuart, ed. *The Routledge Critical Dictionary of Post Modern Thought.* [1998] New York: Routledge, 1999.

Wallach, Alan. *Trouble in Paradise: Twenty-Four Essays on the Social History of American Art.* Leiden: Brill, 2025.

Wolf, Bryan Jay. *Romantic Re-Vision: Culture and Consciousness in Nineteenth Century American Painting and Literature.* Chicago: University of Chicago Press, 1982. [pp. 203, 191]

Chapter 18 West as America, 1991

Bolton, Richard, ed. *Culture Wars: Document from the Recent Controversies in the Arts.* New York: New Press, 1992.

Hills, Patricia. "The Naked Body, Censorship and the NEA," *Art New England* 13 (August/September 1992): 14-16, 50.

Hills, Patricia. "Censorship and Propaganda in Art and Visual Culture" in Hills 2000 [pp. 408-23]

Kramer, Hilton. "Has Success Spoiled the Art Museum: On the De-aestheticization of the Art Museum." *The New Criterion* (September 1991).

Morgan, Charlotte. "Censorship and Self-Censorship in Museums" (2014). See https://www.academia.edu/9677417/Censorship_and_self_censorship_in_museums

Nemerov, Alex. "Doing the 'Old America': The Image of the American West, 1880-1920" in Truettner 1991. [p. 309]

Truettner, William H. ed. *The West as America: Reinterpreting Images of the Frontier, 1820-1920.* Washington: National Museum of American Art, 1991. [Essays by Nancy K. Anderson, Elizabeth Johns, Patricia Hills, Howard R. Lamar, Alex Nemerov, Julie Schimmel, and William H. Truettner.]

Editors, American Art. "Showdown at the "West as America," *American Art* 5:3 (Summer 1991), pp. 1-11.

Wallach, Alan. "The Battle over the West as America" in *Exhibiting Contradiction: Essays on the Art Museum in the United States.* Amherst, MA: University of Massachusetts Press, 1998.

Chapter 19 The Boston Massacre, 1999

Anonymous, "Museum Reels from Backlash Over Firing Curators," *The Beacon Hill/Back Bay Chronicle*, August 31, 1999, pp. 1, 7-8.

Bean, Alex. "MFA's Huckster Loses Round One to Art Glitterati," *Boston Globe* September 15, 1999, p. D1.

Beggy, Carol. "Stebbins Resigns from MFA." *Boston Globe*, November 18, 1999, D1 and D8.

Giuliano, Charles. *Museum of Fine Arts Boston: 1870-2020.* North Adams, MA: Berkshire Finc Arts, 2021.

Hartigan, Patti. "Malcolm Rogers Has Left the Building," *Boston Globe*, August 25, 2015.

Hills, Patricia. Papers. Archives of American Art, Smithsonian Institution. [A large file contains copies of all the letters, emails, newspaper articles, and personal written notes pertaining to the Boston Massacre.]

Kaufman, Jason Edward. "Staff Sacking Unleashes Fury." *The Art Newspaper*, 10:95 (September 1999), pp. 14-15. [Includes an interview with Malcolm Rogers.]

Kramer, Hilton. "Now Banned in Boston: A Decent Art Museum," *New York Observer*, August 23, 1999, p. 1.

Raysson, Michael. *The Art of Organizing: The Boston Museum of Fine Arts Union Drive.* New York: Hard Ball Press, 2020.

Chapter 20 Building Community, Expanding Boundaries, 1980s-90s

Patricia Hills Papers. Archives of American Art, Smithsonian Institution.

Chapter 21 Older and Wiser, 1990s-2014

Patricia Hills Papers. Archives of American Art, Smithsonian Institution.

Chapter 22 Travels with My Art, 1981-2006

Hills, Patricia. Personal Journals.

Chapter 23 Berlin Sojourn, 2013

Hills, Patricia. Personal Journals.

http://berkshirefinearts.com/06-24-2013_letter-from-berlin-first-impressions.htm

http://berkshirefinearts.com/06-29-2013_second-berlin-letter-bonnie-wood.htm

http://berkshirefinearts.com/07-08-2013_letter-from-berlin-3-anish-kapoor.htm

Chapter 24 Alice Neel, 1973-Present

Hills, Patricia. *Alice Neel.* New York: Abrams, 1983.

Hoban, Phoebe. *Alice Neel: The Art of Not Sitting Pretty.* New York: St. Martin's Press, 2010.

Neel, Andrew. *Alice Neel.* Documentary Film, 2007.

Chapter 25 May Stevens, 1974-present

Baranik, Rudolf and May Stevens. *in words.* New York, privately published in conjunction with the exhibition EXISTENTIAL/POLITICAL at Exit Art, 1994.

Craven, David. *Poetics and Politics in the Life of Rudolph Baranik.* Humanities Press: Atlantic Highlands, NJ, 1997.

Drobnick, Jim. *Rudolf Baranik's Dictionary from the 24th Century.* (New York: Bee Sting Press, 1990).

Heresies: A Feminist Publication on Art and Politics (1977-1993)

Hills, Patricia. Papers, Archives of American Art, Smithsonian Museum. [Contains transcripts of interviews.]

Hills, Patricia. "Foreword: Recent Concerns, Recent Work," in *May Stevens: Ordinary * Extraordinary, a Summation 1977-1984* Boston: Boston University Art Gallery, 1984.

Hills, Patricia. "May Stevens: Painting History as Lived Feminist Experience," in Burnham, Patricia M. and Lucretia Hoover Giese. *Redefining American History Painting.* New York: Cambridge University Press, 1995)

Hills, Patricia. *May Stevens.* Petaluma, CA: Pomegranate Press, 2005.

May Stevens and Rudolf Baranik Foundation Archives. [Contains audio tapes, video tapes, correspondence, writings, catalogues and brochures.]

Chapter 26 Jacob Lawrence, 1983-Present

Gates, Henry Louis, Jr. *The Black Box: Writing the Race.* New York: Penguin Random, 2024.

Hills, Patricia. Papers, Archives of American Art, Smithsonian Institution. [Contains transcripts of interviews.]

Hills, Patricia. *Painting Harlem Modern: The Art of Jacob Lawrence.* Berkeley: University of California Press, 2009.

Wheat, Ellen Harkins. *Jacob Lawrence: American Painter.* Exh. Cat. Seattle: University of Washington Press, 1986. [Contains essay Patricia Hills, "Jacob Lawrence's Expressive Cubism."]

Wilkerson, Isabel. *The Warmth of Other Suns: The Epic Story of America's Great Migration.* New York: Vintage Books, 2011.

Chapter 27 Diversity, Equity, Inclusion, 2015-2025

Buskirk, Martha. "Interviews with Sherri Levine, Louise Lawler, and Fred Wilson," *October* 70 (Fall 1994): 99-112. [Reprinted Hills 2000, pp. 427-430.]

Locke, Steve. "Guston, Whiteness, and the Unfinished Business of the Vile World," *Art Forum* (December 2020).

Museum of Fine Arts, Boston, Handout for Philip Guston exhibition, 2022.

Museum, publication of the American Alliance of Museums, recent issues.

Small, Zachery. "U.S. Museums See Rise in Unions Even as Labor Movement Slumps." *New York Times* [updated February 22, 2022].

Chapter 28 My Last Hurrah, 2015-25

Hills, Patricia. "My Advocacy for the Digital Catalogue Raisonné." *Panorama* 9:1 (Spring, 2023). [Internet publication]

Hills, Patricia and Abigael MacGibeny. www. eastmanjohnson.org

MacGibeny, Abigael and Patricia Hills, "Dealing with Historical Titles: The Case of the Eastman Johnson Catalogue Raisonné," *Nineteenth Century Art Worldwide* 20, no. 3 (Autumn 2021). [Internet publication]

Chapter 29 Losing Kevin, 2015-2025

Hills, Patricia. Personal Journals and Family Papers

"Guy Kevin Whitfield," Obituary, *New York Times,* August 29, 2021.

ACKNOWLEDGMENTS

I want to thank the many people who set me on my course to enter the art world as a curator, teacher, and scholar: Grace Morley, William S. Lieberman, Leo Steinberg, and John I. H. Baur. I especially want to express my gratitude to Henry Louis Gates, Jr., the director of the Hutchins Center for African and African American Research at Harvard. It was Gates who reassured me that being a white woman did not preclude me from studying Jacob Lawrence. Gates always emphasized that good scholarship is what counts, no matter who does it.

The following friends and colleagues read through the whole manuscript in its early stages, gave me needed feedback, and I am grateful: David Brody, Deborah Gardner, John Murphy, and X Bonnie Woods. Those who corrected facts for specific chapters include Theodore E. Stebbins, Jr., Patricia Johnston, Amy Lighthill, Dan Ranalli, and Michael Mendillo. I especially want to call out Abigael MacGibeny, who partnered with me in creating the Eastman Johnson Catalogue Raisonné, the topic of Chapter 28. Those who read single chapters, cheered me on, and encouraged me toward rethinking the book's structure are: Jordan Chaim, Martha Potter De Barros, Kathryn Delmez, Vivien Fryd, Barbara Gallati, Charles Giuliano, Melanie Hall, Andrew Hemingway, Stephanie Heydt, Christina Hills, Katherine Howe, Amy Lighthill, Mary Lubin, Lisa Peters, Sheila Schwartz, Gwendolyn Du Bois Shaw, Alan Wallach, Sally Webster, Alona Wilson, Tom Wolf, and Sylvia Yount.

Colleagues at Boston University who supported me over the years include Fred S. Kleiner, Keith N. Morgan, Cheryl Crombie, and Susan Rice.

In addition to the above, other good friends have contributed to my understanding of what it means to live and work in 20th- and 21st- century times and to develop an independent voice. They are Richard Anderson, Rudolf Baranik, David Hall, Carrie Hamilton, Patricia Johnston, Gwendolyn and Jacob Lawrence, Lucy Lippard, Alice Neel, Emma Rhoads, Jake Rosen, Lois Rudnick, May Stevens, Alan Wallach, as well as my former graduate students who brought new ideas to the seminar table.

Thanks also go to a superb editor, Joe Maniscalco. And to Tim Sheard of Hard Ball Press for shepherding my prose through the final editing and publishing process. As Stephen King has said, "Editors are always right."

Of course, I thank my parents—Hartwin A. Schulze and Glennie Gorton Baker—who raised me, taught me, and supported me. My first husband Fred Hills taught me to write. My second husband Kevin Whitfield not only taught me the nuances of writing, but urged me to think deeply about the contradictions inherent in a society of inequality and unbalanced social justice.

I want to thank my children—Christina Hills, Bradford Hills, Andrew Whitfield, and my stepchildren Mary Whitfield and Emily Whitfield—who taught me to have patience and empathy toward the needs of growing children and teenagers. And thanks to my niece and nephews Jeanne Jackson, Syth DeVoe, Hall McCormick, and my granddaughter Magenta Rose Brown.

Finally, I want to give a huge thanks and my gratitude to my sister Abigail Gorton and her husband John Biddiscombe, who along with Christina, Bradford, and Andrew, supported me during difficult times. With love to you all.

This book is dedicated to Kevin.

ABOUT THE AUTHOR

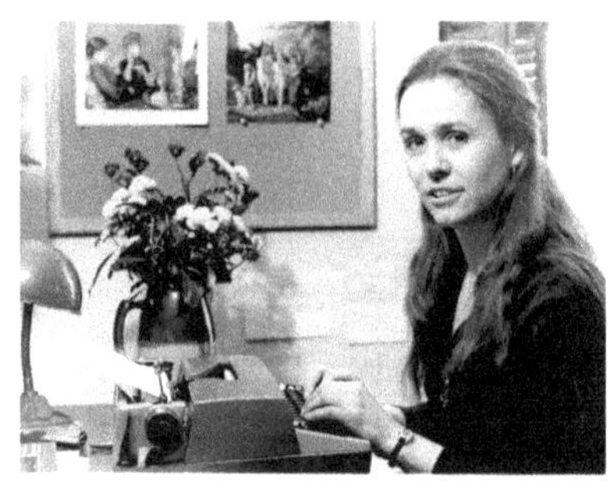

Photograph by Jeanne Hamilton, 1973

Patricia Hills, Professor Emerita, Department of the History of Art and Architecture at Boston University, was given The Distinguished Teaching of Art History Award in 2011 by The College Art Association. The Association recognized that Dr. Hills's scholarship in American art and visual culture and African American art has helped to define the field of American art history.

Professor Hills has published books, catalogue entries, and essays on 19th- and 20th-Century American art, African American artists, and art and politics. Her recent books are *Modern Art in the USA: Issues and Controversies of the 20th Century* (2001), *May Stevens* (2005), and *Painting Harlem Modern: The Art of Jacob Lawrence* (2009).

Images and Photos are posted on: www.patriciahills.com

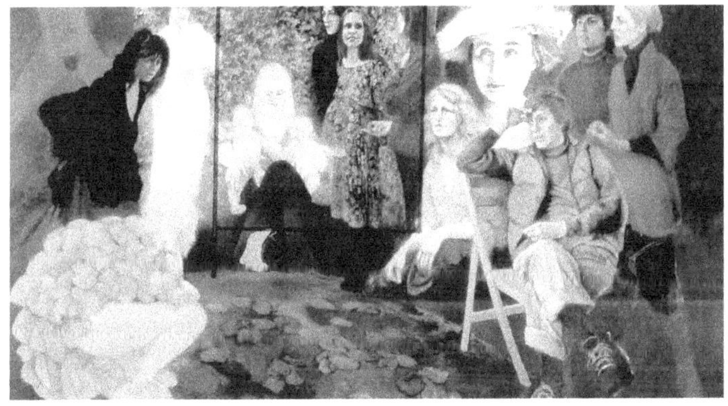

May Stevens, *Mysteries and Politics*, 1978. Acrylic on canvas, 78 x 142 inches. The San Francisco Museum of Modern Art, gift of Mr. and Mrs. Anthony Grippa. The figures represented are, clockwise, Betsy Damon, Pat Steir, painting of Mary Beth Edelson's torso, photograph of Stevens' mother holding the artist as a baby, Poppy Johnson holding her twin babies, Carol Duncan, Patricia Hills pregnant with Andrew, Stevens (face averted), Suzanne Harris, painting of Rosa Luxemburg, Amy Sillman, Elizabeth Weatherford, and Joan Snyder seated on a chair.

FIND MORE POWERFUL STORIES AT HARD BALL PRESS

- Union organizing

- Labor history & memoirs

- Fiction & Poetry

- The Shop Steward detective series

- Bilingual children's stories

LINK TO HARD BALL PRESS WEBSITE:

https://www.hardballpress.org/